# MASTERY OF

# REGENTS' READING EXAMS

## Third Edition

### LINDA L. ARTHUR, PH.D.

**KENDALL/HUNT PUBLISHING COMPANY**
4050 Westmark Drive          Dubuque, Iowa 52002

Images on pages 2, 8, 48, from JupiterImages Corporation.
Images on pages 60, 98, 348 from Eyewire.
Image on page 228 © 2007 PhotoDisc, Inc.

ISBN 13: 978-0-7575-3853-7

Printed in the United States of America
10  9  8  7  6  5  4

# TABLE OF CONTENTS

**Chapter Six, continued**

# PREFACE

I am pleased to offer the third edition of *Mastery of Regents' Reading Exams*. The text is designed for students enrolled in Regents' Reading review courses at the college level. New to this edition are the following:

- Simulated Diagnostic Exam
- Test Anxiety Scale
- Chapter on Reading Rate
- Timed Readings
- More vocabulary exercises

Other features of the text include:

1) general information about the reading portion of the Regents' Reading Exam;
2) explanations of the reading skills required to master Regents' Reading Exams;
3) exercises to practice the required reading skills;
4) ten Simulated Exams that provide more opportunities for practice in particular skills; the exams are designed to be practical assessment tools with
   a. perforated pages for quick removal
   b. scantrons with diagnostic charts of skills for each test; a category for Main Idea, whether it is Stated or Unstated, is included.
5) practical test taking strategies for success on this type of exam;
6) answer keys for chapters and for simulated exams;
7) the exams have been piloted in the Regents' Reading Review classroom; and
8) particular tests emphasize a particular skill (please refer to the end of each skills chapter)

Of special interest is the *Graphics Answer Key* that maps answers in a visual format. Used in the classroom the Graphics Answer Key becomes versatile. Answers to questions in the Simulated Diagnostic Exam through Simulated Exam Three are graphically displayed and mapped.

a. Instructors can make transparencies of the graphics and use them in the classroom as a teaching aid. Visual learners may be aided during classroom discussion through the use of such transparencies.

b. Simulated Exams Four through Ten are intentionally left unmapped so that the student may practice this strategy.

c. Because some students are anxious when they take tests, they sometimes read over an obvious answer or clues to an answer. These graphic illustrations will point students to the answers and give them a starting point for further discussion.

The format of the book is aimed at maximizing student success and encouraging students to become successful readers. Most selections are 250 to 300 words. Passages are drawn from college textbooks and other college-level materials. Selections include narrative and expository materials—the latter representing topics from the social sciences, humanities, business, current events, natural sciences, pop culture, and health sciences.

**DEDICATION**

*This textbook is dedicated to my daughter, Catherine Sermo Smith*

# UNIT ONE

OVERVIEW OF THE REGENTS' READING EXAM

EXPLANATION OF READING SKILLS

PRACTICE EXERCISES

TIMED READINGS

# CHAPTER ONE

## A BRIEF OVERVIEW OF THE REGENTS' READING EXAM

College reading instructors would probably agree that the most often-asked question from you, the student, the first day of a Regents' Reading class is, "Why do I have to take this test?" This question is a valid one, but it is usually followed up by a statement such as, "I'm a sophomore; I know how to read." How to respond to this kind of statement is up to the instructor, but to adequately answer the question of why a regents' exam has been created, one can refer to the Board of Regents' policies for particular states. The information presented below is from the state of Georgia, but other states may adhere to the same kind of policies.

According to the policy statement of 1972, the Board of Regents of the University System of Georgia announced that system institutions must ensure that students receiving degrees possess minimum literacy competence. Literacy competence may be defined as "certain minimum skills of reading and writing." Students' scores on the exams are used to determine whether they have the minimum levels of reading and writing competency for graduation.

A policy issued in the academic year 2003–2004 states that

> *Students with SAT-I Verbal scores of at least 510 or ACT Reading scores of at least 23 will be considered to have fulfilled the reading comprehension requirement of the Regents' Test and do not need to take the reading portion of the Regents' Test.*

When students should first sit for the exam depends on various factors. Colleges and universities may allow students to take the Regents' Reading Exam after they have successfully completed the first writing class. Some students might want to wait until they have finished their second writing class to give them more time to improve their reading ability. Also, institutions may have specific guidelines. Other universities allow the student to take the test after having earned 30 semester hours of degree credit. Students who do not pass the test must continue taking the test each term until they are successful. Students are advised to check with the Testing Office to understand their institution's regulations and guidelines.

It is interesting to note that in Georgia the passing rates for first-time examinees are published. For example, for the academic year 2002–2003, 87.1% of the students from Georgia Southern University who completed the reading portion of the Regents' Test passed (University System of Georgia website). Obviously, this means that a college with a pass rate of 87.1% would have 12.9% of that same population designated as "repeaters"—some of whom may ultimately take a review course. This leads us to another question frequently asked by students: "Why do I have to take this reading class?" The answer to that question varies from institution to institution; however, most institutions require a student to take the reading review class after attempting a certain number of hours (if the exam has not yet been passed).  At Georgia Southern University the policy from the undergraduate catalogue reads: "If a student has earned 45 semester hours of degree credit, the student must take a review or remedial course each semester in attendance until the test [has] been passed." (p. 48).

It is true that many students enrolled in review courses are frustrated, but what if the university system offered no review classes?  After taking the test several times, some repeaters may welcome the opportunity to have some academic assistance so that they have the optimal chance of achieving a passing score.

In regard to the format of the Regents' Reading Test, the Board of Regents states:

> The reading Test, which has an administration time of one hour, is a 54-item, multiple-choice test that consists of nine reading passages and five to eight questions about each passage. The passages usually range from 175 to 325 words in length and treat topics drawn from a variety of subject areas (social science, mathematics and natural science, and humanities).  Students' responses to the items of the Reading Test are recorded on machine-readable answer sheets so that these responses can be read and scored by computer. A standard score is used to describe the Reading Test performance of each examinee. This score is derived by translating the student's total raw score (number-right) on the test to a Rasch scaled score with a range from 0-99.  The minimum passing score on this scale is 61.
>
> (University System of Georgia, website)

The following raw scale score is found on the University System of Georgia's Regents' Testing Program website (www.gsu.edu/~wwwrtp/form231.htm).

**The following table may be used to compute scale scores for this practice test.**

Raw Score to Scaled Score Conversion Table
for Form 23 of the Regents' Reading Test

| Raw Score** | Scaled Score | Raw Score | Scaled Score |
|---|---|---|---|
| 1 | 6 | 31 | 53 |
| 2 | 13 | 32 | 54 |
| 3 | 18 | 33 | 55 |
| 4 | 21 | 34 | 56 |
| 5 | 24 | 35 | 57 |
| 6 | 26 | 36 | 58 |
| 7 | 28 | 37 | 59 |
| 8 | 30 | 38 | 60 |
| 9 | 31 | 39 | *61 |
| 10 | 33 | 40 | 62 |
| 11 | 34 | 41 | 63 |
| 12 | 35 | 42 | 64 |
| 13 | 37 | 43 | 66 |
| 14 | 38 | 44 | 67 |
| 15 | 39 | 45 | 68 |
| 16 | 40 | 46 | 70 |
| 17 | 41 | 47 | 72 |
| 18 | 42 | 48 | 74 |
| 19 | 43 | 49 | 76 |
| 20 | 44 | 50 | 78 |
| 21 | 45 | 51 | 82 |
| 22 | 46 | 52 | 86 |
| 23 | 46 | 53 | 93 |
| 24 | 47 | 54 | 99 |
| 25 | 48 | | |
| 26 | 49 | | |
| 27 | 50 | | |
| 28 | 51 | | |
| 29 | 52 | | |
| 30 | 53 | | |

*minimum passing score

From the table you can see that a passing score is 61 for this form of the Regents' Reading Test (this form, Form 23, has been "retired"). The number answered correctly is 39, which means that you can answer fifteen questions incorrectly and pass with a minimum score. Other forms of the test still require a student to achieve a score of 61, but for a passing score, the number correct might change; for example, on one form students may need to answer 40 correctly, while on another form they may need 38 correct answers to be successful.

## OVERVIEW OF READING SKILLS

Reading is an active process that comprises many interrelated skills and abilities. Reading is not just a passive, laborious act. Instead, it is a process that requires quite a bit of energy on the part of the reader: it requires critical thinking. The ability to comprehend text material depends on several factors, such as 1) the background (prior knowledge) the reader brings to the printed page; 2) the reader's vocabulary base, including strategies for unlocking the meanings of unknown words; and 3) the reader's ability to interpret, evaluate, and synthesize the material in a meaningful way.

It is obvious that reading has not taken place unless you read with understanding. Merely knowing most of the words does not mean you are a successful reader. To be truly successful on the Regents' Reading Exam, you must understand the words within the sentences, the sentences within the paragraphs, the paragraphs within the passages. In addition to this, an understanding of the relationships between various components of the passage is necessary. The abilities required for the Regents' Reading Exam are referred to as higher-level reading skills—and these skills must be taught. If you have not previously been instructed in these skills areas, then it is unlikely that you have magically acquired them on your own. This may be the major reason why many students will benefit from taking the Regents' Reading review course—they will have the opportunity to perfect their higher-level reading skills.

There are four basic skills areas you will need to master for the reading portion of the Regents' Exam: vocabulary enhancement, literal comprehension, inferential comprehension, and analysis. In the chapters that follow, you will find a description of the skills and exercises designed to practice them.

---

REMEMBER: *There are four basic skills areas students need to understand in order to enhance their being successful on the Regents' Reading Exam:*

> *Vocabulary in Context*          *Literal Comprehension*
> *Inference*                               *Analysis*

## OTHER STRATEGIES FOR REGENTS' READING EXAMS

Consider these strategies for improving your score on the reading portion of the exam:

First, because there are nine passages on the test and 60 minutes is allowed, give yourself about six (6) minutes to spend on each passage. Practice limiting yourself to six minutes before you sit for the exam to get a sense of how long it takes you per selection.

Second, you can answer many literal comprehension questions in the same time it takes you to answer one main idea question. Within a passage, if there is a main idea question that is difficult to answer, skip it and come back to it after you have answered the "easier" questions. Answering the literal questions first may help you formulate an answer for the main idea. If you still cannot answer the main idea and are spending too much time on it, skip it and come back to it later if you have time. (*Note*: there are probably no more than five to six main idea questions on the entire test, so this strategy will not defeat you; it should help you.)

Third, since the test score is based on number right, do not leave any items blank. An educated guess is better than leaving a blank and knowing for certain you will get the answer wrong.

Fourth, it is better not to read the questions before you read the passage. If you read the questions first the last time you took the test, then you already know that strategy did not work for you. Two negative consequences could occur from reading the questions before reading the selection: one, you could read the question wrong which will "color" how you read the passage; and two, you could obsess on one question and not absorb other critical information in the passage. Therefore, read the passage first as quickly as you can while concentrating, then look at the questions.

Fifth, when you come across inference questions, do not skip them. There are too many of them to skip without penalizing yourself; rather, utilizing the strategy you have learned in this text, look for clues that will give you the answer.

Sixth, to answer Vocabulary and Analysis questions, rely on the signal words and indicators you learned in this textbook.

Seventh, because material for the exam is chosen from a variety of disciplines across the curriculum, you already have some prior knowledge about various topics. The more you read your college textbooks before taking the exam, the more prior knowledge you will have—and the more vocabulary you will recognize. While taking the exam, depend on any background information you possess about a subject. The more you know about a topic, the faster you will be able to process the information presented on the Regents' Reading Exam.

## A NOTE ABOUT TEST ANXIETY

Because some students are affected by test anxiety, a test anxiety scale along with suggestions for helping yourself are provided in Appendix A.

# CHAPTER TWO

## VOCABULARY (18% to 24%)

Each passage on the Regents' Reading Exam may include at least one underlined word that you must analyze. This means that a total of nine to thirteen questions of the test may entail vocabulary. To achieve mastery of the vocabulary items on the test, you must be prepared to identify the meanings of words as they are used in passages. Since a dictionary is not allowed into the testing situation, the student will rely heavily on his or her ability to use context clues.

It is not a good idea to answer a vocabulary question hurriedly—some of you may feel you already know the definition of a word. However, a word can have many different meanings or shades of meaning depending on the way it is used in the sentence, so automatically choosing the first recognizable answer may not benefit you. In addition, students sometimes make a mistake by staring just at the underlined word, ignoring the words that surround the vocabulary word. If you isolate the word, you may miss a clue that actually gives you the meaning.

Context (the words, sometimes the sentences, around the underlined word) frequently clarifies the meaning of the unknown word. Often, especially on the reading portion of the Regents' Exam, a familiar word is used in an unfamiliar sense; therefore, you need to analyze the "situation" of the unknown word a little closer. Most of the time, if you add some context to the isolated underlined word, you will be able to formulate an approximate meaning because the added context will provide clues.

Context clues (the clues which help you determine the meaning of the word) may be found very close to the underlined word on the Regents' Reading Exam. They may be in the same sentence, the sentence before the underlined word, or the sentence after the underlined word. Therefore, it is best not to view the word in isolation but to read *all the words and sentences surrounding the unknown word*, the context.

In addition to unlocking the meaning of the underlined word, you will also be required to recognize the words given as answer choices. When taking the Regents' Reading Exam, have you ever thought that you comprehended the underlined word only to look at the answer choices and not recognize one word listed? Because these options are given in isolation, context will not be of any help. There are, however, several strategies that will aid you, and they are discussed in this chapter.

*Exercise 1.* Consider for a moment these vocabulary words that are in isolation (they have no context). How many of them can you define? Write a definition for the words, tear out this page, then place this sheet under your desk; you will return to it later.

obi                    _____

lucid                  _____

raw score              _____

meticulous             _____

charismatics           _____

condiments             _____

garrulous              _____

penury                 _____

oxidized               _____

ebullient              _____

## Context Clues

How can the reader determine the meaning of an unknown word by using a strategies that focus on context clues?  Writers very often

### 1.  DIRECTLY DEFINE A WORD/DESCRIBE A WORD

> Decorative *obi*, or wide sashes, are worn with kimonos during festive occasions.

Direct definition may be signaled by punctuation as in the example above.  The commas alert the reader that the definition "wide sashes" is nearby.

---

**REMEMBER:**  *When you encounter an underlined word on the Regents' Reading Exam and do not know the meaning, look for these:  commas, colons, dashes, parentheses, or brackets.*

*Phrases/words that alert the reader that a definition of the unknown word is nearby are:*
  *-any form of the verb **to be***
  *-**or** (equating two things)*
  *-the phrase **that is,***
  *-the word **since***
  *-the word **because.***

---

**Example A**.  That concept is very lucid now *because* the professor used a visual aid.

Notice that the word "because" signals that the definition/description is about to be given: the "professor utilizing a visual aid" would certainly make concepts more clear.  Therefore, the underlined word lucid must mean *clear*.

**Example B**.  The final score is derived by translating the student's raw score *(*number of correct answers*)* on the test to a scaled score.

Note that the information within the parentheses actually defines the underlined word; therefore, raw score means *number of correct answers*.

Authors might even

### 2.  DIRECTLY EQUATE TWO OR MORE THINGS BY USING THE WORD "AND" OR BY LISTING

**Example A**.  My cousin is an extremely <u>meticulous</u>, detailed, orderly, and
conscientious individual.

Since the word "and" equates things, <u>meticulous</u> must be similar in meaning to the words
*detailed*, *orderly*, and *conscientious*.

Third, writers may

### 3.  GIVE AN EXAMPLE OF THE WORD

**Example A**.  The behavior of <u>charismatics</u> *such as* Hitler or Jim Jones
has long been studied by sociologists and psychologists as well as
historians.

Although you may not be familiar with Jim Jones (a minister who enticed approximately
900 of his followers to commit suicide), you have most likely heard of Hitler.  Since you
know that Hitler had a huge following and that people surrounding him obeyed his every
wish, you may deduce that a charismatic is *someone with a magnetic personality*.  By the
way, the word "charisma" (from which "charismatic" derives) does not always connote
something good; it may also connote something or someone evil.

**Example B**.  <u>Condiments</u> like mustard, salt, and pepper are abundant in
developed countries.

Because you are given common words (*mustard, salt, pepper*) you have an excellent idea of
what a condiment is.

---

**REMEMBER:**  *Definition by example may be signaled by these words and phrases:* ***such as,
like, as, the following, for example,*** *or* ***for instance.***

---

In addition, writers

### 4.  CONTRAST THE WORD WITH ONE YOU ALREADY KNOW

**Example A**.  *Whereas* Stefani is very *quiet*, Kaley is extremely <u>garrulous</u>.

Since you know the meaning of the word *quiet*, then by contrast you know the meaning of

<u>garrulous</u>, talkative!   Your signal word, of course, is "whereas," which tells you there is a contrast within the sentence.

> **Example B**.  The festivities during Carnival in Rio de Janiero, Brazil give some tourists the impression that Brazil is a wealthy country.  *On the contrary*, the majority of the population live in a state of <u>penury</u>.

You know the meaning of the word "wealthy," and you know that *on the contrary* is a contrast phrase; you also know that the opposite of wealthy is poor.  What is the noun form of the adjective poor?  Yes, poverty.  Thus, <u>penury</u> means poverty.

---

**REMEMBER:**  *Contrast context clues are signaled by these words and phrases:*
***whereas, or, but, however, although, though, on the contrary, unlike, conversely, or on the other hand.***

---

Next, writers can

### 5.  PRESENT A CAUSE-EFFECT SITUATION

> **Example A**.  Josef left the metal bat out in the rain; *so*, when he went to retrieve it he found that it had <u>oxidized</u>.

You have all learned from your basic science class that metal will rust if left out in the weather.  So, <u>oxidized</u> must mean *rusted*.  The **CAUSE** (leaving the bat out in the rain) results in the **EFFECT** (the bat rusted).

---

**REMEMBER:** *Definition by cause-effect may be signaled by these words and phrases:*
***because, so, thus, consequently, therefore, since, if....then.***

---

Sixth, writers may

### 6.  HINT AT THE MEANING THROUGH LONG EXPLANATION

> **Example A**.  Mikya was a cheerleader.  Her smile, her enthusiasm,

her lively actions, her excitement about the upcoming game always attracted people. I never knew such an <u>ebullient</u> girl.

How would you define <u>ebullient</u>?

In regard to the context clue Long Explanation, you are alerted to the meaning of an unknown word through a pattern called "description." The explanation is often several sentences in length and is usually loaded with adjectives or other "describing words." What are the "describing words" in Example A? The words "smile" and "enthusiasm," for example, tell you what Mikya's personality is like. Are there any other words that give you a clue as to what <u>ebullient</u> means?

---

**REMEMBER**: *Definition by Long Explanation is signaled by the pattern of organization called Description. The explanation is often several sentences in length and full of adjectives.*

---

*NOTE*: In addition to these five basic context clues, the student should always consider COMMON SENSE as well. If a sentence states: "The butterfly <u>flitted</u> from bush to bush," with the underlined word being <u>flitted</u>, common sense tells us there are not that many things a butterfly can do. As a result of using your common sense, you are indeed able to narrow down the options.

---

*Exercise 2.* Do you remember the list of words under your desk? Pick it up again and consider the words once more. Now write a definition for those words that were in isolation. How many of them do you know now? Can you see how context really aids you in determining the meaning of an unknown word?

*obi*                     _____

Decorative <u>obi</u>, or wide sashes, are worn with kimonos during festive occasions.

*lucid*                   _____

That concept is very <u>lucid</u> now *because* the professor used a visual aid.

*charismatics*                    _____

The behavior of <u>charismatics</u> *such as* Hitler or Jim Jones has long been studied by sociologists and psychologists as well as <u>historians</u>.

*condiments*                      _____

<u>Condiments</u> like mustard, salt, and pepper are abundant in developed countries.

*raw score*                       _____

The final score is derived by translating the student's <u>raw</u> <u>score</u> *(*number of correct answers*)* on the test to a scaled score.

*meticulous*                      _____

My cousin is an extremely <u>meticulous</u>, detailed, orderly, and conscientious individual.

*garrulous*                       _____

*Whereas* Stefani is very *quiet*, Kaley is extremely <u>garrulous</u>.

*penury*                          _____

The festivities during Carnival in Rio de Janiero, Brazil give some tourists the impression that Brazil is a wealthy country. *On the contrary*, the majority of the population live in a state of <u>penury</u>.

*oxidized* _____

Josef left the metal bat out in the rain; *so*, when he went to retrieve it, he found that it had <u>oxidized</u>.

*ebullient* _____

Mikya was a cheerleader. Her smile, her enthusiasm, her lively actions, her excitement about the upcoming game always attracted people. I never knew such an <u>ebullient</u> girl.

*Exercise 3.* Are you ready to try more words in isolation? Take a stab at these; then, tear them out and place them under your desk.

1. pungent      _____

2. shrouded      _____

3. disheveled      _____

4. circa      _____

5. facilitate      _____

6. succulent      _____

7. regress      _____

8. eluding      _____

9. audible      _____

10. imminent      _____

*Exercise 4.* In this exercise, there are three steps. First, you are to read the sentence and write a meaning for the underlined word. Second, you are to recognize the key word, phrase, and/or punctuation that alerted you to the meaning. Third, you are to write the context clue that aided you.

1. A <u>pungent</u> odor came from the bushes where we spotted a skunk.

meaning of <u>pungent</u>: strong

key words/phrases/punctuation: skunk

context clue:

2. The dark-<u>shrouded</u> shapes, dressed as ghosts, appeared from around the corner to join the other Halloween trick-or-treaters!

meaning of <u>shrouded</u>: costume

key words/phrases/punctuation:

context clue:

3. Her <u>disheveled</u> appearance made us think she had just woken up: unbuttoned clothing, sleepy eyes, and strands of hair whipping in all directions.

meaning of <u>disheveled</u>: messy, sloppy

key words/phrases/punctuation:

context clue:

4. The time frame in regard to when the antique Chinese chest was built was not clear—<u>circa</u> WWI or even earlier.

meaning of <u>circa</u>: Approx. date

key words/phrases/punctuation:

context clue:

5.  Most teachers <u>facilitate</u> learning; however, a few make it difficult to learn.

meaning of <u>facilitate</u>:

key words/phrases/punctuation:

context clue:

6.  The peach I bought at a fruit stand off Georgia Interstate 16 was <u>succulent</u> and juicy—the best I have ever eaten.

meaning of <u>succulent</u>:

key words/phrases/punctuation:

context clue:

7.  When it comes to their careers, many young adults progress; but, when it comes to their relationships, some <u>regress</u>!

meaning of <u>regress</u>:

key words/phrases/punctuation:

context clue:

8.  The prisoner was incredible at <u>eluding</u>, evading, and all together avoiding law enforcement officers.

meaning of <u>eluding</u>:

key words/phrases/punctuation:

context clue:

9. The captain of the regiment was shouting, face purple, his voice barely <u>audible</u> above the uproar.

meaning of <u>audible</u>:

key words/phrases/punctuation:

context clue:

10. For days the citizens of Savannah hunkered down in their homes, their apartments, their residence halls. According to the broadcasts, today was the day. It seemed that the hurricane was <u>imminent</u> off the coast of Tybee Island: winds were increasing, small trees were being uprooted, power lines were swaying, and the sky was darkening.

meaning of <u>imminent</u>:

key words/phrases/punctuation:

context clue:

*Exercise 5.* Remember that list sitting under your desk? Take a look at it now. You can probably define all of those isolated words now. Write the definitions next to the word.

*Exercise 6.* In this exercise, there are three steps. First, you are to read the sentence and choose the meaning of the underlined word by circling it. Second, you are to recognize the key word, phrase, and/or punctuation that alerted you to the meaning. Third, you are to write the context clue that aided you.

Myra's past was well-documented; Bill's, on the other hand, was <u>dubious</u>.

1. The word <u>dubious</u> most nearly means

a. sketchy.
b. irresistible.
c. certain.

key words/phrases/punctuation:_____

context clue: _____

2. The puppy heard the <u>lash</u> of her master's voice, so she scurried back to the safety of the doghouse.

As used in the sentence, <u>lash</u> is best defined as

a. whip.
b. sharpness.
c. sweetness.

key words/phrases/punctuation:_____

context clue: _____


3. A <u>craft</u> of indescribable type, the *Catherine Sermo* was long, low-sided, multi-oared, and blunt-prowed. The muddy waters of the Cape reached within six inches of her rail.

The word <u>craft</u> most nearly means a

a. ship.
b. piece of artwork.
c. form or shape.

key words/phrases/punctuation:_____

context clue: _____


4. Ian was not <u>enthused at</u> the prospect of paying for such an expensive textbook he would never even glance at again.

As underlined in the sentence, the phrase <u>enthused at</u> can be defined as

a. excited about.
b. angered about.
c. responsible for.

key words/phrases/punctuation:_____

context clue: _____

5. Many immigrants arrive at the shores of the United States hungry, penniless, and destitute.


Destitute, as underlined, signifies

a. pathetic.
b. sympathetic.
c. poor.


key words/phrases/punctuation:_____

context clue: _____


6. The slaying or killing of the lamb was a ritual of some ancient tribes.


As utilized in the sentence, slaying means

a. preparing.
b. killing.
c. raising.

key words/phrases/punctuation:_____

context clue: _____


7. When the young boy stepped on the rattlesnake, he suppressed the urge to run.

The word suppressed most nearly means

a. succumbed to.
b. submitted to.
c. curbed.

key words/phrases/punctuation:_____

context clue: _____

8. Althea continued to work at the humane society, though she received no <u>remuneration</u> like cash, county check, or cashier's check.

<u>Remuneration</u> can be defined as

a. reason.
b. training.
c. payment.

key words/phrases/punctuation:_____

context clue: _____


9. In New York City some women are learning to <u>fend off</u> attackers. They are taking martial arts and enrolling in courses on how to handle a handgun. Some women are attending the police academy that offers educational courses for citizens. Others are now carrying pepper spray.

The phrase <u>fend off</u>, as underlined, most nearly means

a. keep away.
b. go along with.
c. destroy.

key words/phrases/punctuation:_____

context clue: _____


10. The woman <u>implored</u> the judge to be fair in the distribution of the property for her child's sake.

As used in the sentence, <u>implored</u> signifies

a. asked.
b. told.
c. begged.

key words/phrases/punctuation:_____

context clue:

*Exercise 7.* Using context and your knowledge of grammar and parts of speech, determine an appropriate "fit"; then fill in the blanks with the correct word. Choose from the list provided.

|  |  |  |
|---|---|---|
| doubt | impressive | psychiatrists |
| everyone | dreams | meant |

     The Victorians had dream books, which said quite straightforwardly that to dream of a black cat (1)_____ good luck, or that to dream of a violet meant love. At the other extreme, psychologists and (2)_____ have used dreams as a help in analyzing their patients. But no one now accepts that one person's (3)_____ can mean the same as another's dreams. Everybody dreams. This has been experimentally established beyond any (4)_____ . Some people have almost complete recall of their dreams; most of us remember a few elements of our dreams, and occasionally recall in great detail a dream which seems to be especially (5)_____, especially important. And almost (6)_____ has the feeling that some dreams, at least, have something interesting to say to us.

                                      -Parker, p. 7

|  |  |  |
|---|---|---|
| school board | evacuated | continental |
| confronted with | disastrous | interned |
| levied upon |  |  |

     After 1885, thousands of Japanese men came to the (7)_____ United States from their homeland, often via Hawaii. Following on the heels of harassment, acts of violence, and legal restrictions (8)_____ _____Chinese immigrants, it should be no surprise that the 22,000 Japanese who had come to America by 1900 were (9)_____ _____ a variety of challenges.
     The "Yellow Peril" had become such a specter that in 1906 the San Francisco (10)_____ _____ ruled that Japanese American school children must attend special schools. [It was later revealed that only 93 children out of a school population of 25,000 were Japanese.]
     The insecurity of Japanese life in America hardened when the two nations went to war. The surprise attack by Japan upon Pearl Harbor had (11)_____ results for Japanese citizens of the United States. By the spring of 1942, 70,000 American citizens of Japanese ancestry, as well as some 40,000 nonresidents, were forcibly (12)_____ from their homes on the West Coast and (13)_____ in several "relocation centers."
                                          -Solberg, pp. 326-329

*Exercise 8.* Read the passage below from *The Lord of the Rings: The Return of the King* and answer the vocabulary questions that follow.

> Pippin looked out from the shelter of Gandalf's cloak.  Sleepily he tried to reckon the times and stages of their journey, but his memory was <u>drowsy</u> and uncertain.  There had been the first ride at terrible speed without a halt, and then in the dawn he had seen a pale gleam of gold, and they had come to the great empty house on the hill.  And hardly had they reached its shelter when the <u>winged shadow</u> had passed over once again, and men wilted with fear. This was the second, no, the third night since he had looked into the Stone.  And with that <u>heinous</u> memory he woke fully, and shivered.  Pippin <u>cowered back</u>, afraid for a moment, wondering into what dreadful country Gandalf was bearing him.                -Tolkien, p. 3

1. The word, <u>drowsy</u>, as underlined in the passage, is best defined as

1. asleep.
2. foggy.
3. clear.

2. The phrase <u>winged shadow</u> connotes a creature that is

1. angelic.
2. religious.
3. frightful.

3. <u>Heinous</u>, as used in the passage, most nearly means

1. repulsive.
2. glorious.
3. sleepy.

4. The phrase <u>cowered back,</u> used in the last sentence, can best be defined as

1. pulled away.
2. moved toward.
3. shrank away from.

Read the passage below adapted from *Nefertiti Resurrected* and answer the vocabulary questions that follow.

In the study of ancient Egypt, Queen Nefertiti is perhaps better known than her husband, the heretic king Akhenaten. It is said that even in the ancient world, her beauty was famous. She was more than a pretty face, however, for she seems to have taken an <u>unprecedented</u> level of importance in the Amarna period of Egypt's history. In artwork, her status is evident and indicates that she had almost as much influence as her husband. For example, she is <u>depicted</u> nearly twice as often as her husband, at least during the first five years of his reign. Indeed, she is once even shown in the pose (with sword dripping with blood) of a pharaoh <u>smiting</u> the enemy, a job traditionally reserved for males.

We know that Akhenaten and Nefertiti had six daughters, but it was probably with another royal wife called Kiya that the king sired his successors. Nefertiti also shared her husband with other royal wives, but undoubtedly, Akhenaten seems to have had a great love for his Chief Royal wife. They were shown as inseparable in early artworks, many of which showed their family in loving and <u>utopian</u> scenes. At times, the king is shown riding with her in a chariot, kissing her in public and allowing her to sit on his knee.

In the end, it was the figure of Nefertiti that Akhenaten had carved onto the four corners of his granite <u>sarcophagus</u>, providing protection to his mummy inside.

Towards the end of Akhenaten's reign, Nefertiti disappeared from historical Egyptian records and her burial place has never been found. What could have happened to her? Though not all researchers agree with her, Joanne Fletcher from the University of York in England announced that she and her team may have identified the actual mummy of the Queen. She said that the mummy had deteriorated badly; that the skull was pierced with a large hole, and the chest hacked away. Worse still, the face, which would otherwise have been excellently preserved, had been cruelly <u>maimed,</u> the mouth and cheek no more than a gaping hole.

So controversy swirls around Nefertiti. At best, someday we may know more about this <u>intriguing</u> queen, but until then we can only make guesses about her life, as well as her death.
                                                                 -Internet address and Discovery Channel

5. In the passage the underlined word, <u>sarcophagus</u>, most nearly means

1. palace.
2. temple.
3. coffin.
4. pyramid.

6. In the passage the underlined word, <u>maimed</u>, most nearly means

1. thrown aside.
2. wrapped.
3. painted.
4. mutilated.

7. In the passage the underlined word, <u>depicted</u>, most nearly means

1. illustrated.
2. denounced.
3. lowered.
4. ignored.

8. In the passage the underlined word, <u>smiting</u>, most nearly means

1. slicing.
2. welcoming.
3. showing mercy.
4. scolding.

9. In the passage the underlined word, <u>unprecedented</u>, most nearly means

1. low.
2. extraordinary.
3. insignificant.
4. marginal.

10. In the passage the underlined word, <u>intriguing</u>, most nearly means

1. corrupt.
2. fascinating.
3. malicious.
4. pretty.

## OTHER STRATEGIES FOR UNLOCKING THE MEANING OF UNKNOWN WORDS

There are two major reasons students do not do as well as they want to on the vocabulary portions of the exam.

First, there may be too many technical words within the passage. Notice how difficult the following passage is to read:

> The term fossil has been variously used, but is here interpreted to be an evidence, direct or indirect, of existence of organisms in prehistoric time. An exact definition as to what constitutes a fossil, or an upper limit of prehistoric time, is difficult to establish. Are the remains (of a mastodon or hairy mammoth) fossils, when they are still well enough preserved that the meat can be eaten rather palatably, even though the animals lived in the Pleistocene? The upper fringe of prehistoric time is a difficult and sometimes arbitrary area in the definition of the term fossil.
>
> -Peterson, p. 74

Look how many terms are not "common" to the English vocabulary! Though an anthropologist may have not trouble comprehending this excerpt, I doubt too many individuals would be comfortable reading this selection. In fact, they may have to read it twice to get the gist of the passage. Why is this particular passage so difficult?

1. Most of the highlighted words and phrases are "technical"—that is, not words in common, everyday usage.
2. Ordinary words that you might know are not used in their "regular" way.
3. Because the unknown words force a reader to hesitate and break the flow of comprehension, a reader has to read the same sentence over again, thus wasting time and making the "read" a frustrating experience.

Second, students sometimes complain that even though they can get a good sense of the meaning of the underlined word from context, they do not know some of the meanings of the answer choices (which appear, of course, in isolation). Consider this instance:

**Example**: As underlined in the third paragraph, the word <u>hireling</u> most nearly means

    1. employer
    2. mercenary
    3. venal
    4. mercantile

When considering the example, you may have an idea from the context (not provided here) that <u>hireling</u> means someone who is hired. So, number 1 as a choice can be eliminated. However, what happens if you do not know the meanings of #2, #3, or #4? It will be almost impossible to choose correctly.

What should a student do to overcome these dilemmas? In actuality, you will most likely **NOT** encounter such an overloaded, "technical" passage as the one above on the Regents' Reading Exam, though you will encounter some technical words. It is imperative, though, to increase the number of words in your personal database so that while taking the exam you are not forced to hesitate and lose the flow of meaning. The best strategy is to strengthen your general vocabulary *before the exam*. Other than knowledge of Context Clues, there are two effective ways you can enhance your vocabulary.

First, increase your knowledge of word structure (prefixes, suffixes, and roots). You probably came across lists of word parts when studying for the SAT or other standardized tests. The following section will arm you with knowledge of word parts and improve your chances of decoding the unknown words you encounter on the Regents' Reading Exam.

Second, it is worth a student's time to do as much vocabulary buildup as possible months before the exam on his/her own. Make lists or stacks of index cards (of words you want to incorporate into your existing vocabulary base) when reading current articles in magazines, listening to words used in conversation, listening to words used in lectures, reading novels, or reading the newspaper. You may be surprised how quickly your knowledge base expands.

## Word Structure

Where did English words originate? Most words used in our language are not originally English; they derive from Greek or Latin.

English words can be made up of three parts:

1. a prefix that appears in front of the base element (root)
2. a root that is the base element of the word
3. a suffix attached at the end of the base element (root)

Consider the word, *sympathetic*, in respect to where it originated and how it can be broken down into word parts:

|  | **Prefix** | **Root** | **Suffix** |
|---|---|---|---|
|  | *sym* | *pathe* | *(t)ic* |
| *meaning*: | *same* | *feeling* | *pertaining to* |
| origin: | **(Greek)** | **(Greek)** | **(Greek)** |

Referring to the Affixes/Roots Chart 1 below, what would you think the following word means?

|  |  |  |
|---|---|---|
|  | *apathetic* |  |
| *a* | *pathe* | *(t)ic* |

Write a meaning here:

## Chart 1. Useful Affixes/Roots

| | |
|---|---|
| a- | without |
| ab- | away from |
| ad- | toward |
| am- | love |
| anim | life |
| anthrop | mankind |
| annu | yearly |
| anti- | against |
| -ate | to cause |
| auto- | self |
| aud | hear |
| bene | good |
| biblio | book |
| bio | life |
| cide | killing |
| cogn | know |
| con-, com | together |
| contra- | against |
| cred | believe |
| dic, dict | say |
| equ, equi | equal |
| ex- | out |
| extra- | over and above |
| gamy | marriage |
| gen | people, race |
| graph | write |
| habit | dwell |
| hom | man |
| in-, im- | not |
| inter- | between |
| -ic | pertaining to |
| -ist, -er, -or, -ant | one who |
| -less | without |
| -logy | study of |
| mal- | bad |
| matri, mater | mother |
| mort | death |
| multi- | many |
| non- | not |
| omni- | all |

Chart 1., continued

| -ous | full of |
|------|---------|
| -pathe, pathy | feeling |
| per | through |
| poly- | many |
| port | carry |
| potent | power |
| post- | after |
| pre- | before |
| pseudo- | false |
| re- | again |
| sca | climb |
| somn | sleep |
| spect, spic | see |
| sub- | under |
| sui | self |
| super- | over and above |
| sym-, syn- | same |
| ten | hold |
| terre | earth |
| -tion | act of |
| trans- | across |
| ven, ventu | come |

As you can readily see, by changing the prefix you can totally change the meaning of a word. To illustrate further, consider words with the root, *cide*. You know the meaning of *suicide*, but did you know that the prefix *sui-* means "self"? And *cide*, of course, means "killing." Therefore, the word is interpreted as "self-killing," or "killing of self."

If you changed the prefix, *sui-*, the meaning of the word would change. How many different words can be made with the root, *cide*?

*Exercise 9.* Consulting Chart 1 or using your existing knowledge of vocabulary, give a meaning for these words that have *cide* as their root.

1. aborticide          _____

2. biocide             _____

3. elephanticide       _____

4. fratricide          _____

5. insecticide         _____

6. genocide            _____

7. homicide            _____

8. matricide           _____

9. pesticide           _____

10. parenticide        _____


Do you see the power of this strategy?  You have already increased your knowledge of words related to the root, *cide*, tenfold!

*Exercise 10.*  Referring to Chart 1, assign meaning to the "nonsense" words below and then try to choose the correct meaning from Column B.

**Column A**                        **Column B**

_____1. abanthrop                  a.  P.S.

_____2. antimort                   b.  sympathetic

_____3. equipathetic               c.  everlasting

_____4. mortate                    d.  supervisor

_____5. beneless                   e.  emotional

_____6. multigamy                  f.  the world

_____7. extrapathy                 g.  kill

_____8. postgraph                  h.  bigamy

_____9. superspector               i.  a hermit

_____10. omniterre                 j.  bad

*Exercise 11.* Integrating knowledge of prefixes, roots, and suffixes as well as context clues, write a meaning of the affix and base element, and then give a meaning for the underlined word.

1. Famous people are always wearing sunglasses, making their eyes <u>inconspicuous</u>.

in-:_____

spic:_____

meaning of word: _____


2. His hateful comments seemed to roll off her back; she was <u>impervious</u> to them

im-:_____

per:_____

meaning of word: _____


3. Some tyrants, such as Attila the Hun, believe they are <u>omnipotent</u>.

omni-:_____

potent: _____

meaning of word: _____


4. Grandmama couldn't see the instructions on her medicine bottle, so she got out her <u>spectacles</u> and placed them on her nose.

spec: _____

meaning of word: _____


5. I asked my friend for the hundredth time not to <u>intervene</u> in my affairs.

inter-:_____

vene: _____

Meaning of word: _____

6. My sister Tootsie hurt my feelings, but I finally realized her intentions were <u>benign.</u>

ben: _____

meaning of word: _____

7. When Theron went to the red-carpet ceremony, he was able to get a few <u>autographs</u> of celebrities.

auto-: _____

graph: _____

meaning of word: _____

8. The crowd's anger was "mild" at first, but then <u>escalated</u> into violent, mob mentality.

sca: _____

meaning of word: _____

9. Over time, Steve has searched for the Fountain of Youth, having a desire to be <u>immortal.</u>

im-: _____

mort: _____

meaning of word: _____

10. When Henry VIII claimed that he would replace the Pope, many at court thought his announcement <u>incredulous</u>.

in-: _____

cred: _____

-ous: _____

meaning of word: _____

## Identifying Vocabulary Questions

It is easy to recognize vocabulary questions on Regents' Reading Exams since the word itself is underlined in the question and in the passage. Use your scanning skills to quickly locate the underlined word in the passage. Question stems may be worded as follows:

-"(the underlined word), as used in the passage, most nearly means . . ."
-"As used in paragraph three, (the underlined word) is best defined as . . ."
- "(the underlined word) may be defined as . . ."

Now, go to Simulated Exam One, Six, or Ten to test your new Vocabulary in Context skills and your knowledge of Word Structure.

# CHAPTER THREE

## LITERAL COMPREHENSION (18% to 24%)

This kind of question requires you to recognize specific details. There will be about ten to thirteen literal comprehension questions on the Regents' Reading Exam. In regard to literal questions, a reader can find the answer to the question asked by merely looking back at the passage. Many literal comprehension questions ask for a name or a number, and it is only a matter of seconds before the student can point to the exact information in the passage (usually Arabic numbers or words that begin with a capital letter). In fact, Wassman and Rinsky say that an average reader scans approximately 1,000 words per minute. Perhaps this is the reason most students answer literal comprehension questions faster than any other type of question: their eyes will pick up numbers and capital letters very quickly, providing them with "literal" answers.

Once you have read the passage, you may come upon a literal comprehension question. The most efficient way to find the specific information is to put your index figure at the top of the passage (in the middle of the passage) and move it straight down the middle to the end of the passage. As your index finger moves down the page, your eyes will glimpse capital letters (which will answer *who, where,* and *what)*, numbers (which will answer *when, how many,* and *how much)*, and underlined words (which designate vocabulary questions) in a matter of seconds. (*Note*: According to some reading experts, scanning the traditional way of moving your eyes from left to right may slow you down when reading columned material.)

You should have confidence when answering the literal comprehension questions on the Regents' Reading Exam; after all, you have been answering these kinds of questions for many of your school years.

## Identifying Literal Comprehension Questions

Literal comprehension questions themselves may be recognized by the following words and phrases which appear in the question stem:

| *who* | *what* | *where* | *how much* | *how many* |
|-------|--------|---------|------------|------------|
| *when* | *according to the passage, what....* | | | *which of the following....* |

*Exercise 1.* Read the brief paragraphs (found in a textbook on disasters) and answer the literal comprehension questions that follow. Notice how quickly you are able to find the answer.

It is not easy to rank catastrophic forest fires. But, as far as human casualties are concerned, the 1871 Peshtigo fire in Wisconsin must be viewed

as one of the worst on record.  The hot and dry summer left the huge forests
in a dangerous dry state.  Lumbering operations, aided by the construction of
railroads, had penetrated the great forest leaving behind large amounts of debris.
Fires in the interior began to merge, and an ominous glow reddened the night sky.
Holbrook, using minimum figures, estimates the regional total deaths at 1,152.

-Ebert, pp. 206-207


1.  What is the name of one of the worst forest fires on record?

2.  Where was the fire?

3.  About how many people died in the fire?

4.  What did lumbering and railroad companies leave behind them after their work was
done?


        The perception of most people is that volcanoes call forth beautiful,
symmetrical cone volcanoes as typified by Mount Fuji in Japan; however,
volcanoes are also viewed as violent destroyers of people, towns, and nature.
In several instances volcanoes killed thousands of humans, and such killer
volcanoes stand out in the memory of humankind: Mt. Pelee (1902), on the
Caribbean island of Martinique, within a few minutes wiped the town of St.
Pierre off the map and killed more than 30,000 people; and more recently in
1985, the giant volcano Nevado del Ruis obliterated the town of Armero in
Colombia killing more than 20,000.                          -Ebert, p. 25

5.  What volcano may people recall when thinking of symmetrical, cone-shaped volcanoes?

6.  What is the name of the volcano that killed more than 30,000 people?

7.  How many people did Nevado del Ruis obliterate?


        On August 7, 1978, the news media all over the U.S. announced that
President Carter had declared a state of emergency at Love Canal in the city
of Niagara Falls, New York.  As early as 1836 the site of Love Canal had been
surveyed because of its favorable setting for the construction of a canal that
would circumvent an escarpment.  The canal was to become the site for an

electrical power plant. The construction project failed, however, and with growing industrialization in the area came increasing amounts of waste materials.

The Love Canal site was studied as a potential dumping location. Hooker Company obtained permission to discard chemical waste into the canal; this operation started in 1942. Between 1942 and 1952 about 21,800 tons of various chemicals were placed into the old canal bed.

In 1953, the Niagara Falls Board of Education obtained the canal zone from Hooker Company for the price of one dollar. Hooker was quite aware of the potential dangers presented by the thousands of tons of chemical waste. The Board of Education built a baseball diamond situated directly on the canal property. Then, several hundred residences were built along new streets that paralleled the canal.

Strong chemical odors were reported in the neighborhood around the canal as early as the mid-1950s: smelly, oily substances oozed out of low-lying spots; damp basement walls emitted a strong smell of chemicals, and a heavy odor hung over the area on warm windless days.

Convincing correlations between birth defects, kidney diseases, leukemia, respiratory illnesses, and a higher-than-average occurrence of cancer in the vicinity of seepage areas are still under study.                                    -Ebert, pp. 278-284

8. List several of the illnesses caused by the Love Canal incident.

9. Who was the president during this time period?

10. How much did Love Canal cost when Hooker Company sold it to the Board of Education?

11. When did chemical waste dumping begin at the Love Canal?

12. In what state is Love Canal located?

13. Name one way in which the people of Love Canal knew there was an environmental problem.

14. How many tons of chemicals were placed in the canal?

15. Who built a baseball field at Love Canal?

The frequency of tornadoes in the U.S. falls within a range of 500 to 600 per year; however, some years had a much greater number. Some of the worst years were 1967 with 912 tornadoes and 1973 when more than 1,100 were reported. For some regions in the U.S. the threat of tornadoes is an ever-present fear.

On the average the largest number of tornadoes occur in the southern plains of Texas, Oklahoma, and Kansas. Even though the total number of annual tornadoes in the United States is large, the statistical probability that a particular place will be visited by this deadly storm is quite small.

-Ebert, p. 110

16.   According to the passage, on average how many tornadoes occur in the United States per year?

_____

17.  In what year did the most tornadoes make landfall in the United States?_____

18.  What three states see the most tornadoes?_____

_____

19. True/False: It is stated that the probability that a tornado will hit a particular place is high.

_____

20. How many tornadoes hit in 1967?_____

*Exercise 2.* Tear this page from your textbook. Read the passage and make ten literal comprehension questions for it. Next, hand your questions to a classmate and have them answer the questions.

As a result of policies initiated by President Nixon in the early 1970s, American Indians were accorded more political and economic sovereignty, proving their success in their own capitalistic endeavors. Perhaps their greatest step toward economic self-sufficiency has been tribal gambling casinos across the nation, resulting in $6 billion in profits in 1995. By implementing the white man's free-enterprise strategies, the tribal council of the Fort Apache Indian Reservation in Arizona earns millions annually from their own land management policies and highly successful ski resort. The Choctaw in Mississippi provide jobs not only for their own people but for 1,000 non-Indians who enter the reservation to work in factories making plastic utensils for McDonald's restaurants, electrical wiring assemblies for automobile plants, and greeting cards.          -Solberg, p. 319

1._____

Classmate's answer:

2._____

Classmate's answer:

3._____

Classmate's answer:

4._____

Classmate's answer:

5._____

Classmate's answer:

6._____

Classmate's answer:

7._____

Classmate's answer:

8._____

Classmate's answer:

9._____

Classmate's answer:

10._____

Classmate's answer:

*Exercise 3*. Now, try some paragraphs from the social sciences. Read the sentences and circle whether or not the literal information is true or false (taken from Kestner and Henslin).

> First identified in 1981, HIV attacks and disables the immune system of the human body, leaving the victim exposed and vulnerable to any number of "opportunistic" diseases that eventually kill. Worldwide, over 20 million people have already died from AIDS, and an additional 50 million people carry the AIDS-related virus. Most recently, the highest levels of new HIV infection in the U.S. are among heterosexuals, particularly females.            -pp. 343-344

1. True/False: The highest levels of new HIV infection in the United States are among heterosexual males.

2. True/False: Worldwide, 50 million people have already died from AIDS.

> According to the data, there is a clear distinction between the perception of increased violence and the actual levels of violence coded in the 15 years of WWF's Wrestlemanias. Interestingly, the National Television Violence Study, the largest study of media content ever undertaken, released its finding in April 1998. One of those findings was that there was no change in the overall level of violence in reality programming across the three years studied. That study, however, did not examine cable programming, the outlet of most professional wrestling.
> What has clearly increased is the popularity of professional wrestling over the last three years. The WWF alone holds approximately 200 live events each year in major arenas. Cable ratings of both the WWF and the WCW have increased to the point that professional wrestling draws over 35 million viewers each week.
> -p. 457

3. True/False: 35 million viewers watch professional wrestling each week.

4. True/False: Over the three years studied, violence in wrestling increased.

5. True/False: The popularity of wrestling has decreased due to the violence.

> Much of the early research on personality characteristics and the incidence of stress-related illness has centered on *Type A* and *Type B* personality types. Characteristics of *Type A* behavior include

competitiveness (viewing everyday events as competitions, whether
it's driving on the freeway or playing a game of cards), time urgency
(a persistent drive not to waste time, doing more than one thing at a time,
becoming impatient with delays), and anger or hostility (the tendency to
take everything personally, to view challenges as personal affronts). Type B
behavior, on the other hand, is characterized by greater passivity and lower
levels of competitiveness and hostility. The easy-going Type B is slow to
anger, and displays greater levels of patience.                      -p. 485

6. True/False: Research on stress has ignored the concepts of *Type A* and *Type B*
   personalities.

7. True/False: *Type As* might get angry at their computers if they do not generate
   information quickly enough.

8. True/False: *Types Bs* frequently show anger.

9. True/False: Competitiveness is a characteristic of a *Type A* personality.

10. True/False: You can describe a *Type B* personality as someone who is laid-back.

*Exercise 4.* Read the two passages below and answer the literal comprehension questions
that follow.

> Mass media reflects women's changing role in society. Although
> media images that portray women as mere background objects remain, a
> new image has broken through. This new image illustrates a fundamental
> change from submissive to dominant in social relations. *Xena, Warrior
> Princess*, is an outstanding example of this change.
> Lara Croft, an adventure-seeking archeologist and star of *Tomb
> Raider* and its many sequels, is the essence of the new gender image. Lara
> is smart, strong, and able to utterly vanquish foes. With both guns blazing,
> she is the cowboy of the twenty-first century. She is the first female protagonist
> in a field of muscle-rippling, gun-toting macho caricatures.              -p. 80

1. The example of Xena is given in the first paragraph. Xena is a

a. mass media broadcaster.
b. warrior princess.
c. lonely housewife.

2. The passage states that images of "women as background objects"

a. still exist.
b. are nonexistent.
c. are unimportant.


3. In the passage, Lara Croft is compared to a(n)

a. archeologist.
b. stereotypical female.
c. cowboy.


4. According to the passage, Lara Croft carries

a. guns.
b. a spear.
c. a chip on her shoulder.


"Impression Management" is not limited to individuals. Families, corporations, colleges, in fact probably all groups, try to manage impressions. So do governments. When on September 11, 2001, Arab terrorists hijacked four commercial airliners and flew three of them into the World Trade Center in New York City and the Pentagon in Washington, D. C., the president was in Florida, speaking at a grade school. For his safety, the Secret Service rushed him into hiding, first to a military base in Louisiana, then to another base in Nebraska. Bush first addressed the nation from these secluded locations. To assure the people that the government was still in control, it wouldn't do for the president to speak while in hiding. He had to get back to Washington. The perceived danger to the president was ruled less important than his presence in the White House. To reassure the public, Bush was flown to Washington, escorted by U.S. Air Force F-16 fighter jets, where that same evening he addressed the American people from within the symbol of power, the Oval Office.     -p. 120


5. It is stated in the passage that Impression Management is

a. limited to individuals.
b. the Secret Service's most important task.
c. most likely a concern for all groups.

6. According to the passage, the president was hidden

a. at the White House.
b. in Florida.
c. at two military bases.

7. Who hijacked commercial airliners on September 11, 2001?

a. the Secret Service
b. terrorists
c. some disgruntled members of the U.S. Air Force

8. Where was the World Trade Center located?

a. New York City
b. Nebraska
c. Louisiana

9. When terrorists hijacked four commercial airliners, the president was

a. in a bunker in Nebraska.
b. at an elementary school in Florida.
c. in the air being escorted by two F-16 fighter jets.

10. In order to give the impression that President Bush was taking care of matters he

a. traveled to New York City.
b. remained at the elementary school.
c. addressed the American public from the White House.

## Identifying a Referent

In addition to detailed questions you may be asked to identify referents. (You may encounter only one or two of these.)  A referent is a word that refers to or alludes to another word in the passage.  That is, referents are used to point the reader back to their origins within the passage.  On the Regents' Reading Exam pronouns are used quite often as referents. You will also find words like *first* and *second* or *former* and *latter* used as referents. Consider this example:

> When we read a book such as *Lord of the Rings: The Fellowship of the Ring* or *Harry Potter and the Sorcerer's Stone*, there is little chance of our mistaking the power struggle between good and evil: the first proclaims the threat of evil to the fellowship; the <u>second</u> relates a threat to Harry and his friends.

On the Regents' Reading exam the word *second* would be underlined. The question would most likely be formed like this:

The underlined word, <u>second,</u> as used in the passage, refers to

1. *Lord of the Rings.*
2. *Harry Potter and the Sorcerer's Stone.*
3. good.
4. evil.

To what is the word *second* referring? Option 2.


*Exercise 5.* Recognizing referents: Write to whom or to what the underlined word is referring.

1. On Saturday, Catie went to her physician for a checkup. It was a routine visit. Let's suppose, however, that the next week she went to the dentist for a cleaning. During that visit, her dentist remarked that her hair was rather long, then took out a pair of scissors and offered to give her a haircut. In the former scenario, everything seemed customary; in the <u>latter</u> scenario, her dentist violated background assumptions: assumptions about how a dentist should act.

<u>Latter</u> refers to:_____


2. To be truly successful on the Regents' Reading Exam, you must understand the words within the sentences, the sentences within the paragraphs, the paragraphs within the passages. In addition to this, an understanding of the relationships between <u>these various components</u> of the passage is necessary.

<u>These various components</u> refers to:_____

## Practice in Scanning

*Exercise 6.* Tear out this page. On the next page there is a page from a Publication List. You will have 90 seconds to scan for and write down the answers to the questions below so work quickly. Your instructor will tell you when to begin.

1. Who wrote *History of Rock & Roll*?_____

2. Which textbook has the most pages?_____

3. Is there a textbook on animal nutrition?_____

4. How many books are written by two authors (indicated by a hyphen)?_____

5. When was *Precalculus* published?_____

6. How many books are about geology?_____

7. What is the name of the literature textbook?_____

8. Was *Hazard South, Kentucky* published in 2004 or 2005?_____

9. How many books have CD supplements?_____

10. Based on this list, what kind of binding is most often used?_____

# Publication Listing

| Author | Title | Discipline | Page Count | Binding | Pub Date |
|--------|-------|------------|-----------|---------|----------|
| WISCONSIN FAST PLANTS PROGRAM | FAST PLANTS SPIRAL: SPANISH | TEACHER RESOURCES | 172 | WC | 08/24/04 |
| JOHNS-BERGLUND | FLUENCY: STRATEGIES | READING | 128 | PF | 02/14/05 |
| CRONIN | FORENSIC PSYCHOLOGY | PSYCHOLOGY | 148 | SW | 08/16/05 |
| HARRIS ET AL | FT: GEOLOGY OF NATIONAL PARKS | GEOLOGY | 896 | FT | 08/30/05 |
| COAST LEARNING SYSTEMS (GEOLOGY) | GEOLOGY BX/ROCKS 0-7575-0479-5 | GEOLOGY | 0 | SW | 03/23/05 |
| MILLER-WRIGHT | GEOLOGY DEATH VALLEY | GEOLOGY | 138 | PF | 11/10/04 |
| HARRIS ET AL | GEOLOGY OF NATIONAL PARKS CD | GEOLOGY | 0 | SW | 08/30/05 |
| COAST LEARNING SYSTEMS (GEOLOGY) | GEOLOGY TX 0-7575-0479-5 | GEOLOGY | 200 | PF | 03/04/05 |
| COAST LEARNING SYSTEMS (GEOLOGY) | GEOLOGY VD 0-7575-0479-5 | GEOLOGY | 0 | SW | 03/01/05 |
| K/H TOPO | GEORGE LAKE, NEBRASKA 4C | REFERENCE | 0 | | 06/23/05 |
| AHF (HARD) | GRADE 1 BIG BOOK 0-7872-6759-7 | HEALTH AND FITNESS | 16 | WC | 06/24/04 |
| K/H TOPO | HAZARD SOUTH, KENTUCKY 5C | REFERENCE | 0 | | 06/23/05 |
| LARSON | HISTORY OF ROCK & ROLL | PERFORMING ARTS | 322 | WC | 02/02/04 |
| LARSON | HISTORY ROCK & ROLL CD | MUSIC | 0 | | 01/22/04 |
| LARSON | HISTORY ROCK CD 0-7575-1527-4 | MUSIC | 0 | SW | 02/25/05 |
| LARSON | HISTORY ROCK TX 0-7575-1527-4 | PERFORMING ARTS | 322 | WC | 05/20/05 |
| HEALTHY LIFESTYLE CHOICES | HLC PROGRAM: GRADE 1 | PHYSICAL EDUCATION | 222 | BI | 08/31/05 |
| HEALTHY LIFESTYLE CHOICES | HLC PROGRAM: GRADE 2 | PHYSICAL EDUCATION | 266 | BI | 08/31/05 |
| HEALTHY LIFESTYLE CHOICES | HLC PROGRAM: GRADE 3 | PHYSICAL EDUCATION | 242 | BI | 09/26/05 |
| HEALTHY LIFESTYLE CHOICES | HLC PROGRAM: GRADE 4 | PHYSICAL EDUCATION | 196 | BI | 09/26/05 |
| HEALTHY LIFESTYLE CHOICES | HLC PROGRAM: GRADE 5 | PHYSICAL EDUCATION | 230 | BI | 09/26/05 |
| HEALTHY LIFESTYLE CHOICES | HLC PROGRAM: GRADE 6 | PHYSICAL EDUCATION | 226 | BI | 09/27/05 |
| HEALTHY LIFESTYLE CHOICES | HLC PROGRAM: GRADE K | PHYSICAL EDUCATION | 236 | BI | 08/31/05 |
| RAUBER ET AL | IM PAK: SEVERE WEATHER | METEOROLOGY | 296 | PL | 04/08/05 |
| JURGENS | IM: ANIMAL FEEDING | ANIMAL FEEDING AND NUTRITION | 742 | SW | 09/23/05 |
| WALKER-BROKAW | IM: BECOMING AWARE | INTERPERSONAL COMMUNICATION | 316 | SW | 07/25/05 |
| ROSS | IM: CELL BIOLOGY & CHEMISTRY | ALLIED HEALTH | 128 | SW | 06/22/05 |
| READENCE ET AL | IM: CONTENT AREA LITERACY | READING | 100 | SW | 08/16/05 |
| ZIMMER | IM: ESSENTIAL MATHEMATICS | MATH | 0 | SW | 08/18/04 |
| COAST LEARNING SYSTEMS (GEOLOGY) | IM: GEOLOGY LAB | GEOLOGY | 80 | SW | 02/03/04 |
| OSSIAN | IM: INSIGHTS...GEOLOGY | GEOLOGY | 84 | SW | 07/26/05 |
| GAYTON-VAUGHN | IM: LEGAL ASPECTS ENGINEERING | ENGINEERING | 124 | | 07/28/04 |
| STASZKOW | IM: MATH SKILLS | MATH | 202 | SW | 09/29/05 |
| WHEELER-WHEELER | IM: MODERN MATHEMATICS | MATH | 224 | SW | 06/18/04 |
| SHANKMAN | IM: PHYSICAL GEOGRAPHY LM | GEOGRAPHY | 230 | SW | 03/12/04 |
| MUNEM-YIZZE | IM: PRECALCULUS | CALCULUS | 780 | SW | 01/15/04 |
| MAKAY | IM: PUBLIC SPEAKING | SPEECH | 318 | SW | 09/12/05 |
| BOLNER-POIRIER | IM: RESEARCH PROCESS | INFORMATION RESEARCH | 112 | SW | 08/05/05 |
| BLIMLING | IM: RESIDENT ASSISTANT | COUNSELING | 90 | SW | 08/09/05 |
| MCKEAGUE | IM: STEP BY STEP LITERATURE | LITERATURE | 196 | SW | 06/28/04 |
| NIELSEN | IM: STRUCTURE & FUNCTION | BIOLOGY | 102 | SW | 09/17/04 |
| BSCS | IM: TEACHING TOOLS CD | BIOLOGY | 0 | | 08/30/04 |
| MILL-MORRISON | IM: TOURISM SYSTEM | HOSPITALITY | 282 | SW | 08/09/05 |

*Exercise 7.* Try your scanning skills again. Tear out this page. Using the material provided from the dictionary on the next page, scan for specific information. Words you are to scan for are in italics. You will have 100 seconds. Your instructor will tell you when to begin.

1. What are the guide words for this dictionary page?_____

2. How many entries are there for *Murray*?_____

3. Where is *Murfreesboro*?_____

4. How many definitions are given for the word *muscle*?_____

5. What part of speech is the word *muscid*?_____

6. From what language does the word *muriate* derive?_____

7. *Muscat* is the capital of what country?_____

8. What is a *muscadine*?_____

9. On what peninsula is *Murmansk*?_____

10. Is the *Mures* a river or a mountain?_____

hard, unsafe, or disagreeable to do or deal with —*vt.* 1. to kill (a person) unlawfully and with malice 2. to kill inhumanly or barbarously, as in warfare 3. to spoil, mar, etc., as in performance [a song *murdered* in the rendition] —*vi.* to commit murder —*SYN.* see KILL[1] —☆get away with murder [Slang] to escape detection of or punishment for a blameworthy act —murder will out 1. a murder or murderer will always be revealed 2. any secret or wrongdoing will be revealed sooner or later —**mur′der·er** *n.* —**mur′der·ess** *n.fem.*

**mur·der·ous** (-əs) *adj.* 1. of, having the nature of, or characteristic of murder; brutal [a *murderous* act] 2. capable or guilty of, or intending, murder ☆3. [Colloq.] very difficult, disagreeable, dangerous, trying, etc. —**mur′der·ous·ly** *adv.* —**mur′der·ous·ness** *n.*

**mure** (myoor) *vt.* mured, mur′ing [ME. *muren* < MFr. *murer* < LL.(Ec.) *murare*, to provide with walls < *murus*, wall: see MURAL] same as IMMURE

**Mu·res** (moo resh′) river flowing west from the Carpathian Mountains into the Tisza in SE Hungary: 470 mi.

**mu·rex** (myoor′eks) *n.*, *pl.* **-ri·ces′** (-ə sēz′), **-rex·es** [ModL., name of the genus < L., the purple fish < IE. base *mus*, whence MOUSE, Gr. *myax*, sea mussel] any of a genus (*Murex*) of flesh-eating snails, found in warm salt waters and having a rough, spiny shell: some species yield a purple substance formerly valued as a dye

**Mur·frees·bor·o** (mur′frēz bur′ō, -bə-) [after Col. Hardy *Murfree* (1752–1809)] city in C Tenn.: site of a Civil War battle (1863): pop. 33,000

**mu·ri·ate** (myoor′ē āt′, -it) *n.* [Fr. < *muriatique*: see MURIATIC ACID] [Now Rare] a salt of hydrochloric acid; chloride; esp., potassium chloride, used as a fertilizer

**mu·ri·at·ic acid** (myoor′ē at′ik) [Fr. *muriatique* < L. *muriaticus*, pickled < *muria*, brine < IE. *meuro-* < base *meu-*, damp, musty, whence MOSS, MIRE] hydrochloric acid: now only a commercial term

**mu·ri·cate** (myoor′ə kāt′) *adj.* [< L. *muricatus*, pointed, shaped like a purple fish < *murex*, MUREX] rough, with short, sharp points: also **mu′ri·cat′ed**

**mu·rid** (myoor′id) *n.* [< ModL. *Muridae* < *Mus* (gen. *Muris*), type genus < L., MOUSE] any of a family (*Muridae*) of rodents, including the old-world rats and mice

**Mu·ri·el** (myoor′ē əl) [prob. < Celt., as in Ir. *Muirgheal* < *muir*, the sea + *geal*, bright] a feminine name

**Mu·ril·lo** (moō rē′lyō; *E.* myoo ril′ō), **Bar·to·lo·mé Es·te·ban** (bär′tō lō me′ es te′bän) 1617–82; Sp. painter

**mu·rine** (myoor′in, -in) *adj.* [L. *murinus* < *mus* (gen. *muris*), MOUSE] of the murids, or family of rodents including the rats and mice —*n.* a murine rodent

**murk** (murk) *n.* [ME. *mirke* < ON. *myrkr*, dark, akin to OE. *mirce*, dark] darkness; gloom —*adj.* [Archaic] dark or dim

**murk·y** (mur′kē) *adj.* **murk′i·er**, **murk′i·est** [ME. *mirky*] 1. dark or gloomy 2. heavy and obscure with smoke, mist, etc. [the *murky* air] —*SYN.* see DARK —**murk′i·ly** *adv.* —**murk′i·ness** *n.*

**Mur·mansk** (moor mänsk′) seaport on the NW coast of Kola Peninsula, U.S.S.R., on the Barents Sea: pop. 279,000

**mur·mur** (mur′mər) *n.* [ME. *murmure* < OFr. < L.. a murmur, roar, muttering < IE. echoic base *mormor-, *murmur-*, whence Sans. *marmara-*, Gr. *mormurein*] 1. a low, indistinct, continuous sound, as of a stream, far-off voices, etc. 2. a mumbled or muttered complaint 3. *Med.* any abnormal sound heard by auscultation; esp., such a sound in the region of the heart —*vi.* 1. to make a murmur 2. to mumble or mutter a complaint —*vt.* to say in a murmur —**mur′mur·er** *n.* **mur′mur·ing** *adj.*

**SYN.**—murmur implies a continuous flow of words or sounds in a low, indistinct voice and may apply to utterances of satisfaction or dissatisfaction [to *murmur* a prayer]; mutter usually suggests angry or discontented words or sounds of this kind [to *mutter* curses]; to mumble is to utter almost inaudible or inarticulate sounds in low tones, with the mouth nearly closed [an old woman *mumbling* to herself]

**mur·mur·ous** (-əs) *adj.* characterized by or making a murmur or murmurs —**mur′mur·ous·ly** *adv.*

**mur·phy** (mur′fē) *n.*, *pl.* **-phies** [< *Murphy*, Ir. surname] [Old Slang] a potato

☆**Mur·phy bed** (mur′fē) [after W. L. *Murphy*, its U.S. inventor (c. 1900)] a bed that swings up or folds into a closet or cabinet when not in use

☆**Murphy game** [? after a 19th-c. confidence man of that name] any confidence game in which the victim is persuaded to pay in advance for something never received

**Murphy's Law** a facetious or satirical proposition stating that if there is a possibility for something to go wrong, it will go wrong

**mur·rain** (mur′in) *n.* [ME. *moreine* < OFr. *morine* < L. *mori*, to die: see MORTAL] 1. any of various infectious diseases of cattle 2. [Archaic] a pestilence; plague

**Mur·ray** (mur′ē) [< the surname *Murray* < ? Celt., as in W. *mor*, the sea] 1. a masculine name 2. (George) Gilbert (Aimé), 1866–1957; Brit. classical scholar & statesman, born in Australia 3. Sir James Augustus Henry, 1837–1915; Brit. lexicographer, born in Scotland 4. Lind·ley

(lind′lē), 1745–1826; Eng. grammarian, born in America

**Mur·ray** (mur′ē) river in SE Australia, flowing from the Australian Alps into the Indian Ocean: 1,596 mi.

**murre** (mur) *n.*, *pl.* **murres, murre**: see PLURAL, II, D, 1 [< ?] any of several swimming and diving birds (genus *Uria*) related to the guillemots and auks

**murre·let** (-lit) *n.* [prec. + -LET] any of a number of small auklike birds found chiefly on N Pacific islands

**mur·rey** (mur′ē) *n.* [ME. *murry* < OFr. *moree*, a dark-red color < ML. *moratum* < L. *morum*, a mulberry] a purplish-red color; mulberry —*adj.* of this color

**mur·rhine** (mur′in, -in) *adj.* [L. *murr(h)inus* < *murr(h)a* < Iran., as in Per. *mori*, glass ball] of an ancient Roman semiprecious stone, variously believed to be jade, fluorite, etc., used for making vases and drinking cups

**Mur·rum·bidg·ee** (mur′əm bij′ē) river in SE Australia, flowing west into the Murray: c. 1,000 mi.

**mur·ther** (mur′thər) *n.*, *vi.*, *vt.* *obs. or dial. var. of* MURDER

**mus.** 1. museum 2. music 3. musical 4. musician

**Mus. B., Mus. Bac.** [L. *Musicae Baccalaureus*] Bachelor of Music

**Mus·ca** (mus′kə) [L., a fly: see MIDGE] a S constellation

**mus·ca·dine** (mus′kə din, -dīn′) *n.* [altered < *muscadel*, var. of MUSCATEL] an American grape (*Vitis rotundifolia*) growing in the SE U.S., with small leaves, simple tendrils, and small clusters of large, spherical, musky grapes

‡**mus·cae vo·li·tan·tes** (mus′ē väl′ə tan′tēz, mus′kē) [L., flying flies] specks that appear to float before the eyes, caused by defects or impurities in the vitreous humor

**mus·ca·rine** (mus′kə rin, -rēn′) *n.* [< ModL. (*Amanita*) *muscaria*, fly (agaric) < L. *muscarius*, of flies < *musca*, a fly: see MIDGE] an extremely poisonous alkaloid, C₅H₁₅O₃N, found in certain mushrooms, rotten fish, etc., esp. affecting voluntary muscle movement

**Mus·cat** (mus kat′) capital of Oman; seaport on the Gulf of Oman: pop. 7,500

**mus·cat** (mus′kət, -kat) *n.* [Fr. < Pr. < It. *moscato*, musk, wine, lit., having the smell or flavor of musk < LL. *muscus*, MUSK] 1. a variety of sweet European grape from which muscatel and raisins are made 2. *same as* MUSCATEL (sense 1)

**Muscat and Oman** *former name of* OMAN (sense 2)

**mus·ca·tel** (mus′kə tel′) *n.* [ME. *muscadelle* < OFr. *muscadel* < Pr. or < It. *moscadello*, orig. dim of Pr. *muscat*, It. *moscato*, MUSCAT] 1. a rich, sweet wine made from the muscat 2. *same as* MUSCAT (sense 1) Also **mus′ca·del′** (-del′)

**mus·cid** (mus′id) *adj.* [< ModL. *Muscidae*, name of the family < L. *musca*, a fly: see MIDGE] of the family (Muscidae) of two-winged insects that includes the common housefly —*n.* a muscid insect

**mus·cle** (mus′'l) *n.* [Fr. < L. *musculus*, a muscle, lit., little mouse (from the fancied resemblance between the movements of a mouse and muscle), dim. of *mus*, MOUSE] 1. any of the body organs consisting of bundles of cells or fibers that can be contracted and expanded to produce bodily movements 2. the tissue making up such an organ 3. muscular strength; brawn ☆4. [Colloq.] power or influence, esp. when based on force or threats of force —*vi.* -cled, -cling ☆[Colloq.] to make one's way or take control by sheer strength or force or threats of force (usually with *in*)

**mus·cle-bound** (-bound′) *adj.* 1. having some of the muscles enlarged and less elastic, as from too much exercise 2. not flexible or adaptive; rigid

**muscle sense** *same as* KINESTHESIA

**mus·co·va·do** (mus′kə vä′dō, -vä′-) *n.* [Sp. *mascabado* (or Port. *mascavado*), unrefined, of inferior quality < Sp. *mascabar*, to depreciate] the dark raw sugar that remains after the molasses has been extracted from the juice of the sugar cane

**Mus·co·vite** (mus′kə vīt′) *n.* 1. a native or inhabitant of Muscovy; Russian 2. an inhabitant of Moscow —*adj.* 1. of Muscovy; Russian 2. of Moscow

**mus·co·vite** (mus′kə vīt′) *n.* [formerly called *Muscovy glass*: see -ITE[1]] the common, light-colored mica, KAl₂Si₃O₁₀(OH)₂, used as an electrical insulator

**Mus·co·vy** (mus′kə vē′) 1. former grand duchy surrounding and including Moscow, that expanded into the Russian Empire under Ivan IV 2. *former name of* RUSSIA

**Muscovy duck** [altered (after prec.) < MUSK DUCK] any of a number of varieties of domestic duck (*Cairina moschata*) characterized by a large crest, red wattles, and its wheezy sound

**mus·cu·lar** (mus′kyə lər) *adj.* [< L. *musculus* (see MUSCLE) + -AR] 1. of, consisting of, or accomplished by a muscle or muscles 2. having well-developed or prominent muscles; strong; brawny 3. suggestive of great physical strength; vigorous; powerful —**mus′cu·lar′i·ty** (-lar′ə tē) *n.* —**mus′cu·lar·ly** *adv.*

**muscular dystrophy** a chronic, noncontagious disease characterized by a progressive wasting of the muscles

**mus·cu·la·ture** (mus′kyə lə chər) *n.* [Fr. < L. *musculus*] the arrangement of the muscles of a body or of some part of the body; muscular system

*Exercise 8.* Read the passages and answer the literal comprehension questions.

The most notorious perpetrators of frontier violence were the outlaws and gunmen, like Belle Starr, Billy the Kid, Butch Cassidy and the Sundance Kid, the Dalton Gang, and Frank and Jesse James. These outlaws held up stagecoaches and trains, robbed banks, and stole horses and cattle. Frank and Jesse James—who ironically were the sons of ministers—learned outlaw strategy as Confederate guerrillas during the Civil War. They are most renowned as bank and train robbers; they staged at least 26 daring robberies between 1866 and 1881 in Missouri, taking in half a million dollars.

The most popular accounts of Western banditry, however, appear to be grossly exaggerated and romanticized. Bat Masterson, who, according to legend, killed 30 men in gunfights, actually killed only three. Billy the Kid, who supposedly killed one man for each of his 21 years of life, also apparently killed only three.

-Martin, et al., p. 471

1. The most notorious frontier violence was committed by

a. cattle rustlers.
b. outlaws and gunmen.
c. Confederate soldiers.

2. It is stated in the passage that the James brothers were sons of

a. a minister.
b. Confederates.
c. Belle Starr.

3. How many robberies did the James brothers stage in Missouri?

a. 30
b. 21
c. 26

4. How much money did the James brothers steal from 1866 to 1881?

a. 5,000,000
b. 500,000
c. 5,000

The son of President George Herbert Walker Bush, George W. Bush received his college degree from Yale University and Master of Business Administration from Harvard Business School. He served as an F-102 pilot for the Texas Air National Guard during the Vietnam War, before beginning his career in the oil and gas business in Texas. He later served as managing general partner of the Texas Rangers baseball team until he was elected Governor of Texas in 1994.

During the 2000 presidential campaign, George W. Bush described himself as a "compassionate conservative" committed to the principles of limited government, personal responsibility, strong families, and local control. The events that took place on September 11, 2001, however, have re-shaped the whole direction of his presidency.                    -Martin, et al., p. 902

5. According to the passage, President George Herbert Walker Bush and George W. Bush are the same person.

a. True
b. False

6. It is stated in the passage that George W. Bush served in Vietnam.

a. True
b. False

7. During the presidential campaign, George W. Bush referred to himself as a compassionate conservative.

a. True
b. False

8. According to the passage, during the 2000 campaign George W. Bush believed in federal control.

a. True
b. False


9. George W. Bush played for the Texas Rangers baseball team.

a. True
b. False


10. The author of the passage states that the events of September 11, 2001 have re-shaped the direction of George W. Bush's presidency.

a. True
b. False


Now, go to Simulated Exam Four or Ten to practice your newly acquired Literal Comprehension skills.

# CHAPTER FOUR

## INFERENTIAL COMPREHENSION (33% to 41%)

An inference is an educated guess based on available clues. Because the Regents' Reading Exam includes many questions that require you to infer (in fact, 18 to 22 may be this type), you should not ignore these questions. Inferential Comprehension question stems require you to not only use your ability to identify the main idea of a passage or paragraph but also to use your inductive and deductive reasoning skills to make general inferences. To answer inference questions on the Regents' Reading Exam, you must synthesize and interpret material that is presented in a passage. Since these analytical skills take more time, you will not be able to answer them as quickly as Literal Comprehension questions. When reading for Inferential Comprehension (assuming your rate is 300+ wpm), your reading rate will decrease to a range of 150–300 words per minute (Wassman & Rinsky), much slower than the rate to read for specific details. Skimming or scanning is not useful in this instance because the answer is not something you can simply pick out. Therefore, you need to practice this skill until it becomes second nature to you.

Inferential Comprehension is best understood if you contrast it to Literal Comprehension. As mentioned, identifying specific or literal information is a relatively easy task. You, as a student, have been locating information in stories and passages since elementary school: Who is the hero? Where does she live? How much time did it take her to catch the criminal? What was the criminal charged with? When did she receive the medal of bravery from the mayor? Teachers at every grade level have asked you these types of detailed questions. In the previous section you learned that *who, what, when, where,* and *how much* are classified as indicators of Literal Comprehension questions. The answers to Literal Comprehension questions are easily found in the passage; you can actually go back and pinpoint the answer if you have to because the answer is directly stated. But what if you are asked, "Why did the hero become a crime fighter?" or "Why did the criminal commit such a heinous act?" Unless you are given the answer directly in the passage, you will have to make an educated guess—and you need to base your estimation on clues you find in the selection. You cannot wildly guess or let your imagination take over. The better you are at picking out clues, the better chance you have of making the correct inference. On the Regents' Reading Exam, *why* and *how* questions often indicate you are being asked to prove your ability to infer.

> REMEMBER: *The more actual evidence you can gather, the more accurate your inference will be.*

According to Arthur and Dallas (2003),

> Inference skills are not only necessary to interpret college
> text material adequately but also to interpret daily situations
> correctly.  Most students do not realize how much they already
> employ inference in their everyday life circumstances.  In fact,
> it is inferring incorrectly that may lead to breakdowns in
> communication and even personal relationships.        -p. 189

Consider this example:

> Lillie and Catie had just met and, believe it or not, they met through
> a young man in whom they both had an interest.  Even so, they liked
> each other immediately.  As yet, the young man had not shown any
> inclination to ask either of them out.  Since Catie lived alone, Lillie
> tried her best to visit at least once a week.  One Saturday, Lillie
> telephoned Catie to let her know she was on her way over.  When
> she arrived, she found the door open.  So, Lillie knocked briefly and
> walked in. Catie was on the phone with her back to the door, and
> when she turned around and saw Lillie she jumped.  She motioned
> Lillie to have a seat; at the same time, Catie lowered her voice as she
> talked on the phone.  Still keeping her voice lowered, she walked into
> her bedroom, and closed the door.

What can you infer from the clues you glean from this scenario?  Mentally check the
statements that would apply:

_____Catie is talking about Lillie.
_____Catie is angry with Lillie.
_____Catie is speaking of personal matters.
_____Catie is speaking to the young man.
_____Catie has paid her phone bill.
_____Someone is in Catie's bedroom.

In this instance, it is very tempting to check that "Catie is speaking to the young man," but
can we really infer that with any degree of confidence when we were given the information
that he has shown no interest in either young woman?   There are two inferences you can
make with a good deal of confidence.  These are statements that have reasonable support:

1. "Catie has paid her phone bill," that is, Catie would not ordinarily be speaking
into a phone that was not working; and

2. "Catie is speaking of personal matters." We do know that in most cases people lower their voices when speaking of personal matters. (It is possible that Catie has lowered her voice because she does not want to disturb someone who is sleeping or studying. However, the reader has been given the information that Catie lives alone; from the information we have been given, when Lillie telephoned Catie, there was no mention of Catie already having company.)

If you chose another answer, go back to the scenario and try to highlight the evidence for your answer. Make sure you have strong clues for your answer. It seems from the clues given that none of the other inferences can be supported with a high degree of confidence. If you checked any of the other statements, perhaps you are allowing your imagination to work overtime. On the Regents' Reading Exam, be careful not to let vivid thoughts overwhelm you so that you assume too much.

> **REMEMBER:** *If you are having trouble detecting clues, authors provide hints through words, phrases, sentences, and information they offer. Words have negative and positive connotation which convey an author's meaning and intent.*

## Identifying Inference Questions

You can identify inference questions by looking at the stem of the question. Recognizing this type of question is possible by using the following words and phrases as indicators:

> *probably     possible     maybe     most likely     conclude     imply     suggest     infer*

On the Regents' Reading Exam inferential questions will most likely read as follows:

> The reader might conclude that . . .
> We can deduce that . . .
> The passage implies that . . .
> The selection suggests . . .
> The author most likely believes . . .
> It can be inferred that . . .
> The writer would probably agree that . . .
> With which of the following statements would the author most likely agree?

REMEMBER: *You will be asked 18 to 22 inference questions on the exam. That is, this type of question is asked most frequently. Be sure you understand the strategies for answering inferential comprehension questions.*

As mentioned, inference questions take longer to answer than Literal Comprehension questions do, but practicing Inferential Comprehension questions now will train you to look for clues, and it will become second nature to you before you sit for the exam.

*Exercise 1.* Tear out this page as well as the next page. Test your inference skills by reading the sentence, considering the clues, deciding upon a reasonable inference, and writing it in the blank provided. Be sure to write a statement about which you feel confident. Next, exchange your worksheet with your classmate and ask him to write his inference in the space provided. Are both inferences similar? Are both written statements inferences that most people would make?

1. Adam Edward has three cats, two dogs, and one hamster named Hamstring.

Inference: _____

Classmate's inference:

2. When you enter Scott's apartment, you are immediately struck by all the art work on the walls, some signed by Scott himself.

Inference: _____

Classmate's inference:

3. When we first began our trip not one of us ever imagined that we would not only experience Mickey Mouse but encounter swamp alligators as well.

Inference: _____

Classmate's inference:

4. Nik certainly knows a lot about kangaroos and koala bears; he even speaks with an accent.

Inference: _____

Classmate's inference:

5. Malkmus says that children should be seen and not heard.

Inference: _____

Classmate's Inference:

6. Parinya's mother buys one antique piece every time she visits a foreign country.

Inference:_____

Classmate's inference:

7. If you ever have the chance to visit Tyler's place, you will be amazed at the amassing of tires, wheels, carburetors, radiators, and various other engine parts lying around the property.

Inference:_____

Classmate's inference:

8. Brooklyn has many Middle Eastern restaurants.

Inference:_____

Classmate's inference:

9. On St. Patrick's Day celebrations are in full swing in Dublin, Ireland as well as in Dublin, Georgia!

Inference:_____

Classmate's Inference:

10. Quintus, standing in the prow of the Roman war ship, was eagerly peering through swirling fog ahead, toward a glimpse of high white cliffs. Suddenly he lurched onto the heaving deck as a great wave hit the galley. He grabbed at the painted eagle on the prow and lost his footing. Green water sloshed over him, and he collapsed with a clatter of shield, sword, and armor on the wet deck. The galley slaves, though straining at their oars to keep the boat headed for shore in this rising wind, nevertheless snickered.          -Seton, p. 11

Inference
#1:_____

Inference
#2:_____

Classmate's inference #1:
Classmate's inference #2:

*Exercise 2.* Read the passage below. First, answer the inference questions by circling the correct answer, and then write the clues from the passage that led you to your answer.

Why does anyone volunteer to fight in a war, especially someone who would not otherwise be called upon? There are approximately 400 documented cases of women who served in the ranks of the Civil War, both North and South. But, why did these women fight?

*Photo Natl Archives*

*Private Lyons (aka Rosetta) Wakeman.*

The most telling story is that of fighting lady, Rosetta (Lyons) Wakeman. She was the oldest child in a large family, and by necessity she worked under brutal conditions on the family farm in upstate New York. She left home at 19, and instead of taking a job as a laundress or a domestic for pennies a day, she dressed as a man and hired onto a canal boat as a coal handler.

When she learned she could earn $13 per month in the army, she enlisted as a private in the 153rd New York State Volunteers. She saved her army pay and sent home large sums of money and generous gifts.

In the army she enjoyed the freedoms not possible to her as a woman. And, she was having the time of her life. She wrote, "I enjoy myself first rate. . . I have had plenty of money to spend and a good time asoldiering. I find just as good friends among strangers as I do at home."

Her true identity was never discovered, not even when she visited male friends in other regiments who knew her from home, or even when she was hospitalized with dysentery. When she died in a New Orleans Army hospital, she was buried as a soldier. She rests at Chalmette National Cemetery with a soldier's headstone.       -Smithsonian

1. The reader can infer that Rosetta's family was

a. middle class.
b. poor.
c. well off.

Clues:_____

_____

2. We can conclude that the main reason Rosetta joined the army was because she was

a. patriotic.
b. adventurous.
c. interested in making more money.

Clues:_____

_____


3. It is stated in the passage that Rosetta

a. had a good experience while in the Army.
b. was treated very badly by male friends in other regiments.
c. was teased unmercifully because she was female, but she was well-liked.

Clues:_____

_____


4. The reader can conclude that during the Civil War women

a. were treated as equal to men.
b. were inducted into the Army much like today.
c. had limited rights in the job market.

Clues:_____

_____


*Exercise 3*. After reading the passage below, write two inferences along with the clues that led you to your answer. Then, write three facts about the information presented.


After compiling data from thousands of biological and behavioral studies of humans and animals, UCLA researchers identified a broad pattern, they termed "tend and befriend," that women use to cope with stress. Stressed-out women are likely to seek social contact rather than indulge in the "fight-or-flight" behavior that has long been considered the principal way both sexes cope with stress. This newly discovered pattern shows that females of many species, including humans, respond to stressful conditions by seeking social contact and support from others (especially other females) and by nurturing their young. Befriending methods range from talking on the phone with relatives or friends to such simple social contacts as asking for directions when lost.

In one study, when the typical father came home after a stressful day at work, he responded to stress by wanting to be left alone, enjoying peace and quiet away from the stress of the office. When office-related stress was particularly acute, a typical response would be to react harshly or create conflict with his wife or children, the UCLA report said. When the typical mother in the same study came home from work bearing stress, she was more likely to cope with her bad day by focusing her attention on nurturing her children.

The different ways that men and women respond to stress may also help researchers understand why men are more vulnerable to the adverse health effects of stress. "Because the tend-and-befriend regulatory system may, in some ways, protect women against stress, this biobehavioral pattern may provide insights into why women live an average of seven and a half years longer than men," the report said.

The study will be published in an upcoming issue of the American Psychological Association's journal.

                                                                                   -Beasley, Internet

1. Inference:_____

Clues:_____

2. Inference:_____

Clues:_____

3. Fact:_____

4. Fact:_____

5. Fact:_____

*Exercise 4.* After reading the passage below, write three inferences along with the clues that led you to your answer. Then, write five facts about the information presented.

In Japan, animation is considered a high art, and no artist is more esteemed than film director Hayao Miyazaki. A few years ago, Miyazaki's masterwork,

*Spirited Away*, became the biggest box-office hit ever in Japan, pulling in a staggering $214 million over eight months and displacing *Titanic* in the Japanese record books. A coming-of-age fantasy about a little girl working in a resort frequented by gods and ghouls, *Spirited Away* became the first animated film to win the Golden Bear award, the top prize at the Berlin International Film Festival in April.

Miyazaki isn't new to international acclaim. The 61-year-old animator has been in the top ranks of the world's innovative artists since the 1980s. He didn't start out that way, though. Miyazaki studied economics and political science at the elite Gakushuin University in central Tokyo, graduating in 1963. He then spent years doing TV animation for low wages at Toei Animation Company. He got his first big break in 1979, when he directed the now classic film *Lupin III*. Soon after, film critics began dubbing him the Walt Disney of Japan.

The specters in *Spirited Away* are far more pleasing to the eye than other Japanese animation icons, such as Pokemon. Nor does this film or previous works—such as Miyazaki's 1997 release *Princess Mononoke*—follow the formulaic plots of anime, which rely on violence, gore, and thinly-clad female characters. Miyazaki's themes reject the crass materialism of modern society and focus instead on self-reliance and quiet determination. He also weaves a fair amount of humanism into his works.

Since 1985, Miyazaki has been associated with Studio Ghibli, an animation studio fully dedicated to producing his works. Although Miyazaki isn't a young man, he shows no signs of slowing down.

Miyazaki once said that he measures the success of his films not by box-office receipts but by whether his young fans today would want to show his works to their children 20 or 30 years from now. Given the appeal of his films to adults and children around the world, that seems a sure bet.          -*Business Week*, Internet

1. Inference:_____

Clues:_____

2. Inference:_____

Clues:_____

3. Inference:_____

Clues:_____

4. Inference:_____

Clues:_____


5. Inference:_____

Clues:_____


6. Fact:_____

7. Fact:_____

8. Fact:_____


*Exercise 5*. After reading the passage below, write five inferences along with the clues that led you to your answer. Then, write five facts about the information presented.


In Nepal, the Kumari Devi is an ordinary prepubescent four to seven-year-old girl from the lower caste of the Sakya community who is chosen to live her young days in Katmandu's god-house. From that time she is confined in the small house of magnificent intricate carvings, never to touch the ground with her feet. During her tenure in the god-house, the government trust fund bears her entire expenses including that of her caretakers. From time immemorial the practice of worshiping an ordinary pre-pubescent girl as a source of supreme power has been an integral part of both Hinduism and Buddhism. Indeed, the Kumari Devi is a source of worship and great affection.

The selection of the Living Goddess is a highly elaborate ritual. According to tradition, young girls who have an 'appropriate' horoscope are screened on the basis of 32 attributes of perfection, including color of eyes, shape of teeth, and even voice quality. They are then are taken to a dark room, where terrifying tantrik rituals are performed. The real goddess is one who stays calm and collected throughout these trials. Finally, the Kumari must choose items of clothing and decoration worn by her predecessor.

Under normal circumstances, her days in the god-house come to an end with her first menstruation. She then changes back to the status of normal mortal and the search of a new Kumari begins. It is said to be unlucky to marry an ex-Kumari.

-based on visitnepal.com

1. Inference:_____

Clues:_____

2. Inference:_____

Clues:_____

3. Inference:_____

Clues:_____

4. Inference:_____

Clues:_____

5. Inference:_____

Clues:_____

6. Fact:_____

7. Fact:_____

8. Fact:_____

9. Fact:_____

10. Fact:_____

## Finding the Main Idea

On the Regents' Reading Exam you will be required to find the main idea of a passage or a paragraph—in most cases when it is not directly stated. If the main idea is stated, good places to skim for it are the first sentence of the first paragraph or in the last paragraph. If, however, the main idea is not directly stated, you will need to rely on your inference skills to determine a main idea.

Perhaps the most effective way to find the main idea is to compile all the details in the passage first. (*Note*: on the Georgia Regents' Reading Test you are allowed to jot down notes on the test.) Follow these suggested steps:

Step 1.  Look at all your details and try to either group them or identify what they have in common.

Step 2.  Before looking at the question options, analyze the commonality of the details.

Step 3.  Write one sentence describing what the main idea is.

Step 4.  Check the options to determine which one is closest to your written main idea. Practice this strategy as many times as you can before the actual test. You will become more at ease with finding the main idea the more you practice this method.

*Exercise 6.* Using Steps 1 through 3 in the four-step method above, write a main idea for the following paragraphs taken from *King In Hell*.

A.      Bothwell thrust open the study door and the smile on his face froze. His glance swept past Janet and came to rest on the equally startled face of Queen Mary Stuart. She was the last person he had expected to find here, and his previous attempts to see her flashed before him. Slowly the shock wore off, and his thoughts came in rapid succession. How would she receive him? How did she really feel about his having broken prison? Would she be angry because he had attempted to leave the country without her permission?      -Balin, pp. 120-121

Step One.  List details:_____

_____

_____

Step Two.  Commonality of details:

_____

Step Three.  Write one sentence describing the main idea of the paragraph.

_____

B.        Bothwell rose and pulled Queen Mary to her feet.  She clung to him; dry sobs caught in her throat.
          "We had best hurry," he said.  "The others will be wondering where we are."
          They found their way back along the passageway and climbed the stairs hand in hand.  In the courtyard, Mary paused to fix her hair and straighten her gown while Bothwell went for the horses.
          He lifted her to the saddle, his hands lingering on her waist.  "You will never forget me," he said.
          Tears shimmered in her eyes as she gazed at him, heartbreak on her face.  "No, I will always remember your arms, the touch of your hands, the feel of your lips on mine—and this day."                                    -Balin, pp. 225-226

Step One.  List details:_____

_____

_____

Step Two.  Commonality of details:

_____

Step Three.  Write one sentence describing the main idea of the paragraph.

_____

C.        Bothwell waited until midnight before going to Mary.  It was a risky business, since the palace was filled with noblemen come to town for Parliament, but tonight his recklessness knew no bounds.  Mary was expecting him and had left the door to her private passageway unlatched.
          She ran to him and threw herself into his arms.  She whispered in his ear,

"Now we can be wed."

      Incredulous, he released her and stepped back. "Are you crazy? I already have a wife."

                                        -Balin, p. 410

Step One.  List details:_____

_____

_____

Step Two.  Commonality of details:

_____

Step Three.  Write one sentence describing the main idea of the paragraph.

_____

*Exercise 7.* Adding Step Four, choose a main idea for the paragraphs based on the main idea sentence you wrote.

    A.    India, which has had disappointing results with its voluntary family planning programs, enacted more forceful measures in the mid-1970s, such as the compulsory sterilization of some government workers with more than two children. Several Indian states passed laws requiring sterilization and/or imprisonment for those couples who bore more than two or three children. A male vasectomy program was also vigorously pursued, with transistor radios and money being given as an incentive to those agreeing to have the sterilization operation.

                                        -Seitz, pp. 54-55

Step One.  List details:_____

_____

_____

Step Two.  Commonality of details:

_____

Step Three.  Write one sentence describing the main idea of the paragraph.

_____


Step Four.  Which one of the options below matches your main idea statement in Step Three above?  Choose the correct answer.


The central focus of the paragraph is that

a.  Indians do not like children.
b.  the Indian government awards transistor radios to men who have vasectomies.
c.  India has resorted to forceful measures to stem its population growth.


B.       If you are like most people, you will take credit for the good grade and find some external reason for the bad grade.  You failed the test because it was unfair, the instructor didn't like you, you didn't get a chance to study, the person next to you during the test needed a bath badly and distracted you, or you were sick.  There are many possible reasons for poor performance that don't threaten one's self-image.                                                          -Kestner, p. 437


Step One.  List details:_____

_____

_____

Step Two.  Commonality of details:

_____

Step Three.  Write one sentence describing the main idea of the paragraph.

_____

Step Four.  Which one of the options below matches your main idea statement in Step Three above?  Choose the correct answer.

The main idea of this paragraph is that

a. it is the instructor's fault if a student doesn't make good grades.
b. most people look for reasons for poor performance so that one's self-image isn't threatened.
c. if you are like most people, you take responsibility for your academic failures.

---

REMEMBER: *To find a main idea that is not directly stated, find what the details have in common; then, write one sentence to describe that commonality.*

---

Practice finding the main idea by looking at different photos, pictures, or single-panel cartoon drawings and writing captions for them.  Writing a caption is much the same as generating a main idea.   After practicing this skill, you can then transfer the skill to written text.

## Identifying Main Idea Questions

You can identify main idea questions by recognizing certain key words in the stem of the question:

What is the *central theme* of the selection?
What is the *focus* of paragraph two?
Which of these statements best expresses the *central idea* of the excerpt?

The *best statement of the main idea* is . . .
This passage *primarily* deals with . . .
The author's *main point is that*. . .
The *best title* for this selection is . . .
What is the *main idea* of the *passage*?
What is the *main idea* of *paragraph* five?

Now, practice your Inference skills by taking Simulated Exam One, Two, Five, or Nine.

# CHAPTER FIVE

## ANALYSIS (18% to 24%)

Most analysis questions are not questions that ask about the content of the passage, but rather focus on the technique and organizational patterns the authors use to get their points across. Analysis questions are concerned with *how the passage is written* (tone, style, patterns of organization) or *why the selection was written* (author's purpose). When reading for analytical information, you will probably read at the same rate as reading for inferential questions: 150 to 300 words per minute.

## Identifying Analysis Questions

You will notice that analysis questions are very straightforward:

> What is the tone of the passage?
> The author's attitude is one of . . .
> What is the author's style?
> What is the author's purpose in writing the selection?
> The purpose of the passage is . . .
> The author gets his point across through the use of. . .

REMEMBER: *Analysis questions emphasize how and why the author wrote the passage.*

Next, you will find a description of each type of analysis question and lists of options for answering each type.

## Tone, Attitude, and Style

As we all know, an individual's mood can be shown through facial expressions, gestures, and body language. But how is mood, tone, or attitude portrayed through the written word? In passages, the most efficient way a writer can relate the tone is through his or her word choice.

As Arthur and Dallas (2003) state:

> By using a certain tone—whether it be sarcastic, angry, resentful, complaining, and so forth—an individual can get an attitude across. In writing, the tone, or the writer's attitude, is conveyed through his or her choice of words. When reading, it is possible to detect the tone by being cognizant of the wording. There is a big difference in meaning if a writer uses the word "liked" as compared to using the word "enamored." The writer is letting us know that in the second instance, the feeling is a lot stronger.
>
> -p. 170

On Regents' Reading Exams you can detect tone and attitude by noticing the words and phrases the author has chosen to use as well as noticing the way in which the subject matter is approached.

Below you will find a list of words to describe tone and/or attitude that may appear as options on Regents' Reading Exams:

### TONE AND ATTITUDE OPTIONS

| | |
|---|---|
| angry | hateful |
| apathetic | impartial |
| argumentative | indifferent |
| bitter | informal |
| compassionate | informative |
| complaining | ironic |
| complimentary | mocking |
| critical | neutral |
| defensive | nostalgic |
| depressing | objective |
| despairing | optimistic |
| distrustful | pessimistic |
| doubtful | resentful |
| dramatic | sarcastic |
| empathetic | sentimental |
| enthusiastic | somber |
| formal | sincere |
| hopeful | skeptical |
| hopeless | subjective |
| hostile | suspenseful |
| humorous | tragic |

Be aware that questions of this type are very straightforward and not meant to trick you: "What is the author's tone? What is the tone of the passage? What is the writer's attitude toward . . . ?"

*Exercise 1.* In each sentence you will detect a tone or attitude. Choose the best answer by circling it.

1. Get away from me! You've stolen all my money and left me with nothing!

a. sentimental
b. angry
c. pessimistic

2. My goodness, Miss Hogarth, don't you look smashing today?

a. neutral
b. serious
c. complimentary

3. Mildred told me she doesn't care whether you go or not, and neither do I.

a. indifferent
b. suspenseful
c. sarcastic

4. With their home blown away by the typhoon and no relatives to care for them, the Yamaguchis were devastated.

a. distrustful
b. defensive
c. despairing

5. Though Nita Bordeaux didn't like the way the young girl was costumed, she still gave her 10 points for her skating ability.

a. subjective
b. impartial
c. sincere


6. Florian believes that there is always a rainbow around the next corner.

a. empathetic
b. optimistic
c. nostalgic


7. You can't send me to boarding school; I won't have any friends! I'll die there!

a. dramatic
b. critical
c. informal


8. This is an announcement regarding Amtrak to Atlanta. The 9:00 p.m. train is delayed; it will be departing at 9:25 p.m. Please have your boarding pass ready.

a. enthusiastic
b. hopeless
c. informative


9. My flight was miserable: no food was served, the economy section was crowded, and the seat was cramped.

a. doubtful
b. complaining
c. argumentative


10. Many Americans doubt there will be a return of the Democrats to the White House.

a. ironic
b. mocking
c. skeptical

*Exercise 2.* Decide on the tone in these short paragraphs. Then write the words that led you to decide the correct option.

1.      This chapter is designed primarily for school psychologists, social workers
        and counselors. The method for dealing with difficult discipline problems in the
        schools is based on a communications-based family-systems approach entitled
        "Brief Family Intervention."                                          -Valentine, p. 11

The tone of the paragraph is

a. depressing.
b. academic.
c. hopeful.


Words chosen by author to convey tone:_____

_____


2.                  Historically, most psychologists have looked at inappropriate behavior
        in students from a one-person and/or medical model. They assumed that some
        process inside the child's brain caused him to act inappropriately. They believed
        that if they could get inside his head and change whatever was going on, they
        could change the child. They tried to work with the child, usually in individual
        counseling or therapy, to change his inappropriate behavior. Even if they believed
        that the family had something to do with the child's behavior, they usually worked
        with the child individually.
                    Family-systems theory brought about a major shift. Psychologists using
        this method no longer look at the child in isolation.              -Valentine, pp. 17-18



The attitude of the author toward the one-person model is

a. sympathetic.
b. objective.
c. critical.

Words chosen by the author to convey attitude:_____

_____

3.          *Cobra* began on July 25, 1945, with a massive bombing attack by over
1,500 heavy bombers.  Since coordination between ground and air was still not
perfected, some bombs fell short, causing a number of American casualties:
111 were killed and 490 wounded.  But overall, the bombing was effective, killing
over 1,000 men of the Panzer Lehr Division; so deafening was the attack that
some of the survivors could not hear for 24 hours afterwards.  Only a dozen
German tanks remained.                                                    -Layton, p. 81

What is the tone of the paragraph?

a.  informative
b.  nostalgic
c.  resentful

Words chosen by author to convey tone:_____

_____

4.          In Japan, company dorm hours were strict.  Each night the gate closed
at ten.  To get in after that, you had to crawl through a low, swinging subgate,
like a pet through a pet doorway.  Anyone going away overnight had to sign out
and state where he was going, the address, the phone number, and the length
of his time away.  Only Sony employees were allowed inside.  Any outsider had
to be received in a lounge by the front door.  Women were not allowed inside at
all.  I asked Kamakura-san, my team's assistant manager, if other American
scholars could visit to see what my workplace was like.  "Sure," he said,
"they're welcome to visit and can stay—up to five minutes."  He wasn't being
sarcastic.                                                              -Katzenstein, p. 49

The tone of the paragraph is

a.  compassionate.
b.  apathetic.
c.  humorous.

Words chosen by author to convey tone:_____

_____

5.          After seeing what workers had to put up with, I was no longer confident
that the "lifetime employment" that many Westerners thought Japanese received
was a benefit.  Now I knew that it was not even uniformly true.  In reality, only
those  who worked for large corporations were guaranteed this (30% of the total
work force), and they were nearly all men.  Since the pension and social security
systems were woefully inadequate, the other 70% of people had to continue to work
to simply support themselves.                                                    -Katzenstein, p. 202

What is the tone of the passage?

a. hopeful
b. critical
c. informal

Words chosen by author to convey tone:_____

_____

        A writer's style will vary according to his or her purposes.  If s/he wants to entertain,
then the style might be informal.  If the author wants to inform and educate, then the style
may be academic and formal.  If the author wants to reach an elite audience, say a group of
physicists, then the style best suited would be scientific.  You may not see very many
questions on an author's style on the Regents' Reading exam, but just in case you come
across one, here are some terms to consider:

| academic | factual | informal | indifferent | romantic |
| argumentative | formal | impersonal | humorous | riveting |

## Author's Purpose

        Obviously, this type of question asks the reader to determine why the author wrote the passage. The question stem will read: "The author's purpose is to . . ." or, more directly, "What is the author's purpose in writing the selection?" You will notice that Author's Purpose options are closely related to the options for Patterns of Organization discussed in the next section. That is because the author uses the optimal writing pattern to make his or her point.

| OPTIONS FOR AUTHOR'S PURPOSE | | | | |
|---|---|---|---|---|
| *to amuse* | *to contrast* | *to educate* | *to illustrate* | *to report* |
| *to argue* | *to criticize* | *to entertain* | *to inform* | *to ridicule* |
| *to condemn* | *to define* | *to explain* | *to narrate* | *to shock* |
| *to compare* | *to describe* | *to expose* | *to persuade* | *to summarize* |

*Exercise 3.* Determine the author's purpose in the short paragraphs. Circle the correct answer.

1.          This radical antislavery mood resulted in violence, including the martyrdom of abolitionist newspaper editor Elijah P. Lovejoy. In 1833, Lovejoy moved to the state of Missouri and began publishing an antislavery newspaper. He continued to publish until 1837 when a pro-slavery mob sacked his office, shot him to death, and threw his printing press into the Mississippi River. Lovejoy's murder sent shock waves throughout the North and South with the news that a white man had been killed in the cause of abolitionism.          -Solberg, p. 71

By using the example of Elijah P. Lovejoy, the author's purpose is to

a. illustrate.
b. contrast.
c. ridicule.

2.          Antislavery newspapers were also published by African Americans, including Frederick Douglass's *North Star*. His anguish as a former slave caused him to reveal the evils of slavery. Douglass was a master of political and moral language, mixing religious and secular thought. The antislavery movement recruited other blacks like Sojourner Truth, Harriet Tubman, and Henry Highland Garnet. Truth toured the North in advocacy of African American and feminist rights. Tubman, known as "the Moses of her people," escaped from

slavery in Maryland in 1849 to begin her work on the underground railroad. Garnet, a former slave and ordained Presbyterian minister, condemned the Constitution as a pro-slavery document. -Solberg, p. 72

By using names and dates in the paragraph, the author is

a. persuading.
b. condemning.
c. informing.

3.     During these hard days, Jenny had the support and love of her brother. Most Sundays Tom arrived at the house early and helped Jenny and her children into the cart. Tom was always aware that he must make these Sundays a pleasure. They would make the journey to his home with Tom singing hymns with the children in order to keep their spirits high. Lizzie enjoyed the day playing with her cousins Betty and Ellen. Richard would help his uncle with the animals, playing with the seemingly endless litters of kittens tumbling around in the cosy warmth of the barn. Jenny relaxed in the farmhouse kitchen, which had after all, been her own home when she was young. Through her mind would flit loving memories of her mother and father bustling around. The return journey saw them in the cart with every spare corner filled with food and before the journey was half done, the children were asleep after a full day of activity, love, and attention. -Mulholland, p. 16

The author's purpose is to

a. narrate and describe.
b. explain and inform.
c. shock and ridicule.

4.     Quintus jerked his chin toward a village he had just discovered to the right of him. There were several round mud houses huddled inside a circular palisade made of sticks. A woman was squatting by the opening in the palisade pounding something in a stone bowl. She wore a shapeless garment that had once been striped and squared with color, but it was very dirty. -Seton, p. 15

What is the author's purpose in writing the selection?

a. to compare Quintus to the woman
b. to describe the village atmosphere
c. to criticize the woman of the village

## Author's Patterns of Organization

To communicate their ideas, their stances on issues, and/or their general beliefs, writers produce written material which is related to and appropriate for their purpose. As stated, the Author's Purpose is closely related to the author's Patterns of Organization. Patterns of Organization refer to the type of passage (or paragraph) the author chooses to write to get his or her point across. It is a good idea to familiarize yourself with the types of passages you will encounter on the Regents' Reading Exam. Some of these types may seem familiar to you; that is because they, in some ways, parallel the context clues we previously discussed. Basically, there are seven kinds of patterns of organization you will find on the exam.

### DESCRIPTION

Usually this type of paragraph presents information (in graphic detail) about an object, person, scene, scenario, or situation by infusing the paragraph with adjectives. Choice of words and phrases impact how well the author portrays the subject. For example, think of the difference between the words, *strong* and *pungent*, in describing the smell of an onion. A more graphic, detailed description can always be generated just by using more imaginative words or phrases. The writer may also evoke a few of the five senses (touch, taste, smell, hearing, sight). Sounds, colors, tastes, textures, or aromas will enhance the feeling or atmosphere the writer is trying to relate. The author's ultimate goal is to reproduce an image that will elicit a response in the reader.

*Example*: In winter, howling winds shipped the scant snowfall across the bleak frozen land. Average yearly temperatures only a few degrees lower triggered the formation of a glacier; a few hot days had little effect. In spring the meager snow that fell on the land melted, and the crust of the glacier warmed, seeping down and out across the steppes. The meltwater softened the soil enough for shallow rooting grasses and herbs to sprout. In the regions near the borders of the ice, where the snow cover was light, the grass supplied fodder for uncountable millions of grazing animals who had adapted to the glacial cold.                                          -Auel, p. 15

Can you point out the adjectives used in this paragraph?
Can you determine the senses evoked and point to the words or phrases which evoke them?


## PERSUASION

The purpose of a persuasive passage is to move the reader to the author's opinion about an issue. To convince the reader, however, the author must present solid arguments and evidence in his or her favor. Because of the necessity to impress the reader, you will find strong language and most likely only one opinion considered to be "right" (the author's). The author will "stack the cards" in his or her favor and will probably not allude to any arguments which would be contrary to the stated position.

> *Example*: Committed but dispirited, most teachers say they are unfairly
> blamed for school shortcomings, undermined by parents, and distrustful
> of their bosses. More than three in four teachers surveyed said they
> were "scapegoats for all the problems facing education...." Teachers
> views ought to matter to a lot of people, Wadsworth said. Parents link their
> children's success to teaching quality, and all states are under federal
> mandate to have highly qualified teachers in every core academic course
> by 2005-06.                                                    -CNN website

How does the author persuade the reader to consider his opinion (i.e., what are his arguments)? What are some of the "strong" words that he uses in this excerpt?


## COMPARISON-CONTRAST

Comparative/contrastive writing involves at least two subjects. While comparative writing focuses on the similarities of persons, places, issues, situations, and so forth, contrastive writing emphasizes the differences. Passages of these types are easily recognizable because several key indicators (signal words/phrases) will more than likely be present:

| INDICATORS OF COMPARISON |
| --- |
| *like    likewise    both    in addition    similar    same    in the same way    analogous* |

*Example*:  Both Maya Angelou and Alice Walker are female voices in the African-American community.  Like Ms. Angelou, Alice Walker is a novelist, poet, and essayist.  In addition, these writers received the same prestigious nomination—a nomination for the Pulitzer Prize.

What/Who is being compared?
What are the signal words that let you know that the paragraph is one of comparison?

| INDICATORS OF CONTRAST | | |
| --- | --- | --- |
| *although* | *differ* | *on the other hand* |
| *but* | *different* | *opposite* |
| *in contrast* | *however* | *parallel* |
| *comparable* | *more than* | *though* |
| *conversely* | *on the contrary* | *unlike* |
| *more, better, worse, worst* | | *words with the suffix " -er"* |

*Example*: The two brothers were as different as night and day, but it was the shorter, dark-haired one who had the lighter heart.  Thonolan's friendly nature, infectious grin, and easy laughter made him quickly welcome any-where.  Jondalar was more serious, his brow often knotted in concentration or worry, and though he smiled easily, especially at his brother, he seldom laughed out loud.  When he did, the sheer abandon of it came as a surprise.
                                                                                    -Auel, p. 19

Who are the two individuals being contrasted?  What are the signal words?

**NARRATION**

One distinguishing feature of a narrative passage is that the reader has a distinct feeling a story is being told—that quite a bit of action (or a significant event) is taking place.  The writer's purpose is to tell a story, hopefully engaging readers so that they want to know "what happens next" to the characters.  Another way to identify a narrative selection is to look for dialogue (designated, of course, by quotation marks).

*Example*: "This has been a hard day for you, hasn't it, Whinney?" Ayla said out loud. She wrapped her arms around the mare's neck and simply held her, the way she would a frightened child. Whinney leaned against her and shook. "What's wrong?" she asked. The cave lion cub was exactly where she had left him. The cub! she thought. Whinney smells the cub. "It's all right, Whinney. That baby cub can't hurt you." Ayla rubbed the horse's soft nose and, putting an arm around the sturdy neck, gently urged the horse into the cave.
                                                            -Auel, pp. 233-234

How do you know this paragraph is narrative text?
What is the most obvious clue?

## DEFINITION

According to Arthur and Dallas (2003),

> A definition paragraph or passage is usually more objective in nature than other passages. The writer will state facts in most cases. You can recognize a definition paragraph or passage by noticing: 1) the repetition of the same topic word and 2) the frequent use of the verb *to be* or verbs such as *comprise, include, contain, consist of, encompass, have,* and so forth. Definition passages sometimes contain an example of what is being defined. The example can, of course, be a person, place or thing.
> 
>                                                            -p. 146

| SIGNAL WORDS AND INDICATORS OF DEFINITION |
|---|

| *comprise*   *include*   *contain*   *consist of*   *encompass*   *have* |
|---|
| *forms of the verb **to be*** <br> *repetition of the topic* |

*Example:* Mentally healthy people are able to deal positively with life's challenges. They are able to cope with stress, remain flexible, and compromise to resolve conflict. They are able to realistically evaluate situations that may occur over a lifespan and limit the

negative impacts of events such as divorce and death.  To be
mentally healthy requires an ability to create solutions that will
allow mental health to be maintained or improved.  The  mentally
healthy are willing to explore personal thoughts and feelings.
                                                                    -Adams, p. 7

What is being defined?
What are the signal words and indicators?

**EXAMPLE**

In the section on context clues, you were instructed that the definition of an
unknown word may be deduced by examples given as clues.  In a passage, one
example or a few examples may be given to illustrate the author's idea.  The author
will usually state a main idea, then use examples as support for his or her argument.
To recognize a passage or paragraph that has Example as its overriding pattern of
organization, look for these words:

| SIGNAL WORDS OF EXAMPLE | | |
|---|---|---|
| *another* | *example* | *illustration* |
| *as* | *for example* | *including* |
| *depict* | *for instance* | *like* |
| *elaborate* | *illustrate* | *represent* |
| *such as* | | |

*Example*: Early Thai verse was written exclusively by the aristocracy
or royalty, the only educated classes able to do so.  Examples of royalty
who were distinguished poets include King Rama I and King Rama II.
King Rama I's *Ramakian,* for instance, is the major historical source of
medieval Thai courtly traditions.  King Rama II–another prominent royal
writer–penned two episodes of the *Ramakian* for classical drama purposes.
                                                        -Royal Thai Government, p. 103

What signal words alert you to the fact that this is an Example paragraph?
Can you name the examples?

**CAUSE AND EFFECT**

Cause and effect passages follow a rationale/consequence paradigm. "Why something happened" (the causes, the reasons) and "what happened as a result" (the consequences) are the focus of this type of passage.

| **SIGNAL WORDS AND PHRASES OF CAUSE AND EFFECT** | | |
|---|---|---|
| *as a result* | *for this reason* | *since* |
| *because* | *hence* | *so* |
| *consequently* | *resulting* | *therefore* |
| *if . . . then* | *first . . .subsequently* | *when . . .then* |

*Examples*:

1. The earth is not absolutely rigid. Consequently, the moon-sun tidal forces produce earth tides. Twice each day the solid surface of the earth rises and falls as much as a quarter of a meter!

2. As a result of the sun's and the moon's tides coinciding, we have high water tides larger than usual. That is, spring tides occur. If the earth is experiencing a spring tide, then there is a higher probability of earthquakes and volcanic eruptions.

-Hewitt, pp. 3-4

Can you name the cause in Example #1?
What is the result?
What is the signal word?

Can you name the cause in Example #2?
What is the result?
What are the signal phrases?

---

REMEMBER: *Since many of these patterns of organization seem to overlap, you may think that two options are correct (for example, description and narration). Always choose the option which is the **overriding pattern of organization***

*Exercise 4.* You are to decide what pattern of organization the author is using to get her/his point across. Read the selection, then write the correct pattern. Then, write the key words/phrases and clues that led you to your answer. The seven patterns are repeated here for you.

**DESCRIPTION**                              **DEFINITION**
**PERSUASION**                              **EXAMPLE**
**COMPARISON**                              **NARRATION**
**CONTRAST**

1.          What is love?  To poets and philosophers, love is magical and mysteri-
   ous.  To psychologists, love is a dependent variable.  Few, if any topics in social
   psychology deal with such a perplexing, joyous, complex, and bewildering emotion.
   Some contend that love is inherently unknowable, and any attempts to quantify it
   are doomed to failure.  What we do know from the social psychological study of
   love is that it is different from liking.                      -Kestner, et al, p. 446

What pattern of organization does the author use to get her point across?

_____

Key words/phrases/clues:_____

_____

2.          Over the past century the types of challenges facing medical researchers
   and healthcare professionals have changed substantially. In the early part of the
   twentieth century, acute infectious diseases such as tuberculosis, influenza, and
   pneumonia led the list of life-threatening illnesses.  The leading causes of death
   and impaired physical functioning in this country today are chronic disorders such
   as diabetes, cardiovascular disease, and cancer.              -Kestner, et al., p. 479

What pattern of organization does the author use to get her point across?

_____

Key words/phrases/clues:_____

_____

3.        All nations should know: America will do what is necessary to
ensure our nation's security. We'll be deliberate, yet time is not on our
side. I will not wait on events while dangers gather. I will not stand by
as peril draws closer and closer. The United States of America will not
permit the world's most dangerous regimes to threaten us with the world's
most destructive weapons. We can't stop short. If we stopped now, leaving
terror camps intact and terror states unchecked, our sense of security would
be false and temporary. History has called America and our allies to action,
and it is both our responsibility and our privilege to fight freedom's fight.
        My hope is that all nations will heed our call and eliminate the terrorist
parasites who threaten their countries and our own.            -Bush, Internet

What pattern of organization does the author use to get his point across?

_____

Key words/phrases/clues:_____

_____

4.        In recent decades, the influx of foreign students has been crucial to the strength
        of U.S. universities and technology companies. For example, *nearly 40 percent*
        of engineering faculty members in the United States are foreign-born. In addition,
        *33 percent* of American Nobel Prize winners are foreign-born!
                                                            -Hockstader, p. A01

What pattern of organization does the author use to get his point across?

_____

Key words/phrases/clues:_____

_____

5.        The fortress of Thessaloniki, Greece oversees the Old Town's placid streets
        and long, tree-lined, congested avenues. Among glitzy and lackluster concrete
        structures, well-heeled Thessalonikians strut their stuff, their hip-clipped cell phones

swinging inches from the beggars and street children sitting below them on the sidewalk.  Golden mosaics, frescoes, and floating domes still gleam in the industrial city's side-street churches.                                                    *-Let's Go Greece,* p. 216

What pattern of organization does the author use to get her point across?

_____

Key words/phrases/clues:_____

_____


6.              Just as twilight was falling on the village, a fisherboy called Urashima was drawing his boat up the pebbled shore after a long day at sea.  Young though he was, his skill with sail, hook, and line equalled that of the best fishermen of the village; and on days when it seemed that the sea was empty of fish and his elders lamented over the poor and unsuccessful season, Urashima never failed to return with something to show for his day's labor.

Urashima started back with his catch when he came upon a circle of children flailing something in their midst.

"It's my turn to beat the drum," cried one, and down came a stick.

"Now, all together," they cried, and sticks and seaweed stocks rained down one after the other.

With its dazed head withdrawn under its solid shell for safety, the turtle, too slow to escape his young tormentors, remained motionless, suffering the barbed pains that every blow darted through his shell to all parts of his body.

"What are you doing?" cried Urashima, moved to anger at their cruelty.

"It is no business of yours, Urashima.  It is our turtle.  We caught it and we can do what we like with it."

"If you give us money, it is yours," the boys said.

Urashima handed over the money, and the children, with derisive shouts and laughter ran off to the village.                                    -McAlpine & McAlpine, pp. 106-107


What pattern of organization do the authors use to get their point across?

_____

Key words/phrases/clues:_____

_____

7.          Research on Mars is helping scientists better understand the life cycles of
deserts on Earth and the potential to tap water resources deep beneath the ground.
"All the pictures of the Martian surface are very similar if not identical to what we
see in the very dry deserts of the Earth," said Farouk el-Baz, a long time adviser to
the United States space agency NASA. "In both places we see these channels that
were formed by rain in the geologic past; we see a mixture of rocks on the surface,
very much like you see here today. "                                          -Sapa, AP

What pattern of organization does the author use to get her point across?

_____

Key words/phrases/clues:_____

_____

To practice the skill of Analysis, try Exam Two through Exam Eight.

# CHAPTER SIX

## READING RATE

Although no studies have been completed regarding reading rate on this exam or what the reading rate should be to finish the exam, instructors familiar with this test can give you good information about timing yourselves. In terms of reading rate, you may not have done well for one of several reasons: 1) you read too slowly; 2) you did not keep track of time; 3) you skipped around and did not allow enough time to go back to unanswered items; 4) you spent too much time on one passage or on one question; 5) you did not read the passage but scanned it for answers to particular questions.

Consider the following to see if any of these ideas will help you:

1. It is a good idea for students to know how fast they are reading. Remember, you have been reading for many years now and probably at the same rate. It may be time for a change. Use the timed readings in this chapter to determine your rate. According to what has been stated about different reading rates for particular skills, it is reasonable to state that students should be reading about 200–250 words per minute. This rate should facilitate comprehension as well as insure that the student finishes the test. (*Note*: reading at 150 words per minute will probably not allow enough time to finish the test.) If you still feel that you need to improve your rate after completing this textbook, consider buying a book of timed readings or ask your reading instructor if s/he has any you could borrow.

2. If you are vocalizing while reading silently, you need to know that this habit will slow you down. "Vocalization" can be described as that little voice in your head that "says" the words as you read. To counter this habit, try "chunking," (i.e., reading words in groups instead of word-for-word). There are natural breaks in language; you are familiar with them because you use them when speaking. When reading, punctuation marks and word groupings (e.g., prepositional phrases) will determine some of the chunks, while your eye fixations and mental acuity will determine others.

For example, **instead of reading this way,**

| At | the | Sugar | Bowl | in | 2002, | the | security | officials |
|----|-----|-------|------|----|----|-----|----------|-----------|
| hired | 500 | snipers | to | patrol | the | top | of | the |
| stadium | to | make | sure | the | fans | were | safe. | |

**Try reading in chunks,**

At the Sugar Bowl in 2002,     the security officials     hired 500 snipers

to patrol the top     of the stadium     to make sure     the fans were safe.

Looking at these two methods of reading, you can see how the second one is more efficient. Any time you can save (without sacrificing good comprehension) is especially helpful on a test like the Regents' Reading Exam.

3. Though we practiced scanning exercises in a previous chapter, it is not suggested here that scanning is the first strategy to use when encountering a passage. When reading a selection for the first time, you should read at your regular rate. Your scanning skills will aid you tremendously after you have read the passage and are going back to scan for specific answers to questions. Remember what was discussed in the Overview in Chapter One. It is better not to read the questions before you read the passage. If you read the questions first the last time you took the test, then you already know that strategy did not work for you. Two negative consequences could occur from reading the questions before reading the selection: one, you could read the question wrong which will "color" how you read the passage; and two, you could obsess on one question and not absorb other critical information in the passage. Therefore, read the passage first as quickly as you can while concentrating, then look at the questions.

4. Since losing your place and having to re-read material takes up precious time, practice using a pencil as a "pacer." You can practice pacing yourself by beginning with a 3 x 5 index card. Slide the index card down the page as you read. This will keep you on track and help you concentrate. Soon you will notice that the index card is slowing you down, and you can switch to your pencil. You will also improve your ability to read smoothly.

5. As your rate increases and you are able to maintain 70% or higher on the comprehension questions, you are preparing yourself for success on the Regents' Reading Exam. Find and add other timed readings to your progress chart (found on page 123) and use the chart not only for recording your timed readings but also as a motivational tool.

## Directions for Timed Readings

*Do not worry about reading to memorize every word of the passage. Just read at your regular pace and get the main points of the selection, retaining as much as you can.*

**Step 1.** Tear out only the page with the passage you will be reading and place it face-down on your desk. Wait for the instructor to begin the timed reading. Put your textbook under your desk.

**Step 2.** Your teacher will time you and record times (in 10-second increments) on the blackboard. When you finish reading, look up at the blackboard and write the last time you see in the space at the bottom of your page. This is the number of minutes and seconds it took you to read the passage.

**Step 3.** Put your passage under your desk. *Because this is a traditional timed reading test, you may not look back at the passage while answering the comprehension questions.*

**Step 4.** Now look in your text and tear out the page that has the appropriate comprehension questions for the passage. Answer them to the best of your ability.

**Step 5.** Grade your test. Write your comprehension score on the passage page.

**Step 6.** Go to the Conversion Table at the end of the chapter and convert the time you recorded to Words Per Minute. Write down the Words Per Minutes at the bottom of your passage page.

## General guidelines for timed readings:

A. If you read *over 250 WPM* and scored 80 or higher on the comprehension test questions, you could read at a *slower* rate.

B. If you read *over 250 WPM* and scored below 70 on the comprehension test questions, *slow down.*

C. If you read *under 200 WPM* and scored 80 or higher on the comprehension test questions, read at a *faster rate.*

D. If you read *under 200 WPM* and scored below 70 on the comprehension test questions, you will want to work on the skills covered in the chapters of this book while gradually pushing yourself to read faster.

# TIMED READING TESTS

**TIMED READINGS: PASSAGE ONE**

She once discussed with Lily her inability to be affected by men. Lily laughed. "Just wait until the right man comes long. Besides, according to your horoscope you'll be married soon."

Ten years ago Lily commissioned Celia's horoscope from an astrologer and several predictions had come true. Perhaps on this trip, it would happen.

They embarked on the *Queen Mary*—Lily, who always knew how to manage these things, sat at the Captain's table. Celia was allotted a table for four. Two, who had been to the States, were from London; the other was an Englishman called Richard Marsdon.

And it happened, just like that, Celia thought. The long, startled look they exchanged. The recognition, *and* bizarre overtones. She was then barely conscious of Richard's handsomeness, except that he was tall and dark, and must be over thirty. She saw only the intense hazel eyes under heavy black brows.

"Your Christian name is Celia," he said. "It's a name which has always attracted me. Not sure why, since I've never known any. But I once bought a recording of a sixteenth-century song about a Celia."

The rest of the voyage was a delicious haze.

One evening they climbed to the boat deck after dinner. With faint astonishment she felt Richard begin to tremble. She did not question, nor did she move as he drew away. But he spoke suddenly in a harsh voice.

"I want you, Celia. As you want me. But I'm afraid. At least, there's a barrier."

She stiffened, the moment shattered. "A barrier? I know you've no wife. Have you a mistress then? Or a mother you adore?"

"Nothing like that. I can't explain the trouble, except it goes deep—and far into the past." He stopped.                                          -Seton, pp. 22-25

**MY TIME:** _____

**WORDS PER MINUTE**_____

**COMPREHENSION SCORE**_____

**TIMED READINGS: PASSAGE ONE**

**TIMED READINGS: PASSAGE TWO**

When we came to a halt before a doorway, Mr. Bekku instructed me to get out. He climbed out behind me, and then as if the day hadn't been difficult enough, the worst thing of all happened. For when Satsu tried to get out as well, Mr. Bekku turned and pushed her back with his arm.

"Stay there," he said. "You're going elsewhere."

I looked at Satsu. I felt myself being dragged backward. I heard women's voices and quite a bit of commotion. I was on the point of throwing myself onto the street when suddenly Satsu's mouth fell open at something she saw in the doorway behind me.

I was in a narrow entryway with an ancient-looking well on one side and a few plants on the other. Mr. Bekku had dragged me inside and now he pulled me up onto my feet. There on the step of the entryway, just slipping her feet into her wooden sandals, stood an exquisitely beautiful woman wearing a kimono lovelier than anything I'd ever imagined. I had no doubt the gown was woven of pure silk, and so was the sash, embroidered in pale greens and yellows. And her clothing wasn't the only extraordinary thing about her; her face was painted a kind of rich white. Her hair gleamed darkly and was decorated with ornaments carved out of amber, and with a bar from which tiny silver strips dangled, shimmering as she moved.

This was my first glimpse of Hatsumomo. At the time, she was one of the most renowned geisha in the district. I was so startled by her appearance that I forgot my manners—not that I had developed very good manners yet—and stared directly at her face. She was smiling at me, though not in a kindly way. And then she said:

"Mr. Bekku, could you take out the garbage later? I'd like to be on my way.

There was no garbage in the entryway; she was talking about me.

-Golden, pp. 36-37

**MY TIME:** _____

**WORDS PER MINUTE**_____

**COMPREHENSION SCORE**_____

**TIMED READINGS: PASSAGE TWO**

**TIMED READINGS: PASSAGE THREE**

*Does anyone really know why they choose to celebrate Saint Patrick's Day? Read the excerpt below to learn about this famous saint.*

British by birth, Patrick was the son of a town counselor. When he was sixteen or seventeen, Patrick was kidnapped and taken to Ireland, where he was sold into slavery and spent the next six years of his life suffering under extreme duress. One night he was told in a dream that he would escape his owner, triumph over many hardships, and finally return to freedom in his homeland. Fueled by this thought, Patrick ran away from his master and traveled two hundred miles to a port, where he begged for passage on a ship to Gaul. The sailors initially denied his request, but mysteriously relented at the last minute. After three days at sea and a month traversing wilderness on foot, Patrick reached his home and was reunited with his family.

Patrick entered the priesthood in France and later became a bishop after years of study. During this time, Patrick began to have visions telling him to go back to Ireland and spread his faith. Conveniently, the missionary bishop in Ireland, Saint Palladius, had recently died, and in 432 Patrick was consecrated in his place. Working primarily in the north, Patrick strove to abolish the sun worship of the Irish Druids. In one celebrated event, Patrick defied the pagan priests by spontaneously kindling an Easter fire on a hillside.

Although he encouraged the Irish to become nuns and monks, Patrick never became one himself. Patrick was remarkably successful in his mission, converting almost the entire island region by region before he died in 461, and helping to re-codify the ancient laws defining slavery. Patrick was buried in Downpatrick, which was an important holy shrine until it was destroyed by the British in 1539.

-Morgan, pp. 40-41

**MY TIME: _____**


**WORDS PER MINUTE_____**

**COMPREHENSION SCORE_____**


**TIMED READINGS: PASSAGE THREE**

**TIMED READINGS: PASSAGE FOUR**

*This excerpt was written by a Georgian, Lewis Grizzard:*

I was in Italy for three weeks. Like most tourists, the first challenge I had to face was the language. To better prepare myself, I bought one of those Berlitz guides of "two thousand helpful phrases."

They were right. The guide would have been very helpful—if I had been having a convulsion. The way to say "convulsion" in Italian is roughly, "Io ho le convulsioni." But who's got time to look it up if they're having a convulsion face down in the pasta?

What I finally did was what most Americans do when they can't speak the language. I started using America-Italian, which means putting a vowel on the end of each English word and waving your arms a lot. For instance, if you want to say, "You are standing on my foot," in Italian, you say, "you-o are-o standing-o on-a my-a foot-a." If you look down and point at your foot, it will help-o.

Once you've mastered the language, it's time to go out.

"Are you going out?" asked the bellman at my hotel in Rome.
"Yes," I replied.

"Be careful," he suggested. "The drivers are very aggressive here."

In a matter of minutes, I had figured it out—it was a game of Demolition-io Derby-o. The buses try to run over the cars. The cars try to run over what seems to be everybody and his Italian brother on a motor scooter. And all three try to run down the helpless pedestrians who are nothing more than human bowling pins. I finally figured out that brakes routinely last 100,000 miles since they're seldom used and the quickest way to become rich is to open a body and paint shop.

-Grizzard, pp. 216-219

**MY TIME:** _____

**WORDS PER MINUTE**_____

**COMPREHENSION SCORE**_____

**TIMED READINGS: PASSAGE FOUR**

**TIMED READINGS: PASSAGE FIVE**

The Japanese wars dragged on for many hundreds of years. The warriors, called the Samurai, and the fighters they commanded, would form groups and set out to fight the enemy. They left behind homes and families with no defense, or protected only by servants of the lowest ranking warrior class. In fact, the Samurai left at home only women, young children, and the frail elderly. War took the Samurai quite a distance from home, leaving its defense in the hands of the women. In historical accounts we find numerous descriptions of women who learned to handle weapons and to defend themselves and their kin. Some women carried into battle a weapon which was a long spear, swung like a scythe from side to side and would more often than not fight to the death. But the more common weapon carried by women was the well known dagger. Every woman of Samurai status carried a dagger and was trained in its use. In battle, a woman would hold the dagger with two hands, with the blade toward the face, and charge the enemy in order to deliver a fatal blow. Were a woman to be attacked within reach of her weapon, she would not hesitate to use it to defend her honor. The woman's dagger was used mainly, though, to carry out suicide. Suicide such as this was parallel to the abdomen slicing of the male Samurai, but it entailed instead the slitting of the throat. We must remember that women who were beaten or defeated in battle were expected to be raped, to become servants, or to be murdered. A woman's honor was paramount to her, and disgrace was seen as a fate worse even than death.

                                                                    -Samuel, pp. 15-17

**MY TIME:** _____


**WORDS PER MINUTE_____**

**COMPREHENSION SCORE_____**

**TIMED READINGS: PASSAGE FIVE**

**Questions for TIMED READING: PASSAGE ONE**

1. The main character in the passage is

a. Richard Marsdon.
b. Lily.
c. Celia.

2. Who originally told Celia she would be married "soon"?

a. an astrologer
b. Lily
c. Richard Marsdon

3. Celia was taking a trip

a. by land.
b. by sea.
c. by air.

4. How did Richard become familiar with the name, Celia?

a. through a novel he read
b. through newspaper headlines
c. through a recording he bought

5. Where was Richard Marsdon from?

a. England
b. London
c. an unnamed island

*True-False:*
_____6. Celia would agree with the phrase "love at first sight."
_____7. Richard Marsdon could be described as a "golden god."
_____8. The reader can infer that Richard Marsdon enjoyed his time with Celia.
_____9. Celia had been affected by men since her teenage years.
_____10. Richard Marsdon probably had a troubled past.

**TIMED READINGS: PASSAGE ONE QUESTIONS**

**Questions for TIMED READING: PASSAGE TWO**

*True-False:*

_____1. The young girls did not expect to be separated.

_____2. The reader can infer that the narrator was taken to work in a textile mill.

_____3. The young girls were probably from a wealthy family.

_____4. Mr. Bekku pulled the girl up on her feet to show respect for Hatsumomo.

_____5. Hatsumomo is a famous geisha.

_____6. The geisha's face was painted a beautiful cream color.

_____7. The young girl was very well-mannered..

_____8. Mr. Bekku is the girls' father.

_____9. The reader can infer that Hatusmomo was spoiled.

_____10. Because Hatsumomo was a geisha, she showed outward kindness to the young girl.

**TIMED READINGS: PASSAGE TWO QUESTIONS**

**Questions for** TIMED READINGS: PASSAGE THREE

*True/False:*

_____1. Patrick was British by birth.

_____2. Patrick knew he would find his homeland again because the bishop told him so.

_____3. Patrick eventually became a monk.

_____4. Patrick's calling was to go to Ireland as a missionary.

_____5. Patrick was not successful in converting the Irish pagans.

_____6. Patrick was buried in Downpatrick.

_____7. It is implied in the first sentence that everyone knows who Saint Patrick was.

_____8. Patrick's childhood was extremely difficult.

_____9. Patrick had a personal interest in having slave laws changed in Ireland.

_____10. Ironically, it was the British who destroyed Saint Patrick's burial place.

## Questions for TIMED READINGS:  PASSAGE FOUR

*True/False:*

_____1.  The author wrote this for the purpose of entertaining.

_____2.  Lewis Grizzard visited Italy.

_____3.  Lewis Grizzard believed that the Italian language guide was very helpful.

_____4.  Grizzard advises that to speak Italian, you need only to add a vowel to the end of each English word.

_____5.  Grizzard is from Georgia.

_____6.  Drivers in Italy are known for their good driving behavior.

_____7.  It is implied in the selection that even Italians believe Rome's streets are dangerous.

_____8.  Grizzard compared the driving scene in Rome to Demolition Derby.

_____9.  Most Italians get around by taxi.

_____10.  According to the excerpt, pedestrians in Rome are in the most danger from traffic.

## Questions for TIMED READINGS: PASSAGE FIVE

*True/False:*

_____1. The Japanese wars lasted for hundreds of years.

_____2. When Samurai left their village to fight, they left their homes well protected.

_____3. We can infer from the selection that Japanese women fought in most of the battles.

_____4. The only weapon a woman was allowed to carry was the dagger.

_____5. Women were trained in the use of their weapons.

_____6. Because women were weak physically, they could only hope to wound their enemy and then try to run.

_____7. According to the selection, the woman's dagger was used mostly for suicide.

_____8. Women were willing to kill or die to defend their honor.

_____9. Ritual suicide was the same among men and women.

_____10. To become a servant was viewed as a fate worse than death for a Samurai woman.

# CONVERSION AND PROGRESS CHARTS

| TIME YOU RECORDED | WORDS PER MINUTE |
|---|---|
| 1:00 | 300 |
| 1:10 | 256 |
| 1:20 | 225 |
| 1:30 | 200 |
| 1:40 | 176 |
| 1:50 | 167 |
| 2:00 | 150 |

| PERCENTAGE: | PASSAGE#1 | PASSAGE #2 | PASSAGE#3 | PASSAGE#4 | PASSAGE#5 |
|---|---|---|---|---|---|
| 100 | | | | | |
| 95 | | | | | |
| 90 | | | | | |
| 85 | | | | | |
| 80 | | | | | |
| 75 | | | | | |
| 70 | | | | | |
| 65 | | | | | |
| 60 | | | | | |
| 55 | | | | | |
| 50 | | | | | |
| 45 | | | | | |
| 40 | | | | | |
| 35 | | | | | |
| 30 | | | | | |

**TIMED READINGS: CONVERSION AND PROGRESS CHARTS**

# UNIT TWO

GENERAL DIRECTIONS FOR THE REGENTS'
READING EXAM

SIMULATED DIAGNOSTIC EXAM

TEN SIMULATED EXAMS

## GENERAL DIRECTIONS FOR THE EXAM*

This is a test of reading comprehension. It is designed to measure your understanding of the material that you read.

The test contains 9 passages. Following each passage is a set of questions about the passage. There are 54 questions on the test.

For each question following a passage, choose the *best* response on the basis of the content of the passage.

Do not spend too much time on any one question. If a question seems very difficult, make the most careful guess you can. *Your score is the number of correct answers* that you give; there is no added penalty for wrong answers.

You will have *60 minutes* to complete the test.

_____
*(University System of Georgia website)

# SIMULATED DIAGNOSTIC EXAM

An Irish proverb states a simple truth: "Even a small thorn causes pain." How often, out of thoughtlessness or lack of attention, do we inflict pain, even though we don't want or mean to? We yearn to live gently, and yet gentleness–especially toward ourselves–seems so difficult in our fast paced lives. When we are frantically trying to abide by a timetable that is at odds with our natural ebb and flow, the ability to breathe deeply and choose our reaction is diminished. Before we know it, a thorny comment is automatically launched.

Lost in the acceleration of our pace is the energy and time for supporting ourselves and our loved ones. But with intention, we can cultivate the art of gentleness. However, we will need to make a strong commitment to living gently and adopt an attitude that supports our decision. And as usual, we'll need to start this attitude adjustment by treating ourselves gently. What a thought!

Of course we expect ourselves to be gentle with others, but aren't we supposed to drive ourselves and be our own severest critic? No. In reality, learning to be gentle with ourselves enhances our ability to treat others with respect. Being unforgiving of ourselves and treating ourselves harshly bruises us and in the long run may cause us to bruise others. By being sensitive to ourselves, we are better and safer friends and family members.

-Thoele, pp. 122-123

1. This passage would be classified as

1. religion.
2. philosophy.
3. science.
4. anthropology.

2. It is implied that most people react

1. after taking a deep breath.
2. purposefully.
3. in haste.
4. with patience.

3. The proverb would best be restated as

1. "thorns are dangerous."
2. "pain is a part of life."
3. "sticks and stones may break my bones, but words can never harm me."
4. "even the most insignificant comment can hurt if said harshly."

4. A main idea for the third paragraph is that

1. we purposefully cause pain in other people's lives.
2. thorny comments are automatically launched.
3. being gentle with ourselves enables us to treat others with respect.
4. we should not be forgiving when someone treats us badly.

5. When the author asks the reader to consider the underlined question in paragraph three, she is being

1. sympathetic.
2. ironic.
3. apathetic.
4. ridiculous.

6. The purpose of this selection is to

1. describe Irish culture and its literary
      elements.
2. entertain the reader by discussing how
      frantic humans get.
3. persuade the reader to be gentler to
      him/herself and others.
4. inform the reader of the latest research
      on stress.

**GO ON TO NEXT PAGE**

**DIAGNOSTIC EXAM, PASSAGE ONE**

*The following is an excerpt from Mother Jones' autobiography written in 1925:*

From 1886 workers in the city of Chicago were involved in a movement for an eight-hour day. The city was divided into two angry camps. The working people were on one side—jobless, hungry, cold, fighting police with bare hands. On the other side were the employers, experiencing neither hunger nor cold, supported by the news-papers and by the police.

Extremists took advantage of the discon-tent to preach their doctrines. Speakers used to address huge crowds on the windy shore of Lake Michigan. Although I never endorsed the philosophy of chaos, I often attended the meetings.

In 1886 a bitterly cold winter set in. Long unemployment resulted in terrible suffering. Bread lines increased. Soup kitchens could not handle the masses. On Christmas day, hundreds of poverty-stricken people in rags, paraded down Prairie Avenue before the mansions of the their employers, carrying a black flag (symbolizing the motto "never surrender"). I thought the parade an insane move as it only served to make the police more savage—and the public less sympathetic.

The first of May ushered in the eight-hour day uprising. The newspapers had done everything to alarm the people. All over the city there were strikes and walk-outs. Employers quaked in their boots. They saw revolution. The workers in the McCormick Harvester Works gathered outside the factory. Bricks were thrown. Windows were broken. Someone turned in a riot call.

The police without warning charged down upon the workers, shooting into their midst. Many were trampled under horses' feet, and young men and young girls were shot.

Time marched on. On November 11, the leaders of the extremists in the eight-hour day movement were hanged. Even though the dead were buried, their cause was not. The struggle for more human conditions in the workplace still lives on.

-Angelfire, Internet

7. It is implied that the extremists' main protest centered on

1. police brutality.
2. unfair newspaper coverage.
3. unemployment.
4. unreasonably long work hours.

8. We can infer that Mother Jones attended the speeches on the lake because

1. she endorsed chaos.
2. her friends were the extremists.
3. she was interested in the movement.
4. she wanted to express her discontent.

**DIAGNOSTIC EXAM, PASSAGE TWO**

9. Mother Jones' attitude toward the parade
on Christmas Day was one of

1. sympathy.
2. skepticism.
3. condescension.
4. understanding.


10 . The protesters paraded on Prairie
Avenue because

1. that was the street where the rich
      employers lived.
2. that was where the soup kitchens were
      located.
3. it was the main avenue in Chicago.
4. the police would not attack them in a
      family neighborhood.


11. The selection is written from the point
of view of

1. the workers.
2. the police.
3. Mother Jones.
4. the newspaper editor.


12. The events depicted in the selection
took place in

1. the early 1900's.
2. before the writer was born.
3. after the death of the writer.
4. the late 1800's.

The great prophet of Islam is Muhammad who was born about 570 AD in Mecca, a city in western Arabia. Muhammad's father died before he was born, and the boy's mother died when he was six years old, so Muhammad was raised in the care of relatives.

Mecca was located along a caravan route used for transporting goods from Asia to Syria and other parts of the Middle East. Muhammad was involved in this trade and became the business agent of a wealthy widow, Khadijah, whom he married when he was about twenty-five (she was forty).

Muhammad appears to have spent much time fasting and praying. In 610 he received a revelation from the angel Gabriel that he was to be the Messenger of God—to recite the words of God for his people. These recitations were later collected into the holy book of Islam, the Koran.

While pagan polytheism was the predominant religious belief of Arabia, there were Christians and Jews there with whom Muhammad had come into contact. Muhammad preached a message that there was but one God, Allah, and Muhammad was his prophet. He warned of a judgment day and urged the Meccans to renounce false idols and to accept the bounty and compassion of the one God. The dominant Quraysh tribe rejected his message. They feared that Mecca would lose its place as a pilgrimage center where numerous gods could be worshiped in an ancient building known as the Kaaba. Muhammad became subject to a boycott. He was nevertheless safe as long as his uncle, who was head of a clan associated with the Quraysh tribe,

offered him protection. But in 619 both his uncle and his wife, Khadijah, died. The new clan leader refused to grant Muhammad protection. In 622 Muhammad and about 70 of his followers decided to flee Mecca and go to Medina which is located about 250 miles to the north.

Muhammad had been invited to Medina to act as a peace arbitrator among the feuding tribes. Medina was a city with three Jewish clans as well as a large Arab population. Muhammad made himself the leader of the Arabs of the city and eventually eliminated the Jews (some by execution) who resisted his efforts at conversion. Later he began attacks on Mecca and in 630 he marched into Mecca with little bloodshed. He granted a general amnesty and made Mecca the center of worship of his new religion. When Muhammad died in 632, Islam was the religion of the greater part of the Arabian peninsula.

-Kehoe, et al., pp. 275-276

13. As is stated in the passage, Muhammad was

1. born in Medina.
2. raised in a caravan.
3. cared for by relatives.
4. left at an orphanage.

14. The Quraysh tribe

1. believed in one God.
2. feared Muhammad.
3. believed in Muhammad.
4. rejected Muhammad's message.

**DIAGNOSTIC EXAM, PASSAGE THREE**

15. The passage implies that Muhammad's uncle

1. was not influential with the Quraysh tribe.
2. cared about Muhammad.
3. thought Muhammad was crazy.
4. was a Christian.

16. Polytheism, as used in paragraph two, most nearly means belief in

1. many gods.
2. multiple wives.
3. Christianity.
4. Islam.

17. We can infer that

1. Muhammad had a large Jewish following.
2. Mecca was more progressive than Medina.
3. Muhammad felt threatened by the Jews of Medina.
4. Islam could never replace polytheism.

18. The author's purpose in writing the selection is to

1. inform.
2. persuade.
3. classify.
4. contrast.

19. The style of writing employed is

1. informal.
2. scientific.
3. academic.
4. argumentative.

**GO ON TO NEXT PAGE**

**DIAGNOSTIC EXAM, PASSAGE THREE**

For many of us, sleep is a fairly routine phenomenon. It is true that the amount of sleep that allows us to function most efficiently may vary across individuals. It is also true that the amount of sleep we experience each night tends to decrease as we move into adulthood and old age.

Most of us are also likely to have found that some nights getting to sleep seems harder than normal. However, most of the time, we probably don't think much about sleep. For some individuals, however, sleep is not typically a routine process.

Insomnia, which is variously described as a lack of sleep, a loss of sleep, or poor sleep, is one commonly reported sleep disorder. Many people who believe that they have problems sleeping turn to sleep medications for help. Mendleson estimated that 20 million prescriptions for sleep medications are written per year, with large numbers of additional people seeking help from over-the-counter medications. However, many psychologists, like Carlson, consider sleeping aids to be one of the main causes of sleeping problems. People develop a tolerance to these medications, requiring larger doses as time goes on.

A second sleep disorder is sleep apnea. A person suffering from sleep apnea stops breathing during sleep, which results in a build-up of carbon dioxide, which causes the person to wake up gasping for air. Sleep apnea may be related to narrow airways, more common in obese people, especially men. The frequency of sleep apnea also increases among the elderly, where the cause is often a malfunction of the brain mechanisms that control respiration. In infants, sleep apnea may be a possible cause of sudden infant death syndrome.

Narcolepsy is another common sleep disorder. It appears to occur because certain components of sleep are activated at inappropriate times. The disorder may run in families. The sudden overwhelming urges to sleep, called sleep attacks, which a narcoleptic experiences at various times during waking hours, constitute the primary symptom of narcolepsy.

-Kestner, et al., pp. 87-88

20. The reader can infer that Mendelson

1. is a professor.
2. believes sleep aids are unnecessary.
3. had a child who died due to sleep apnea.
4. is interested in the number of people taking sleep aids.

21. Contrary to popular thinking, Carlson believes that

1. sleep medications are lethal.
2. sleep medications complicate existing sleeping problems.
3. doses of sleep medications remain the same over time.
4. it is possible to reduce dosages of sleep medications over time.

22. A person with sleep apnea

1. stops breathing during sleep.
2. builds up oxygen while sleeping.
3. remains asleep during the night.
4. has wider airways.

**DIAGNOSTIC EXAM, PASSAGE FOUR**

23. <u>Sleep attacks</u> are best described as

1. tossing and turning.
2. insomnia.
3. narcolepsy.
4. fitfulness.


24. In the passage, the author

1. contrasts types of sleep disorders.
2. attempts to persuade the reader to
        consider his views on narcolepsy.
3. prioritizes sleep disorders.
4. classifies types of sleep disorders.


25. Insomnia can be described as all of the
following *except*

1. sleep walking.
2. loss of sleep.
3. poor sleep.
4. lack of sleep.


**GO ON TO NEXT PAGE**

Verbal abuse is a kind of battering which does not leave evidence comparable to physical battering. It can, however, be just as painful, and recovery can take much longer. The abuser often cloaks his attack in a "what's wrong with you, making a big thing out of nothing" attitude. Often, for the verbally abused woman, there is no other witness to her reality and no one who can understand her experience. Friends and family may see the abuser as a nice guy and, certainly, he sees himself as one.

The victim of abuse lives in a confusing world. In public she is with one man, in private he may become another. Behind doors common occurrences may include: 1) subtle diminishing;  2) angry outbursts; 3) cool indifference;  4) one-upmanship; 5) witty sarcasm;  6) silent withholding; or 7) unreasonable demands.

Many women try every approach to improve their relationship: explaining, overlooking, asking, begging, living their lives independently, or not asking for too much. Nothing seems to work. Evans, a writer in this area, indicates that none of these tactics work because verbal abuse is an issue of control, a means of holding power over another.  The abuser is not interested in making the relationship better: s/he is interested in power over the victim and in a tactic called "crazy-making."

The effects of verbal abuse are primarily qualitative. That is, they cannot be seen like the effects of physical abuse. There are no physical signs of injury—no black eyes or broken bones.  The intensity of anguish which the victim suffers determines the extent of the injury.

Evans states that we should remember three critical aspects of verbal abuse when attempting to analyze it: one, the abuse most often takes place behind closed doors; two, the abuser denies the abuse; and three, physical abuse is always preceded by verbal abuse.                    -Evans, pp. 17-19

26. According to the selection, the general public at first glance considers the verbal abuser as

1. mentally unstable.
2. a physical abuser.
3. a nice guy.
4. somewhat aggressive.

27. In the context of this passage, it is implied that crazy-making (paragraph three) involves

1. the victim making the abuser crazy.
2. the abuser making the victim crazy.
3. women believing men are crazy.
4. friends viewing the couple as
    incompatible.

28. The reader can conclude that the reason women's approaches to improving their relationships do not work is that

1. women do not try hard enough.
2. the victim is too aggressive.
3. the abuser pretends the relationship is
    fine the way it is.
4. the approaches have not been tested
    scientifically.

29. <u>Qualitative</u>, as underlined, most nearly indicates that the effects of verbal abuse

1. cannot be seen.
2. are clearly visible.
3. are hazy and clouded.
4. are indeed minimal.

30. Evans would agree with which of the following statements?

1. Physical abuse may follow verbal abuse.
2. Verbal abuse is always followed by physical abuse.
3. Physical abuse is the same as verbal abuse.
4. Verbal abuse is not as harmful as physical abuse.

31. The main idea of the selection is best expressed by the first sentence of which paragraph?

1. 4th paragraph
2. 2nd paragraph
3. 1st paragraph
4. 3rd paragraph

**GO ON TO NEXT PAGE**

**DIAGNOSTIC EXAM, PASSAGE FIVE**

The American landscape was radically altered by "suburban sprawl." A pioneer in this development was William Levitt, who in 1949 built the first subdivision of homes on Long Island—17,500 of them, all exactly alike. Due to memories of inadequate housing during the war, young married couples stood in line for four days to purchase one of his basic four-room houses which sold for less than $10,000, including everything from landscaping to kitchen appliances. Now the American Dream seemed within the grasp of ordinary Americans: they could now build their own nests.

And nests they were. The home became child-centered, and family size was on the rise. One sociological study reported in the late 1940s that a wife was impregnated every seven seconds. The 37.5 million households in 1945 had increased to 53 million by 1960, largely the result of masses of subdivisions mushrooming across the nation. Moreover, women's magazines like *Ladies Home Journal* began to promote the woman's role as a homemaker, gardener, and den mother. In 1954 *McCall's* coined the word "togetherness" to describe the new commitment to a close family.

Eager for the approval of others, young people were as sedate and conservative in their values as their parents. One observer wrote that the "dedication of bourgeois America to personal security" had produced "a generation with strongly middle-aged values." By 1955 twenty-two percent of all college students majored in business, emulating their parents' desire for the job, the home, and the station wagon filled with kids. One poll in the 1950s revealed that

three of youth's greatest heroes were Joe DiMaggio, Doris Day, and Roy Rogers.
-Solberg, et. al, pp. 245-7

32. It is stated that couples stood in line to purchase basic houses because

1. the homes were cheaper because appliances were not included.
2. they wanted to say they were first to buy a subdivision home.
3. they remembered the inadequate housing situation during the war.
4. they wanted homes with appliances included.

33. The phrase, within the grasp of ordinary Americans, most nearly means

1. Americans could now be ordinary.
2. couples now had more than $10,000.
3. Americans now had a yard.
4. most Americans could now buy their own homes.

34. We can infer from the passage that in the late 1940s the population

1. increased.
2. decreased.
3. stayed the same.
4. was not important.

35. The main idea of the last paragraph is that young people of the 1950s

1. were liberal-minded.
2. majored in business.
3. were like their parents.
4. popularized Joe DiMaggio.

36. The author illustrates his point in paragraph two by

1. contrasting *Ladies' Home Journal* and *McCall's* magazines.
2. telling a story.
3. giving personal testimony.
4. describing the American household.

**GO ON TO NEXT PAGE**

One by one, the names were called out, names of law enforcement officers who died in the line of duty in 1988. And as each name was read, a widow, or a mother, or a child would step forward and place a flower in a gigantic wreath.

Some were stoic, as if they had learned to manage their pain, at least in public. Some wept. Some needed assistance in returning to their seats. Around them, the colleagues of their loved one stood proudly in uniform for two hours, impervious to the soaking rain.

Mourners placed 161 flowers in the wreath, each representing a death that had taken place the year before—the loss of a man or woman who willingly under-took risks most of us would never even consider taking.

As members of "the thin blue line," they risked their lives every day to protect their communities and their nation from the terror and destruction of crime. Yet our nation seems to have simply forgotten their service—and their sacrifice.

Of course, these fallen heroes are remembered by their families and friends. But, as years pass, the newspaper clip-pings yellow and crumble. The flowers so carefully saved from the funeral spray turn to dust.

As Chairman of the National Law Enforcement Officers Memorial Fund, I believe that people do care—but that many of us, busy with our own preoccupations, overlook the need to pay homage to those who give their lives in our service.

Though an estimated 30,000 law enforce-ment officers have died in the line of duty since America's beginnings, we as a nation have created no monument to honor their sacrifices. There's no stately building or peaceful garden dedicated to their memory.
-Clark, pp. 1-2

37. The phrase the thin blue line refers to

1. funeral procession.
2. police force.
3. national law enforcement memorial fund.
4. the margin of risk a police officer takes.

38. Overall, the writer uses which of the following to get her point across?

1. journalistic reporting
2. definition
3. persuasion
4. comparison

39. The word colleagues (paragraph two) most nearly means

1. college mates.
2. relatives.
3. superiors.
4. fellow officers.

40. The tone of the passage is

1. somber.
2. distrustful.
3. suspenseful.
4. impartial.

**DIAGNOSTIC EXAM, PASSAGE SEVEN**

41. Since America's beginnings how many officers have died in the line of duty?

1. 3,000,000.
2. 300.
3. 3,000,
4. 30,000.

42. The writer implies that police officers who have fallen

1. are remembered by no one.
2. should receive more recognition.
3. usually have no family to pay for burial.
4. are given elaborate funereal services.

**GO ON TO NEXT PAGE**

**DIAGNOSTIC EXAM, PASSAGE SEVEN**

Anne Hyde was appointed a maid of honor at the court of Mary, Princess of Orange. There Anne met James, the brother of the princess (and King), for the first time.

It was an unpopular match from the start. Strongest opposition came from James's mother, the Queen Dowager, who did everything in her power to prevent her second son's marriage with a commoner. It was totally unacceptable. Indeed, if James's older brother, King Charles, were to die without an heir, then Anne (a commoner) would become Queen. The Queen Dowager even tried to stop the wedding and reprimanded her son for "having such low thoughts as to wish to marry such a woman." The situation was unthinkable. But James was unmoved. The Queen Dowager's pleadings did nothing but strengthen James's resolve— and, anyway, Anne was already pregnant.

They were married by the chaplain privately around midnight. No sooner had the wedding taken place than James began to have misgivings about his wife and looked for ways to reverse the situation. But James needed grounds to break the marriage. Conveniently, there were rumors that the child was not his.

Princess Mary, who not long before had welcomed Anne into her household, was less than amused and pressed her brother to end the marriage. Even Anne's own father, Edward Hyde, refused to support his daughter. He felt that to incur the wrath of the royal family could easily endanger his own position in the government. Anne's father even suggested to Charles,

the King, that he should send his daughter to the Tower and have her executed by act of Parliament for such behavior.

The King, having reluctantly given his consent to his brother's marriage, would not go back on his word.

-Wallace & Taylor, p. 104

43. Reprimanded her son most nearly means

1. talked to him.
2. scolded him.
3. provoked him.
4. begged him.

44. The Queen Dowager did not want James to marry because she believed

1. Anne was already married.
2. her other son, Charles, was in love with Anne.
3. he was marrying beneath his position.
4. she would lose influence over him.

45. The Queen Dowager's attitude toward Anne was

1. venomous and condescending.
2. loving and caring.
3. sympathetic but strict.
4. undisturbed and indifferent.

**GO ON TO THE NEXT PAGE**

**DIAGNOSTIC EXAM, PASSAGE EIGHT**

46. The passage implies that James was
going to marry Anne

1. to spite the king.
2. for her money.
3. to protest social customs.
4. because she was pregnant.

47. After the marriage, everyone supported
James's desire for annulment *except*

1. Anne's father.
2. the King.
3. the Queen Dowager.
4. Princess Mary.

48. Based on the information given in the
last paragraph, we can conclude that

1. James got the annulment.
2. Anne was sent to the Tower.
3. Anne remained married to James.
4. Anne was executed.

**GO ON TO NEXT PAGE**

**DIAGNOSTIC EXAM, PASSAGE EIGHT**

Whether one calls Australia the world's smallest continent or the largest island, it is a land of fascinating contrasts. Almost the size of the U.S., Australia has a population of under 18 million. Australia is also the only continent inhabited by a single nation, although one in five Australians was born overseas.

In Australia, untamed nature is never far from technological civilization. While this proximity is a major attraction to the visitor, it also poses risks that may not be obvious: sharks may lurk in the blue waters of the golden beaches which stud the coastline; the innocent-looking bush stretching from the roadside is likely to be a treacherous thicket. Hardly a weekend goes by without search parties seeking bush walkers–often allegedly experienced–who have become lost in the maze. Mostly they are found. Also, the Australian countryside rarely radiates mellow serenity. More often it appears harsh and alien at first sight. Indeed, one's first encounter with nature in Australia may evoke a feeling of puzzlement, even dismay. After all, the first Europeans who landed there were shocked when they surveyed their surroundings.

While the major resort areas or the big cities provide maximum creature comforts for the most demanding visitor, trips off the beaten track or to the sparsely populated hinterland, called the Outback, need careful preparation by competent experts, for there the traveler will be left very much alone.

These are sensible warnings only. They are not intended to dampen the traveler's interest in surfing or exploring the bush.

**DIAGNOSTIC EXAM, PASSAGE NINE**

On the contrary, by using common sense and readily available advice, the visitor will enjoy a safe Australian vacation, eventually falling in love with the melancholy beauty of much of the continent.

-Barcs, pp.43-44

49. The purpose of the first paragraph is to

1. persuade the reader to visit Australia.
2. contrast Australia to the United States.
3. prove that most Australians are not born there.
4. give some facts about Australia.

50. Hinterland, as underlined, is best described as

1. urban.
2. relaxing.
3. uninhabited.
4. gloomy.

51. Maze, as used in the second paragraph, is a referent for

1. treacherous thicket.
2. bush walker.
3. studded coastline.
4. technological civilization.

52. The author suggests that the "untamed nature" of Australia

1. is serene.
2. may be dangerous.
3. is unattractive in appearance.
4. swallows up all who try to experience it.

53. In the last paragraph, the writer attempts to

1. dampen the traveler's interest.
2. warn the reader of dangers lurking.
3. ease the reader's mind about visiting.
4. encourage the reader not to visit Australia.

54. In the first paragraph, the reader can infer Australia is unique because

1. it is inhabited by 18 million people.
2. it houses major resort areas.
3. it has more visitors than any other continent.
4. the continent is inhabited by a single nation.

**DIAGNOSTIC EXAM, PASSAGE NINE**

# SIMULATED EXAM ONE

Because human beings are so remarkably adept at using language and because they also are reasonably accurate at predicting how others will respond, they acquire the ability to lie. Children usually have a lot to learn about lying and can easily be caught when they fib. With adults, however, it's not so easy to detect the person who is not telling the truth. Is an employer able to determine whether a job applicant is concealing his or her past? Can police investigators tell whether the suspect is truthful when they claim total innocence? In spite of the pride that many people take at being able to spot liars, even well trained interrogators are not much better at telling who is lying, and who is telling the truth.

Employers and law enforcement personnel may use a polygraph (commonly known as a lie detector) in their <u>quest</u> to gain the truth. Traditional polygraphs measure a person's heart rate, blood pressure, breathing rate, and skin conductivity, based on perspiration. Other forms of lie detectors attempt to measure audible and inaudible frequencies in the words that a person speaks. The assumption behind all of these forms of lie detection is that not telling the truth will create some emotional reactions. Machines that record biological arousal can measure these emotional reactions.

Unfortunately (from law enforcement's point of view) using a lie detector is not that simple. For some people, just being "hooked up" to a machine can cause stress that makes truth versus untruth indistinguishable. Questions asked of the suspect might also be personally embarrassing, causing an emotional reaction in an innocent person.

On the other hand, guilty people may beat the polygraph: some might feel no emotion, and show no autonomic arousal when they lie. <u>Delusional people</u> who have lost contact with reality may actually believe their lies.

It would be nice to have a simple way of finding the truth; unfortunately, there's not one. Research on the validity of polygraph results documents their unreliability.

-Kestner, et al., pp. 376-377

1. According to the passage, polygraphs are more likely to be used by

1. psychologists.
2. law enforcement.
3. personal assistants.
4. judges.

2. The main idea of the passage is that when dealing with liars, law enforcement has found that

1. polygraph results are reliable.
2. autonomic arousal can occur for many reasons.
3. polygraph results are not very reliable.
4. human beings have acquired the ability to lie.

3. The word <u>quest</u> as used in the passage most nearly means

1. search.
2. agenda.
3. road.
4. negligence.

4. Most professionals who utilize lie detectors assume that someone telling a lie

1. does not react emotionally or physically.
2. can be detected easily.
3. can not even answer baseline questions without reacting.
4. responds emotionally when hooked up to a lie detector.


5. The author of the selection would probably agree that

1. an individual's blood pressure changes when s/he is lying.
2. an individual's blood pressure does not change when s/he is lying.
3. an individual's blood pressure goes down when s/he is lying.
4. physical reactions are not considered when measuring whether or not a person is lying.


6. The underlined phrase delusional people is best defined as

1. individuals grounded in reality.
2. individuals who take drugs.
3. individuals grounded in fantasy.
4. individuals interested in facts and statistics.

Frodo took <u>it</u> from his breeches-pocket and handed it slowly to the wizard. Gandalf held it up. "Can you see any markings on it?" He asked.

"No," said Frodo. "There are none; it is quite plain."

"Well, then, look!" To Frodo's astonishment the wizard threw it suddenly into the glowing corner of the fire.

"Wait!" he commanded, giving Frodo a quick look from under his bristling brows. Gandalf got up, closed the shutters, and drew the curtains. The room became dark and silent, except for the clack of Sam's hedge trimmers, now nearer to the window.

For a moment the wizard stood looking at the fire; then he stooped and removed the ring with the tongs, and grasped it in his hands.

"Take it." boomed Gandalf. "It is quite cool. Hold it up. And look closely."

As Frodo did so, he now saw fine lines— lines of fire that formed piercingly bright letters. "I cannot read the fiery letters," said Frodo in a quivering voice.

"No, but I can," replied Gandalf. "The letters are Elvish, of an ancient <u>mode</u>, but the language is that of Mordor, which I will not utter here. But in common tongue they say: *One Ring to bring them all and in the darkness bind them.*

Last night I told you of Sauron, the Dark Lord. This is the One Ring that he lost many ages ago, and he must *not* get it."

Frodo sat silent and motionless. Fear seemed to stretch out a vast hand. "I wish the ring had never come to me."

"So do I," said Gandalf, "and so do all who

live to see such times. But that is not for them to decide. All we have to decide is what to do with the time that is given us."
-Tolkien, pp. 54-56

7. The author implies that Sauron can be compared to

1. the devil.
2. an angel.
3. God.
4. a goblin.

8. From the last two paragraphs, the reader can conclude that

1. Gandalf is not a very powerful wizard.
2. Frodo is too fearful to act.
3. Gandalf is afraid of Sauron.
4. Frodo must make a decision.

9. The passage emphasizes

1. storytelling.
2. religious teachings.
3. persuasive techniques.
4. argumentative writing.

10. The underlined word, <u>it</u>, in the first sentence refers to

1. the wizard.
2. the markings.
3. the ring.
4. Frodo's pocket.

**TEST ONE, PASSAGE TWO**

11.  In this context the word <u>mode</u>, as underlined, most probably means

1.  Elf.
2.  common tongue.
3.  jewelry.
4.  style.


12.  An overriding theme of this selection could be titled

1.  good, evil, and Sauron.
2.  Gandalf, Frodo, and the ring.
3.  Frodo confronts Sauron.
4.  elves have a language of their own.


13.  From the selection, the reader can assume that Sam is

1.  Frodo's friend.
2.  an elf.
3.  the gardener.
4.  a wizard.


**GO ON TO NEXT PAGE**


**TEST ONE, PASSAGE TWO**

The idea, that some stimuli cannot be consciously perceived but can still affect our behavior, first received national attention in the 1950s. James Vicary claimed that when he flashed the messages "Buy Popcorn" and "Drink Coca-Cola" on the movie screen at very short durations during a movie, popcorn and soft-drink sales increased significantly. The idea that people were being unconsciously controlled by subliminal messages became a concern for many, including the Federal Communications Committee.

The issue in the 1980s was the controversy of whether or not subliminal information involving satanic and other antisocial messages was being used to influence teenagers. It was claimed that certain popular heavy-metal groups were imbedding these messages in the music by recording backwards. Parents, clergy, and government officials voiced great concern over subliminal persuasion. A study designed specifically to evaluate the ability of listeners to identify the meaning of backward statements found no evidence that the meaning of the backward speech recordings was understood (Vokey & Read).

The most recent interest in subliminal perception has been generated by the marketing of so-called subliminal audio tapes. These tapes, which appear to contain only relaxing sounds, are claimed to contain subliminal messages for helping people improve things like memory or self-esteem, or to aid in weight loss. The idea is that if one plays the tape while asleep, the subliminal message will have its claimed effect. In a well controlled experiment to test the effects of such tapes, Green-wald and others found no evidence that the subliminal content of the tapes had any effect.                    -Kestner, et al., p. 112

14. Subliminal perception was first discussed in

1. the 1980s.
2. the mid 1990s.
3. the early 1990s.
4. the 1950s.

15. It was claimed that satanic messages were imbedded in

1. federal communications.
2. subliminal audio tapes.
3. music recordings.
4. ads in movie theaters.

16. The author's opinion is that

1. subliminal messaging has little effect.
2. subliminal messaging makes an impact.
3. satanic messages in music are acceptable.
4. audio tapes help people lose weight.

17. In the context of the passage, the
advertising of "Buy Popcorn" and "Drink
Coca-Cola" was

1. traditional in its technique.
2. subliminal in its technique.
3. recorded backwards.
4. put on audio tapes.

18. We can infer that James Vicary

1. owned stock in Coca-Cola.
2. believed subliminal advertising worked.
3. was trying to cheat the public.
4. was a member of the Federal
        Communications Committee.

19. In the second paragraph the word
issue most nearly means

1. edition.
2. offspring.
3. information.
4. concern.

**GO ON TO NEXT PAGE**

**TEST ONE, PASSAGE THREE**

Coming out of China, the Black Death reached the shores of Italy in the spring of 1348 unleashing a rampage of death across Europe. By the time the epidemic played itself out three years later, up to fifty percent of Europe's population had fallen victim to the pestilence.

One form derived its name from the swellings or buboes that appeared on a victim's neck, armpits or groin. Although some survived the painful ordeal, the manifestations of these lesions usually signaled the victim had a life expectancy of up to a week. Infected fleas that attached themselves to rats and then to humans spread this bubonic plague.

A second variation, pneumatic plague, attacked the respiratory system and was spread by merely breathing the exhaled air of a victim. It was much more virulent than its bubonic cousin: life expectancy was measured in one or two days.

The Italian writer Giovanni Boccaccio lived through the plague as it ravaged the city of Florence in 1348. Boccaccio wrote a graphic description of the effects of the epidemic on his city: "The symptoms were not the same as in the East, where a gush of blood from the nose was the plain sign of inevitable death; but it began with certain swellings in the groin or under the armpit. They grew to the size of a small apple or an egg. . . . and were vulgarly called tumors. In a short space of time these tumors spread all over the body. Soon after this, black or purple spots appeared on the body, a certain sign of death.

**TEST ONE, PASSAGE FOUR**

The violence of this disease was that it was highly contagious. No doctor's advice, no medicine could alleviate this disease. Very few recovered; most people died within about three days of the appearance of the tumors."
                                    -The Black Death, Internet

20. According to the passage, once a victim noticed buboes on his body

1. he only had up to a week to live.
2. he would soon be well.
3. his respiratory system would fail.
4. he would only live for two days.


21. In paragraph two, these lesions refers to

1. neck, armpits or groin.
2. manifestations.
3. buboes.
4. pestilence.


22. Virulent, as underlined, is best defined as

1. pneumatic.
2. vicious.
3. controversial.
4. innocuous.


23. According to the passage, in regard to the plague that ravaged Florence, a certain sign of death was

1. a swelling the size of an egg.
2. a gush of blood.
3. an infected rat living in the house.
4. a black spot.

24. We can infer that the Black Death also
ravaged

1. the West.
2. Russia.
3. China.
4. the U.S.

25. Alleviate, as used in the last
paragraph, most nearly means

1. enhance.
2. worsen.
3. propagate.
4. make bearable.

**GO ON TO NEXT PAGE**

**TEST ONE, PASSAGE FOUR**

Ask anyone about wolf vocalizations and the howl invariably springs to mind. It is howling that defines the wolf and fascinates us.

The center of a wolf's universe is its pack and howling keeps the pack together. Some have speculated that howling strengthens the social bonds between packmates; that may be so, but chorus howls can also end in nasty quarrels between packmates. Some members, usually the lowest-ranking, may actually be punished for joining in the chorus. Whether howling together actually strengthens social bonds among wolves, or just reaffirms them, is unknown.

We do know, however, that howling keeps packmates together physically. Because wolves range over vast areas to find food, they are often separated from one another. Of all their calls, howling is the only one that works over great distances. Its low pitch and long duration are well-suited for transmission in forests and across tundra.

When a wolf howls, not only can its pack-mates hear it, but so can any other wolf within range. These other wolves may be members of hostile adjacent packs that are competitors for territory and prey. (Pups, especially those under four months of age, love to howl and will usually reply to any howling they hear, even that of total strangers). In northern Minnesota where wolves are protected from humans, the primary cause of death for adult wolves is being killed by wolves from other packs.

There is one member of the pack who will tend to howl more boldly: the alpha male. The alpha male is the dominant male of the pack and father of the pups. He is most likely to howl and even approach a stranger—often with confrontation on his mind. One sign of this aggressiveness can be heard in his voice: his howls become even lower-pitched.     -Harrington, Internet

26. According to the passage, the boldest of a wolf pack is

1. the pregnant female.
2. a pup.
3. the lowest-ranking male.
4. the alpha male.

27. According to the passage, howling serves in all of the following ways *except to*

1. keep the pack together physically.
2. locate lost pups.
3. keep hostile wolves away.
4. reaffirm social bonds.

28. In the second paragraph, them, refers to

1. wolves.
2. social bonds.
3. members.
4. lowest-ranking packmates.

29. The main idea of paragraph three is

1. howling keeps the members of the pack in close contact.
2. wolves range over vast areas to find food.
3. wolves live in forest and tundra.
4. wolves are often separated from one another.

**TEST ONE, PASSAGE FIVE**

30. As used in the passage, <u>tundra</u>, most probably means

1. forest.
2. treeless plains.
3. woodland.
4. oceans.

31. The author of this passage uses a style which is

1. informal but informative.
2. formal and informative.
3. scientific and analytical.
4. argumentative and persuasive.

**GO ON TO NEXT PAGE**

**TEST ONE, PASSAGE FIVE**

Cognitive theories of dreaming, like Cartwright's problem-solving theory, view dreams as having important psychological functions. The main function of dreams in Cartwright's theory is to help individuals solve their ongoing problems. Thus, rather than viewing the content or images in dreams as basically random information, Cartwright suggests that the images are selected to tell a story. They relate to recent experiences, especially experiences which have an emotional component.

Dreams during the course of a night's sleep often have repeated images, suggesting that these images are being activated by ongoing concerns rather than by some random process. Dream meaning relates to the status of our ongoing needs, and dreams function to assimilate new data and reorganize related memories.

In times of stress or personal turmoil, when your emotions run high, the same parts of memory are likely to be activated during REM sleep. Thus, the effects of personal concerns on dreams are most likely to be seen by studying people under stress.

Data relevant to Cartwright's theory were provided by studies of dreaming in individuals undergoing a divorce. These studies have shown that depressed people going through a divorce are likely to enter their first REM stage earlier than nondepressed individuals, and to stay in REM longer. The work of Cartwright and her colleagues also suggests that by incorporating what is stressing you into your dream and experiencing the emotions that go with these sources of stress, the dream provides a

way to work through and overcome what is troubling you.     -Kestner, et. al., pp. 86-7

32.  We can infer that REM refers to

1. Random-Effect-Memory.
2. a stage of dreaming.
3. stress factors.
4. a problem-solving theory.

33.  According to Cartwright, dreams relate to

1. a solitary experience.
2. experiences that have a rational component.
3. recent emotional experiences.
4. random selections from memory.

34.  As underlined in the selection, assimilate most nearly means

1. delete.
2. isolate.
3. disregard.
4. absorb.

35.  The passage states that the effects of personal concerns on dreams are most likely to be seen by

1. examining well adjusted people.
2. testing an individual's memory while awake.
3. analyzing individuals who have been married for many years.
4. studying people under stress.

**TEST ONE, PASSAGE SIX**

36. The central focus of the passage is that

1. dreams attempt to make sense out of
       physiological activities in the brain.
2. dreams provide a way for individuals
       to work through their troubles.
3. Cartwright is the most well-known
       dream researcher.
4. divorced persons have the most
       insightful dreams.

37. The word <u>turmoil</u> most likely means

1. strife.
2. tranquility.
3. divorce.
4. harmony.

**GO ON TO NEXT PAGE**

**TEST ONE, PASSAGE SIX**

Amidst the Medieval and Gothic structures and the unique cityscape filled with a mystique all its own, Florence embraces some of the most exemplary architectural masterpieces created during the <u>Renaissance</u> era. The name, which directly translates as "rebirth," led the way to the development of a new architecture that spanned the 15<sup>th</sup> through the 16<sup>th</sup> centuries. Viewed as the greatest achievement attainable in the arts, these buildings were introduced by Italian architects. The structures were fashioned from a restored interest in classical Roman and Greek theories in art and architecture.

The one man credited with the rise of the Italian style in Renaissance architecture, was a Florentine son by the name of Filippo Brunelleschi. Standing at the threshold of Gothic and Renaissance, Brunelleschi began as a goldsmith and sculptor, but soon after he turned to architecture.

Perhaps one of the structures Brunelleschi is most noted for is the dome of Florence's cathedral. This is a masterful rendering of Brunelleschi's brilliance and ingenuity. With a drum already in place, the Florentine community was faced with the problem of creating a dome structure that spanned the 140-foot diameter base.

Not fearful of such a challenge, Brunelleschi solved this engineering dilemma. Traditional methods were tossed. In their place he created new methods as well as the machinery to execute them. The dome was created around an octagonal section made of twenty-four ribs. To anchor the structure, a "lantern" was placed at the top.

Although Brunelleschi was credited with Renaissance brilliance, this dome was not truly reflective of his own architectural style. In fact, his solutions to the massive structure came from Gothic building principles. This fact only emphasizes Brunelleschi's grandest achievement: he created the first successful merging of both Gothic and Roman building methods.

-Smith

38. <u>Renaissance</u>, as used in the first paragraph, means

1. architecture.
2. era.
3. rebirth.
4. masterpiece.

39. In the context of this passage, the buildings of Florence were based

1. solely on Brunelleschi's theories.
2. on theories of sculpture.
3. on previous Florentine works.
4. on classical Roman and Greek theories.

**GO ON TO NEXT PAGE**

**TEST ONE, PASSAGE SEVEN**

40. According to the passage,
Brunelleschi's grandest achievement was

1. the cathedral itself.
2. merging Gothic and Roman building
      methods.
3. his work as a sculptor.
4. creating a lantern to fortify the dome.


41. The reader can infer that during the
Renaissance, Florence was considered

1. a rural community.
2. a village.
3. a region of city-states.
4. an urban environment.


42. Brunelleschi's attitude toward building the dome was one of

1. fear.
2. enthusiasm.
3. indifference.
4. hopelessness.


**GO ON TO NEXT PAGE**


**TEST ONE, PASSAGE SEVEN**

One needs to recall that the expansionist period into the New World was dominated by different countries at different times. The Portuguese were the first great explorers and began their explorations in the African continent before they went into South America. Then they moved into the area of present-day Brazil; there they introduced the concept of African slavery. The Portuguese influence remained in Brazil; even today, the official language of Brazil is Portuguese.

The Spanish challenged Portugal's dominance and began to dominate the New World in a quest for gold. They solely were influential, controlling South and Central America, Mexico and a vast portion of the present-day United States. The Spanish plundered so much gold from the Native Americans that inflation was the result. There was so much gold in Spain after the Aztecs, Mayas and Incas were conquered that the Spanish actually cast their gold pieces with more gold than the piece was actually worth.

After 1588, with the sinking of the Spanish Armada, the Spanish influence in the New World waned. By this time England and France were competing for a piece of the New World wealth but the days of gold were gone. New commodities would have to replace the fabulous riches of gold.

For the French, dealing with the Native Americans for fur was a mainstay of their economic base; but the English, unlike the Spanish and French, were initially interested in permanent settlements, rather than trading and plundering. Whereas the Spanish and French tended to intermarry among the Native population, English men were accompanied by English women. By their settlement patterns, the European powers each left their legacy, or imprint, in the New World.

-Duke, pp. 7-8

43. Waned, found in the third paragraph, is best defined as

1. decreased.
2. increased.
3. remained constant.
4. fluctuated.

44. A central theme of the passage is that during the expansionist period

1. Spain dominated the New World.
2. the French traded for furs with the Native Americans.
3. the English were marrying Native American women.
4. the New World was dominated at different times by different countries.

45. We can infer from the selection that the Spaniards

1. traded for gold.
2. stole the gold.
3. mined for the gold.
4. married into the tribes for gold.

**TEST ONE, PASSAGE EIGHT**

46. According to the passage, all of the
following statements are true about the
French *except*

1. they married Native American women.
2. they took home vast amounts of gold.
3. fur trading was their economic base.
4. they came to the New World after the
    Spanish.


47. <u>Imprint,</u> as used in the last sentence,
is best defined as

1. indentation.
2. document.
3. legacy.
4. seal.


48. According to the passage, the official
language of Brazil is

1. Spanish.
2. Brazilian.
3. Mayan.
4. Portuguese.


**GO ON TO NEXT PAGE**


**TEST ONE, PASSAGE EIGHT**

The movie, *Gladiator*, though entertaining, does not accurately portray history, particularly when viewed through the roles of Commodus and Lucilla.

Commodus, who became emperor of Rome in 180, was not of average build, dark-haired, nor did he fight with his right hand as in the movie version. In reality, he had a strong physique, sported golden-blond hair, and fought with his left hand. Also, he was not always single: at the age of sixteen, he married Bruttia Crispina (whom he soon after executed for adultery).

In the movie version, Lucilla is the sister that Commodus lusts after. The picture of Commodus as a man starved for affection has some support in historical sources. In *Historia Augusta* the sexual excesses that are typically <u>ascribed to</u> a tyrannical ruler are true of the emperor's behavior. In historical sources, however, Lucilla is the only sister with whom Commodus is *not* accused of incestuous relations.

Not many of the facts of Lucilla's life were revealed in the movie: Lucilla is shown as a once-married mother with a son who is heir to the throne. Historically speaking, Lucilla was fourteen when she married, and she bore three children before she was widowed in her late teens. Her father forced her to remarry immediately. Lucilla had nothing in common with her new husband. Always in consultation with her mother, both Lucilla and her mother bitterly resented the marriage: she was only nineteen, and he was over fifty.

As the movie indicates, Lucilla plotted to kill Commodus in 182. Nothing happened to her in the movie, but we know from history books that she was summarily executed for her part in the plot.

**TEST ONE, PASSAGE NINE**

As for Commodus, in the *Gladiator* he was killed in the arena in front of all of Rome. Actually, he did not die by a gladiator's hand; he was assassinated by assailants of his own court.

One needs to be <u>wary of</u> historical fiction, whether it is read or viewed on screen.                                    -Ward, internet

49. The author makes his point through the use of

1. narration.
2. contrast.
3. description.
4. persuasion.

50. The author's tone is

1. mostly nostalgic.
2. a bit ironic.
3. extremely sarcastic.
4. somewhat persuasive.

51. <u>Ascribed to,</u> as underlined, most nearly means

1. unrelated to.
2. discredited.
3. associated with.
4. inscribed.

52. The reader can infer that Commodus

1. was married for many years.
2. had many children.
3. was never married.
4. was married only for a short time.

53. The main idea of the selection is that

1. Commodus was like a dictator.
2. one needs to be wary of historical fiction.
3. you cannot trust anyone, not even
        relatives.
4. Roman emperors were barbarians.


54. The phrase <u>wary of</u> may be defined
as

1. cautious about.
2. sure of.
3. surprised by.
4. bored with.

# SIMULATED EXAM TWO

Imagine the following scenario. You go to the supermarket one day to buy a half gallon of milk. You are in a hurry and pick up the milk and head over to the express checkout line where it is clearly stated on a sign that the line is for customers purchasing 12 items or less. You get in line and notice that the person in front of you has more than the maximum number of items.

You count the items in that person's cart, all the way up to 18. You look at the sign above the checkout—it says 12 items maximum, and cash only. As you are counting again, the person behind the register starts scanning the items. Then you see the person in front of you pulling out a checkbook. What do you think? Can't they read? Can't they count? You look at the person and say to yourself, "This person is inconsiderate. I have to wait because the person in front of me is a jerk." All these thoughts indicate that you see this person's behavior as evidence of his or her inner traits—bad things are done by bad people, after all.

Now imagine a different scenario. The semester is coming to an end. Being the wonderful person that you are, you have invited all your classmates to your place for a spaghetti dinner. On the day of the dinner, at about 5:00 p.m., you suddenly remember that you are hosting a dinner! You rush to the supermarket to get what you need. You buy four large jars of spaghetti sauce, four boxes of spaghetti, two packets of cheese, five loaves of garlic bread, two bags of tossed salad and a jumbo bottle of salad dressing. You now have 18 items and you rush to the checkout lines. They are jammed with people and their overflowing carts. You glance at the express checkout and see it's empty. So you rush over and quickly start putting your items on the belt. The checkout person scans the first couple of items and just then three people show up behind you with one or two items each.

-Kestner, et al., pp. 438-439

1. Scenario, as used in the passage, is best defined as

1. situation.
2. landscape.
3. view.
4. problem.

2. "You" in the first paragraph is irritated because

1. the cashier scanned the items without counting them.
2. the express lane closed as "you" approached it.
3. there was no milk.
4. someone got in the express lane who had more than 12 items.

3. The author gets his point across through the use of

1. sarcasm.
2. metaphor.
3. irony.
4. figurative language.

4. The reader can assume that "you" is a

1. teacher.
2. student.
3. cashier.
4. bad person.

5. The main idea of the passage is

1. don't do your friends any favors.
2. you can use the express lane under
      certain conditions.
3. a lot of jerks shop at the grocery
      store.
4. we give ourselves the benefit of the
      doubt, but we don't do the same
      for others.

6. From the information we are given in
the second scenario, "you"

1. slows down the express lane.
2. calls the man behind him a jerk.
3. politely gives his place to the people
      behind him.
4. thinks that he, himself, is being a
      jerk.

**GO ON TO NEXT PAGE**

**TEST TWO, PASSAGE ONE**

As a growing number of students traveled to cities like Paris, Bologna, and Salerno in search of the best teachers, they unofficially established themselves in rented halls or rooms, hired the professors, and set the terms and conditions of their apprenticeship. These included the length and content of the lectures, the length of the academic terms, the fines the masters would have to pay for absence, for not covering the text in the required time, or for drawing less than five students to their lectures. At the University of Bologna, formally established by Emperor Barbarossa in 1158, the corporation of students controlled the university.

Not unlike university students of today, the all male medieval students attended lectures, took notes, studied for examinations, and learned the art of oral disputation (questioning and thinking on one's feet). However, there were notable differences. Classes were taught in Latin, the universal language of the Church and scholarship, not in the everyday tongue. Every student who entered the university was expected to be well versed in classical Latin grammar and literature. For lectures, professors read authoritative texts, such as the Bible or the work of Aristotle, and made comments on these texts.

The curriculum consisted of studying the seven liberal arts. Upon the completion of the liberal arts curriculum after three or four years, if the student passed rigorous, comprehensive examinations, he would be awarded a baccalaureate degree. A significant difference between then and now is that students were examined orally and in public.          -Kehoe, et al., pp. 324-325

**TEST TWO, PASSAGE TWO**

7. We can assume from the passage that students during this era

1. were in control of their education.
2. had limited educational opportunities.
3. were more intelligent than students today.
4. never studied for a master's degree.

8. According to the passage, students held professors accountable for all of the following *except*

1. the content of the course.
2. absences.
3. number of students in the classes.
4. writing of supplemental materials.

9. The University of Bologna was established by

1. the Church.
2. the emperor.
3. Aristotle.
4. a corporation of students.

10. According to the passage,

1. the majority of professors were women.
2. men believed women should stay at home and have children.
3. women were not taught Latin.
4. women did not study at university.

11.  A major difference between students today and students of the 1150s is that students today

1.  do not take notes during lectures.
2.  are examined publicly.
3.  are not taught in Latin.
4.  do not attend university.


12.  As used in the second paragraph, <u>oral disputation</u> most likely means

1.  public debate.
2.  private submission.
3.  private agreement.
4.  public broadcasting.


**GO ON TO NEXT PAGE**


**TEST TWO, PASSAGE TWO**

Some of the same questions are asked over and over by Americans who become interested in Japan and things Japanese. Here are two of those questions, along with the answers.

*Hasn't Japan become "Americanized' in recent years?* It was about 125 years ago that Japan opened up to the outside world after a long period of seclusion. From that period (the Meiji era), Japanese delegations traveled everywhere, learning Western forms of every kind of institution: from schooling to transportation to sports. Baseball has been played in Japan for more than a century, for example. So while it is true that there has been a tremendous Western influence exerted in recent years, even as there has been something of a Japanization in the United States, it is not something new. Moreover, Americans are likely to think that such changes are continuous and cumulative, so that every day Japan is somehow less Japanese and more Western; but this has not been the case in the past and is not likely to be so in the future.

*Don't most people in Japan speak English?* The study of English is required in schools, but in the past and even today, a foreign language is studied mostly for the purpose of reading and, to a lesser extent, writing. Speaking a foreign language has not been important. This is because the chances of being able to speak with a foreigner were remote in the past. Also, in Japan what is written has always been valued in a way that speaking has not.      -Condon, pp. 75-6

13.  According to the article, Japan opened up to the world

1.  when the United States was Japanized.
2.  after the first baseball game was played.
3.  over a century ago.
4.  before the Meiji era.

14.  In the context of this passage, Japanization (paragraph two) means that

1.  Japan incorporated ideas from the U.S.
2.  the U.S. incorporated ideas from Japan.
3.  U.S. citizens traveled to Japan.
4.  Japan retained the good from outsiders and disregarded the bad.

15.  The author would probably agree that

1.  Western institutions are better than Japanese institutions.
2.  Americanization of Japan is a new concept.
3.  A complete Americanization of Japan will occur within the next century.
4.  Japan will always remain Japanese.

16.  It can be inferred from the passage that

1.  English has always been taught in
        Japanese schools.
2.  in Japan, English has become more
        important than the Japanese
        language.
3.  if you want to speak English in Japan,
        look for an International School.
4.  English conversation is not widely
        taught in Japan.


17.  The author's style is

1.  formal.
2.  rigid.
3.  chatty.
4.  sarcastic.


18.  The main idea of the passage is that

1.  English is prevalent in Japan.
2.  foreigners sometimes have the wrong idea
        about Japan.
3.  it is difficult for Westerners to visit Japan.
4.  baseball is as popular in Japan as it is in the
        United States.


**GO ON TO NEXT PAGE**


**TEST TWO, PASSAGE THREE**

The Prince swayed as he walked into the Chapel Royal. The two unmarried Dukes on either side of him moved closer. There was a hushed silence throughout the chapel and all attention was focused on two brilliant figures. The Prince swayed again, magnificent in his blue velvet but, as many noticed, looking confused and uneasy; and Caroline of Brunswick, shimmering in her bejewelled white satin with the diamond coronet on her head, looked a true Princess.

But the Prince kept his face turned from her. He was thinking of that other ceremony which had taken place in Mrs. Fitzherbert's house in Park Street. That was a real marriage; this was a farce; and he yearned for Maria, whom he knew he should never have left. If he had left her for marriage to this woman, it would have been a different matter, for this could be blamed on the exigencies of State. But he had deserted her for Lady Jersey whom he was discovering to be worthless.

And here he was at the altar about to be married to a woman he didn't know. He could see no virtue in her. To him she was unattractive, and even the fumes of brandy which dulled his senses could not free him from the future he visualized.

How different that ceremony in Park Street and the ecstasy which had followed.

Is it too late? But of course it was too late. Here he was, kneeling at the altar, and the Archbishop of Canterbury was about to conduct the ceremony.

He stumbled to his feet. He must get away. He could not go on with this. There was a sudden silence in the chapel. All eyes were on the Prince of Wales; all wondered what drama they were about to witness.

-Plaidy, pp. 130-132

19. We can infer from the selection that the Prince did not want to marry Caroline because

1. he was homosexual.
2. Caroline was a foreigner.
3. he was married to Lady Jersey.
4. he wanted to be with Maria.

20. The reader can deduce that the wedding is

1. for royalty.
2. a dream come true for the bride and groom.
3. a simple affair.
4. being held for the common folk.

21. Two brilliant figures (first paragraph) refers to

1. the two unmarried Dukes.
2. Mrs. Fitzherbert and Maria.
3. the Prince and Caroline of Brunswick.
4. Lady Jersey and the Prince of Wales.

22. As underlined in the passage, farce most nearly means

1. fact.
2. fake.
3. luxury.
4. festival.

**TEST TWO, PASSAGE FOUR**

23. The Prince can be described as

1. exultant.
2. argumentative.
3. indifferent.
4. depressed.

24. The last paragraph leaves the reader with a sense of

1. ecstasy.
2. romance.
3. suspense.
4. hope.

·GO ON TO NEXT PAGE

**TEST TWO, PASSAGE FOUR**

Covert behavior falls under the subject of psychology. One question that we face is how can one scientifically study a behavior that is private, <u>implicit</u>, and not publicly observed?

For example, many people are involved in a romantic relationship. In such a relationship, it is very common for a person to express his or her love for the other person. Love is a wonderful emotion to experience, but can it be studied scientifically? In other words, how can we as psychologists test or prove that one person loves another?

As an emotion, love is experienced as a private, internal event in one person. Do you take it on faith, or the other person's word? A scientist studying love would want proof or evidence that can be counted. He would want to define love in terms that may be seen and counted by another person. What could be measured? How about simply counting the number of times that one person tells the other, "I love you"? Or hooking the person up to a machine that measures physiological responses like respiration, heart beat, blood pressure, or skin temperature. Or measuring the frequency of kissing, the amount of money one person spends on the other, or the duration that the couple spends time together. In fact, all of these measures could actually be graphed. Now, you might be saying to yourself, "That is not love; love is more complicated than all that and more personal."

In order to be studied scientifically, love or any other behavior has to be defined in terms that are open, unambiguous, public, and measurable. Therefore, when we think about science we have to remember one important point: science does not have all the answers for us.                    -Kestner, et. al., pp. 4-5

25. The word <u>implicit</u> most nearly means

1. public.
2. illegal.
3. indirect.
4. not complicated.

26. The authors convey their point by

1. defining the field of "psychology."
2. describing a psychological event.
3. giving a testimonial.
4. presenting an example.

27. The reader can deduce from the information in the passage that

1. love does not exist.
2. love may never be studied in purely scientific terms.
3. all feelings are overt.
4. only scientists should study love.

28. In regard to a couple's relation-ship, all of the following can be measured except

1. kissing.
2. loving.
3. time spent together.
4. money spent on one another.

**TEST TWO, PASSAGE FIVE**

29. A main focus of the passage is that

1. love can easily be defined.
2. science can measure covert behavior.
3. an individual should accept love on
      faith.
4. science does not always have the
      answers.


30. Most probably the author is a(n)

1. journalist.
2. psychologist.
3. sociologist.
4. expert on love.


**GO ON TO NEXT PAGE**


**TEST TWO, PASSAGE FIVE**

Anorexia nervosa is an eating disorder that involves the relentless pursuit of thinness through starvation and/or extreme exercise behavior. It can eventually lead to death if it is not treated. It primarily affects females during adolescence and early adulthood, with the most common age (at onset) of 12 to 18; only about five percent of anorexics are male. Anorexia is rarely reported outside the Western industrialized countries of the world. Most anorexics are young, white females who are often bright, talented perfectionists usually preoccupied with feeling in control. Typically, they come from well-educated, middle-income and upper-income families.

Although anorexics avoid eating, they do have a high interest in food. They cook for others, they talk about food, and they may insist on watching others eat. Anorexics have distorted body images, thinking that they will become attractive only when they become skeletal in appearance. As self-starvation continues and the fat content of the body drops to a bare minimum, menstruation usually stops for females.

Numerous causes of anorexia have been proposed including societal, psychological, and physiological factors. The societal factors most often cited are the current fashion trend and glorification of thinness. Psychological factors include motivation for attention, desire for individuality, and denial of sexuality. Physiological causes involve the hypothalamus, which becomes abnormal. There are long-term effects such as infertility, loss of muscle mass, brittle bones, and internal organ damage.

**TEST TWO, PASSAGE SIX**

Death results in somewhere between two percent to ten percent of all anorexics.

-Kestner, et al., pp. 364-365

31. It is suggested in the passage that anorexia is

1. found most often in Asian nations.
2. never found in a nonindustrialized country.
3. particularly evident in countries such as Australia, the United States, and England.
4. widespread throughout the world.

32. Anorexia is rarely found among

1. teenagers.
2. white females.
3. young males.
4. well-educated young women.

33. All of the following are characteristics of an anorexic *except*

1. they have a high interest in food.
2. they become skeletal.
3. if female, they stop menstruating.
4. they have high self-esteem.

34. According to the selection, infertility is an example of a

1. psychological effect of anorexia.
2. physiological effect of anorexia.
3. societal effect of anorexia.
4. mental effect of anorexia.

35. <u>Physiological causes,</u> as cited in the passage, most nearly relate to

1. emotions.
2. physics.
3. mental ability.
4. physical health.

36. The author's tone is

1. factual.
2. emotional.
3. immature.
4. dramatic.

**GO ON TO NEXT PAGE**

**TEST TWO, PASSAGE SIX**

The diversity of American Indian tribes precludes a unification of their religions and their belief systems. Anthropologists have compiled a huge trove of information detailing practices and beliefs of many different tribes. While there is an abundance of popularized versions of Native American spirituality by some researchers, the versions are not the products of the tribes or their members.

The origins of contemporary Native American religion can be traced back 30,000 to 60,000 years with the arrival of the first groups of people from north east Asia. The religion of Native Americans has developed from the hunting taboos, animal ceremonialism, beliefs in spirits, and shamanism embraced by those early ancestors. Since these peoples settled in America slowly and in small groups over several thousand years, we still lack precise immigration knowledge.

The Native American Church, or Peyote Church, illustrates a trend of manipulating traditional Native American spirituality. It incorporates Christianity while moving away from tribal-specific religion. Christianity has routinely penetrated Native American spirituality in the last century. And in the last few decades, New Age spirituality has taken advantage of that trend. New Agers and charlatans alike have radically revised traditional Native American religions: in today's world, "Star Beings" (rather than buffalo) are pondered. Outraged Native

Americans continue to expose those they see exploiting traditional Native American spirituality.

-"Native American Spirituality," internet

37. The word, precludes, in the first sentence most nearly means

1. makes easy.
2. prevents.
3. comes before.
4. comes after.

38. We can infer from the passage that popularized versions of Native American spirituality

1. have not correctly portrayed Native American religions and belief systems.
2. present accurate information about the immigration patterns of Native Americans.
3. do not give enough information to summarize Native American religions.
4. mostly emphasize how Christianity relates to Native American religion.

39. The author believes the Native Americans

1. descend from shamanism.
2. know the history of their migration.
3. migrated from Asia.
4. traveled from North America.

**TEST TWO, PASSAGE SEVEN**

40. The author's attitude toward the Native American Church is one of

1. admiration.
2. skepticism.
3. neutrality.
4. exaltation.

41. The author uses "Star Beings" as an example of

1. the absurdity of New Agers making claims on Native American spirituality.
2. an advertising slogan for Native American religions.
3. traditional shamanistic practices.
4. a famous quote.

42. The purpose of the last paragraph is to

1. describe Christianity.
2. praise New Age spirituality.
3. expose manipulators of Native American spirituality.
4. condone New Agers' actions.

**GO ON TO NEXT PAGE**

**TEST TWO, PASSAGE SEVEN**

With the onslaught of the many 'Crime TV' shows which focus on forensic science, such as *CSI: Crime Scene Investigation*, there has been a dramatic rise in the enrollment in forensics courses at the college level nationwide. One example of this phenomenon is the interest shown by the student body at Purdue University in Indiana.

"Introduction to Forensic Science" is being offered for the first time Fall, 2003. The course introduces students to topics ranging from forensic crime scene techniques to entomology (interestingly, knowledge of the life cycles of insects help investigators determine the time and location of death). In addition, when investigating a crime, forensic scientists often draw upon the fields of biology, physics, botany, and computer science. Trace evidence, court room involvement and new trends in forensic investigations are also covered in the course. Because analyzing and reconstructing a crime often requires expertise from medical examiners, such as psychologists and psychological profilers, students are exposed to guest lecturers in those fields. Neal Haskell, who established the UT Forensic Anthropology Facility to study human decomposition, is one such lecturer.

Other highlights of the course are: 1) opportunities for students to meet professionals in forensics, including crime laboratory investigators from local, state, and federal agencies; 2) provisions for students to review the cases solved by these professional crime scene investigators; and 3) viewings of clips from television shows such as *CSI* and *Justice Files* which illustrate crime investigations in progress.

Aiming to satisfy student curiosity about crime investigations while providing information on the real-life science and technology used to solve crimes, the introductory course promises to be an important addition to the university curriculum.

-Gaidos, internet

43. Entomology is most integral to the field of forensics in regard to determining

1. who the victim is.
2. the time of death of the victim.
3. who the perpetrator is.
4. how the victim died.

44. The course "Introduction to Forensic Science" is being offered

1. at the University of Tennessee.
2. on television.
3. by guest lecturers from the local, state, and federal levels.
4. through Purdue University.

45. The central focus of the passage is

1. *CSI* is the most popular crime TV show.
2. new trends are covered in introductory forensics courses.
3. the enhanced forensic course will be an important addition to the Purdue University curriculum.
4. students view clips of crime TV shows during class.

46. The word <u>onslaught,</u> as used in the first sentence, most nearly means

1. sudden increase.
2. slow decrease.
3. canny advertising.
4. ongoing discussion.

47. The author illustrates his point by using

1. contrast.
2. argumentation.
3. narration.
4. example.

48. The reader can infer that

1. students take forensics classes to earn an easy "A."
2. crime TV shows are the reason students are now interested in forensics classes.
3. guest lecturers have not been invited to forensic classes in the past.
4. traditionally, there has been wide interest in forensics classes across the country.

**GO ON TO NEXT PAGE**

**TEST TWO, PASSAGE EIGHT**

A mass murder of French Protestants in Paris sprang from the attempted murder of one man, Admiral Coligny, during the feast of Saint Bartholomew. The assassination order was given by a powerful woman, Catherine de' Medici, the Catholic king's mother. It was because the attack made on Coligny had failed that Catherine conceived the idea of a general massacre. She saw in this decision a means of preserving her influence over the king. Also, she wanted to prevent the vengeance of the Protestants who were outraged by the attack made on their admiral.

Because the wedding of Henry of Navarre was being held that same week, many Protestants were in Paris, thus presenting the opportunity for mass murder. Toward midnight the troops took up arms in and around the Louvre, and Coligny's home was surrounded. Besme, a man loyal to the Queen Mother, plunged a dagger into the admiral's breast and flung his body out the window.

Coligny was the first victim; his death was followed by the killing of minor leaders and of all Protestants within reach of the soldiery. On the following morning blood flowed in streams; houses of the rich were pillaged regardless of the religious opinions of their owners. Some of the corpses were buried by gravediggers of the Cemetery of the Innocents, but most were thrown into the Seine. The massacre continued even after a royal order to stop, and it spread from Paris into other regions of France.

News of the massacre was welcomed by the pope and the king of Spain. Protestants, however, were horrified; the massacre continued into October, and an estimated 70,000 were killed in all of France. The killings rekindled the ill-will between Protestants and Catholics, and consequently there was a resumption of civil war.

-The Columbia Electronic Encyclopedia & New Advent, Internet

49. We can infer that the King of Spain was

1. a Protestant.
2. related to the pope.
3. a Catholic.
4. married to Catherine de' Medici.

50. The massacre began

1. the week of the wedding of Henry Navarre.
2. a week after the assassination of the admiral.
3. in October.
4. upon the resumption of civil war.

51. Resumption most nearly means

1. end.
2. truce.
3. origination.
4. restart.

52. In paragraph two, the author makes her point through the use of

1. definition.
2. contrast.
3. analytical reasoning.
4. description.

**TEST TWO, PASSAGE NINE**

53. The reader can infer from the passage that Catherine de' Medici gave the assassination order on Coligny

1. because Coligny had ignored her.
2. to make amends with the Protestants.
3. because Henry of Navarre was getting married.
4. because he was a threat to her relationship with her son.


54. Besme was probably a(n)

1. soldier.
2. Protestant.
3. grave-digger.
4. outlaw.

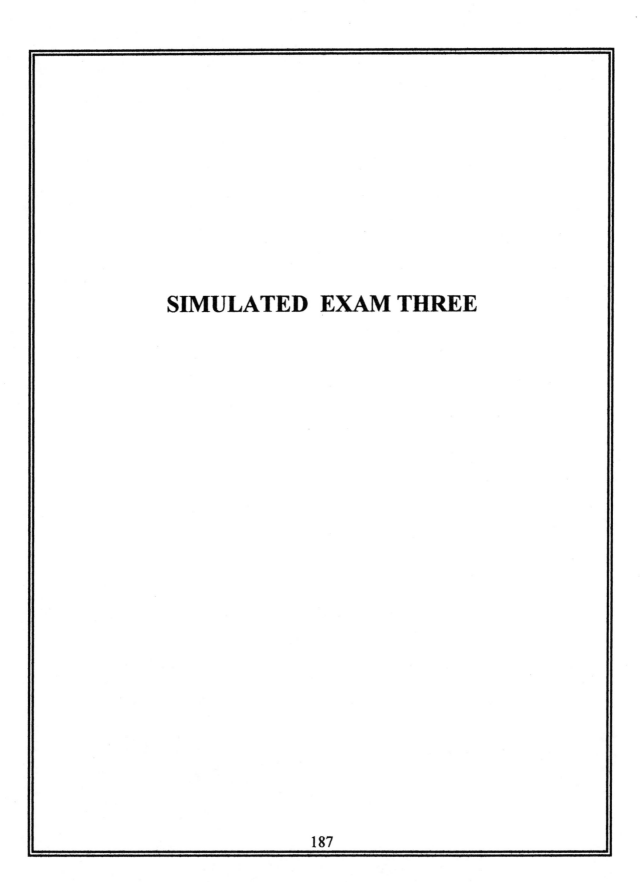

# SIMULATED EXAM THREE

History will record 2001 as a watershed year in the international fight against terrorism. The events of September 11 of that year underlined civilized nations as no other event has. The President's call to arms outlined a global campaign along multiple fronts: Diplomatic, Intelligence, Law Enforcement, and Military, among others.

First, State Department officials immediately began working with foreign officials to forge a coalition to support a response. The President and the Secretary of State met with leaders from more than 50 nations. In addition organizations such as the European Union and NATO took steps to enhance information sharing, to tighten border security, and to combat terrorist financing. Public diplomacy remains in the forefront; the Department of State is aggressively seeking to counter distorted views of the United States overseas.

Second, cooperation among intelligence agencies around the world has expanded to unprecedented levels. Sharing of intelligence about terrorist movements and their planned attacks is an absolute prerequisite for successful interdiction. Such information is extremely valuable in identifying terrorist cells before they have a chance to act.

Third, law enforcement professionals have launched a global dragnet to identify, arrest, and bring terrorists to justice. The FBI has led the law-enforcement engagement, working with all federal, state, and local agencies. To date, more than 7,000 FBI agents have worked diligently to unravel the plans of Al-Qaeda cells.

Last, on September 12, the UN Security Council condemned the attacks and reiterated the inherent right of collective self-defense in accordance with the UN Charter. NATO reiterated that "an armed attack on one or more of the allies in Europe or North America shall be considered an attack against them all." Consequently 136 countries offered a range of military assistance, 89 granted overflight authority, and 76 granted landing rights for U.S. military aircraft.

-U.S. Department of State, Internet

1. The reader can infer that the President

1. understands that he needs support of other nations in the war against terrorism.
2. wants to unilaterally fight terrorism.
3. believes the European Union has done enough to fight terrorism.
4. does not care about the image of the United States overseas when it comes to fighting terrorism.

2. U.S. and foreign officials forged a coalition

1. because of the State Department.
2. to fight terrorism on all fronts.
3. to support a response to the President.
4. to create NATO.

3. Galvanized, as used in paragraph one, is best defined as

1. separated.
2. neutralized.
3. sympathized.
4. roused.

4. The author would probably agree that

1. no Al-Qaeda cells exist except in the
   Middle East.
2. the CIA should head all aspects of
   counter-terrorism efforts.
3. there are Al-Qaeda cells in the United
   States.
4. sharing of intelligence with other
   nations is dangerous.

5. In the last paragraph, the author uses
the UN Security Council's condemnation
as an example of a(n)

1. diplomatic support.
2. military support.
3. law-enforcement support.
4. intelligence support.

6. The phrase collective self-defense most
likely means that if there is an attack on a
European or North American ally,

1. nations will collectively vote on war
   strategies.
2. one nation will respond upon
   agreement from all.
3. only the nation attacked can respond.
4. an attack on one elicits a response from
   all.

7. The word interdiction most nearly
means

1. solutions.
2. accusations.
3. prevention.
4. attacks.

**GO ON TO NEXT PAGE**

**TEST THREE, PASSAGE ONE**

What, then, was the Renaissance and why did it begin in Italy? One can often define an age by contrasting it to another. The Middle Ages revolved around the Age of Faith. The religion of Christianity gave definition to the Middle Ages. The search for salvation was the primary motivation for most people within Christendom. Individuals during the Middle Ages were God-centered.

During the Middle Ages, society was predominantly agrarian. It was ruled by a warrior nobility. The Roman Catholic Church with its priests, monks, and bishops formed the First Estate. The pope was not only a spiritual leader but a powerful political force.

In contrast, the Renaissance was man-centered. It was secular rather than spiritual. This does not mean that religion and salvation were not important, but they were not the focal point of most people's lives.

The Renaissance started in Italy because of four basic reasons. First, Italy exuded an independence and freedom: urban life had never disappeared entirely in Italy, the way it had in the many places in Europe.

Second, for some time, Venice had outfitted the crusaders and was the conduit for the silk and spice trade from India and China. Merchant banking families, like the Medici in Florence, were able to profit from these commercial endeavors and became the ruling elite. These wealthy bankers were able to finance and patronize the arts, providing employment for the famous painters, sculptors and architects of the time.

Furthermore, the Byzantines and Moslems cross-fertilized the urban city-states with their cultural ideas.

Last, Italy had many reminders of the Roman past: the road network, the aqueducts, the public buildings, the monuments.

In conclusion, the freedom of the urban elite, wealth, new ideas, and a standing heritage from the past–all of these factors contributed to a shift in attitude that made the Renaissance.

-Kehoe, et. al., pp.414-5

8. Overall, in paragraphs four through eight, the author makes his point through

1. definition.
2. examples.
3. reasons.
4. sarcasm.

9. The Renaissance period focused on

1. the search for salvation.
2. faith.
3. agrarian issues.
4. man.

10. The word secular, as used in the passage, most nearly means

1. religious.
2. worldly.
3. sectional.
4. mystical.

**TEST THREE, PASSAGE TWO**

11. According to the passage, the Medicis were

1. bankers.
2. crusaders.
3. commoners.
4. artists.


12. The Renaissance started in Italy for all of the following reasons *except that*

1. Italy exuded independence.
2. the common man in Italy supported it.
3. Italy had historical landmarks and
        infrastructures.
4. the Moslems brought in new ideas.


13. In the first paragraph, the author illustrates his point through

1. description.
2. persuasion.
3. religious referents.
4. contrast.


**GO ON TO NEXT PAGE**


**TEST THREE, PASSAGE TWO**

In February, 1895, the Edison "Kinetoscope" was unveiled to audiences in Stockholm, and from that date, Swedes have had a growing interest in cinema. In fact, there are no more stirring phenomena in the entire history of silent film than the Swedish achievements between 1913 and 1921. Although the Swedes allowed the Americans a headstart of at least ten years, from 1913 the world looked to Stockholm for craftsmanship and imagination in cinema.

The beginnings were cautious and some-what ponderous, like many a Scandinavian response to new artistic movements. One man set Swedish cinema on its course. Charles Magnusson had, as a young man of 19, attended the first exhibition of Lumiere films in Malmo in 1896 and resolved to become a cameraman. By 1905 he was starting to make a name as a newsreel photographer of great integrity and courage. In 1909 he joined a youthful company known as Svenska Bio in Kirstianstad (in southern Sweden). From the start, Svenska Bio bolstered its activity by acquiring up to twenty movie theaters, thus providing a ready outlet for its own productions (a tradition that continues to this day in Sweden). Consequently, Kristianstad became the main center of film activity in the country.

Magnusson later became a producer, and his pronouncements reveal him as a rare visionary. He realized that the public must be absorbed in what was happening on the screen: "The action is the motion picture's Alpha and Omega. It should give opportunities for intensely exciting and interesting situations. The film producer must be supreme ruler. He alone decides; but after

he has given the starting signal, he should leave the director in peace. If the director is unworthy of this confidence, he is not fit to be a director."
                                                        -Cowie, pp. 5-6

14. It can be inferred that American silent film began

1. when the world was looking to Stockholm.
2. in 1931.
3. about 1923.
4. around 1900.

15. According to the passage, Svenka Bio was established in

1. Stockholm.
2. Malmo.
3. southern Sweden.
4. northern Sweden.

16. The author suggests that Swedes approach new artistic movements

1. overzealously.
2. timidly.
3. flippantly.
4. seriously.

17. The word, phenomena, used in the second sentence, most likely means

1. definition.
2. silent films.
3. American film work.
4. events.

**TEST THREE, PASSAGE THREE**

18. According to the passage, one of the innovative, enterprising actions Svenka Bio took was to

1. exhibit at Malmo.
2. utilize Edison's Kinetoscope.
3. hire newsreel photographers.
4. buy its own theaters.

19. According to the passage, Magnusson was all of the following *except* a

1. director.
2. cameraman.
3. producer.
4. photographer.

**GO ON TO NEXT PAGE**

**TEST THREE, PASSAGE THREE**

The Harry Potter series is clearly an unprecedented success. *The Sorcerer's Stone, The Chamber of Secrets*, and the *Prisoner of Azkaban* have concurrently occupied the top three positions on the *New York Times* best seller list. They seem to be unparalleled among any other series for children or for adults. Even educators have noted that "after a  decade of despair over a generation lost to video games and television, Harry Potter books have lured huge numbers of school children to the printed page."

Nonetheless, the Harry Potter phenomenon is not without controversy.  In at least eight states, parent protesters want to pull the books from school libraries, or at least stop them from being read in classrooms.  These protesters have argued that the books are harmful to children. The Harry Potter series has been denounced as  "a handbook for witchcraft and violence," "anti-Christian," and "evil and dangerous."  This situation has led to quite a quandary for educators. Because some parents want to ban the same books that have encouraged children to read, school districts seem forced to choose between respecting parental authority and furthering the learning process.

Members of the library profession have questioned the validity of the complaints surrounding the series. Reacting to the controversy, Krug, director of the American Library Association Office for Intellectual Freedom responded with the question "what book did the parents read?"  The implication is that the protestors have not read the books at all and have simply been projecting their own assumptions onto the books without understanding the content.

-Yeager, Internet

20.  In the first paragraph, the Harry Potter series refers to a series of

1.  magazines.
2.  short stories.
3.  books.
4.  films.

21.  The reader can infer from the passage that the Harry Potter series is unique because

1.  it won the *New York Times* award for "best selling series."
2.  the series appeals to elementary school children.
3.  it has already been made into video games.
4.  all three titles were on the bestseller list concurrently.

22.  According to the author, the Harry Potter series protests mainly come from

1.  school children.
2.  parents.
3.  the school board.
4.  teachers.

23.  The author of this article would agree that the Harry Potter series

1.  is controversial.
2.  is harmful but should remain on the bookshelves.
3.  should be banned.
4.  promotes witchcraft and violence.

**TEST THREE, PASSAGE FOUR**

24. The word <u>denounced</u> most nearly means

1. promoted.
2. sold.
3. condemned.
4. ridiculed.

25. Members of the library profession

1. agree with the protesters.
2. question the validity of the Harry Potter
       series.
3. are skeptical of the protestors' complaints.
4. believe the protesters are illiterate.

**GO ON TO NEXT PAGE**

**TEST THREE, PASSAGE FOUR**

During Hoover's presidency attempts were made to aid the economy. The Reconstruction Finance corporation provided $3 billion in loans to some industries, and banks and the Federal Farm Board provided $500 million to farmers. But the two programs were too little and too late. The failure of the economy was blamed on Hoover and not the economic forces. It was his public relations and reactions, however, which hurt his bid for re-election.

Hoover, having realized that part of the economic woes were due to faith in the economy, attempted to restore that faith by having lavish dinners in the White House. The public reacted negatively to the campaign and considered Hoover callous to flaunt lavish dinners when so many were hungry. When the veterans of WWI camped in Washington, D. C. and demanded their veteran's bonus early, Hoover responded by sending MacArthur, Patton, and Eisenhower into the streets with the army, tanks, and tear gas. That spectacle caused Roosevelt to correctly believe that he, himself, would win the election early.

When Roosevelt entered office he and his staff believed drastic measures were necessary to restore faith in the economy and to forestall the worsening depression. One of the first financial acts under the new administration in 1933 was a closure of all the national banks for one week.

The measure could have ignited more panic but instead a festive mood seemed to envelop the country. The intent of the bank closures was to audit the banks, close the weak ones, and shore up the stable banks.

**TEST THREE, PASSAGE FIVE**

One week did not allow a thorough auditing process, but the shakiest banks were closed.                      -Duke, p. 125

26. Why was the economic aid from Hoover not effective?

1. It was given too late.
2. It was not enough money.
3. It was given only to manufacturers.
4. It was too little money, too late.

27. Who was president after Hoover?

1. Patton
2. MacArthur
3. Roosevelt
4. Eisenhower

28. According to the passage, Roosevelt believed Hoover would not win re-election because

1. Eisenhower campaigned against him.
2. Hoover held lavish dinners at the White House.
3. Hoover sent troops against veterans of World War I.
4. Roosevelt had more money with which to campaign.

29. The word lavish, as used in the selection, may be defined as

1. luxurious.
2. delicious.
3. religious.
4. genteel.

30.  We can infer from the passage that
Roosevelt

1.  did not accomplish much in terms of the
         economy.
2.  accomplished more than Hoover did in
         regard to the economy.
3.  was a weak president.
4.  had been a banker before he became
         President.


31.  One result from the closure of the
banks was that

1.  none of the banks were audited.
2.  the public panicked.
3.  all the banks were closed for good.
4.  the unstable banks were closed for
         good.


**GO ON TO NEXT PAGE**


**TEST THREE, PASSAGE FIVE**

When the last millennium was still quite young, a handful of adventurers floated down the river Amstel in hollowed out logs. They built a dam and began to exact toll money from passing traders. In 1275 Count Floris of Holland granted Amsterdam special toll privileges, and in 1300 the town got its first charter.

Amsterdam is a human-sized city, with a compact layout and a resident population of just 750,000. You can cross the city center in half an hour on foot. The mixed, open, tolerant atmosphere is an important part of the city's heritage. Greater Amsterdam is a bustling cosmopolitan region with 140 nationalities represented. Over 44% of Amsterdam's residents are of non-Dutch origin. Amsterdam is a city open to foreign influence in all respects. Flexibility and tolerance of other cultures are keys to Amsterdam's success. Over the centuries, the city has been a haven to many waves of refugees and all have contributed to its style and prosperity. For example, Protestant and Jewish people fleeing to Amsterdam laid the foundations of the diamond cutting industry and brought valuable news of trade routes to the East.

South of the city center is Amstelveen, a 'green municipality' of which only about one-third is built up. Recreational facilities such as parks, sports fields together with water and woods, make up more than 20% of the municipality's surface area. Amstelveen enjoys spacious, low-density housing, and is especially popular with families.

Amsterdam may be a small city, but it packs a big punch. Rembrandt, Van Gogh, and the Royal Concertgebouw Orchestra are all well known. The city is an international meeting-point of culture, business, and science. It is a city that is on the go, but where quality of life still counts.

-Amsterdam Promotion Foundation, internet

**TEST THREE, PASSAGE SIX**

32. The main reason Amsterdam is successful is due to its

1. River Amstel.
2. international flavor.
3. its Jewish population.
4. famous artists.

33. In the second paragraph, the author gets his point across through

1. comparison and contrast.
2. description and definition.
3. narration and persuasion.
4. example and statistics.

34. It is implied that Amstelveen is unique because

1. it is packed with modern housing.
2. 2/3 of the town is commercialized.
3. 2/3 of the town is green.
4. only families are allowed to live there.

35. The phrase packs a big punch most nearly means

1. is impressive.
2. is effective.
3. has political importance.
4. has many artists.

36. The phrase, <u>when the last millennium was still quite young</u>, refers to

1. 1275.
2. recently.
3. the early 1900s.
4. the early 1000s.

37. The author's attitude toward Amsterdam is one of

1. surprise.
2. nostalgia.
3. admiration.
4. sympathy.

**GO ON TO NEXT PAGE**

Have you ever thought about traveling to a country you have held only in your imagination? Or perhaps you would like to return to a country you have already visited? Study abroad programs in the state of Georgia may provide you with that opportunity, and you may draw more benefits from your experience than you thought possible.

There are several myths that surround studying overseas. First, it is natural to wonder whether or not you would be able to afford a study abroad program. In regard to financing, there are many scholarships available. In Georgia, for instance, the HOPE scholarship pays tuition costs and allots money toward book expenses. It is a good idea for students to consult with the International Office or the Financial Aid office at their home institution because most monies from loans can be applied to study abroad and will cover program costs.

Students also have the idea that they have to speak a foreign language to study abroad. The reality is that there are just as many, if not more, programs that are taught in English. The University System of Georgia offers programs to France, Italy, Russia, and Greece which do not require any foreign language skills.

Third, sometimes students are worried that the credits will not fit their curriculum. Because universities have reciprocity agreements, credits transfer easily. The International Office coordinator will work with your advisor to ensure that you receive appropriate academic credit for your over-seas work.

Fourth, the idea of being homesick can be overwhelming. Any professor who has worked with a study abroad program can tell you that you will make new, lifelong friends. Or, you may consider convincing your best friend, who might be attending a university elsewhere, to enroll in the program too.

As you can see, the myths that surround study abroad are just that–myths! They are not the reality.                    -Arthur

38. The author of this article is probably

1. a photo journalist.
2. the president of a college.
3. a study abroad advisor.
4. a travel agent.

39. The purpose of the passage is to

1. entertain.
2. persuade.
3. argue.
4. narrate.

40. The main idea of the passage is that

1. studying abroad does not enhance a
   student's resume.
2. students do not have to speak a foreign
   language to study abroad.
3. students will make lifelong friends
   when they study overseas.
4. myths about study abroad are not the
   reality.

41. The author makes her point by

1. refuting myths about study abroad.
2. describing specific study abroad
      programs.
3. contrasting study abroad to studying
      at a home institution.
4. narrating her own study abroad
      experience.

42. The state of Georgia is used

1. as an analogy.
2. as a symbol.
3. as an example.
4. figuratively.

43. It can be inferred that the author
believes

1. students are not worried about
      receiving academic credit for study
      abroad.
2. many students who want to study
      abroad do not speak a foreign
      language.
3. studying overseas is not a viable option
      for university study.
4. there are no myths that surround study
      abroad.

**GO ON TO NEXT PAGE**

**TEST THREE, PASSAGE SEVEN**

During the past decade, the mountain and hillside ecosystems of the world have become a primary concern of national and international agencies. As a result of the Earth Summit, an increasing number of projects and initiatives are oriented toward global mountain environments.

This emphasis on mountains is not without justification. Mountains and uplands constitute about one-fifth of the earth's terrestrial surface and are directly or indirectly relevant for well over half of the world's population. Although about 10 percent of the world's population live in high mountains, a much larger population, which constitute the bulk of humanity, reside in hilly piedmont regions and adjacent lowlands. This wider population benefits from the supply of mountain food, water, wood, and minerals. The mountains are the water towers of planet earth—indeed without them the Amazon Basin or the Gangetic Plains would transform into deserts. Their massive watersheds are crucial for providing irrigation water, hydro-electric power, and nutrients to populations down stream. Mountains also harbor most of the world's wild species of our major food crops and medicinal plants. Correspondingly, mountains are the homelands of most of the world's remaining tribal groups known for their *in situ* maintenance of plant and animal genetic resources. Along with the Hindu Kush Himalayan Region of Asia, the Andes of South America claims the largest, most diverse, most economically and ecologically important mountain setting in the world.                                    -Rhoades, p. 6

44. The author of this article would probably agree that

1. mountains do not affect the ecosystem to any great degree.
2. the public is not aware of the important role mountains have as a water resource.
3. flatlands are more crucial than mountains and uplands.
4. more people should reside in mountainous areas.

45. When the author writes that the mountains are water towers of planet earth he is making use of

1. figurative language.
2. contrastive phrasing.
3. sarcasm.
4. humor.

46. The author is most likely a professor of

1. biology.
2. geography.
3. ecology.
4. physics.

**TEST THREE, PASSAGE EIGHT**

47. According to the passage, what percent of the earth's land surface is composed of mountains and uplands?

1. 10
2. 20
3. 30
4. 40

48. Most likely, the discussion that follows the last paragraph focuses on

1. international agencies.
2. deserts, such as the Gobi.
3. natural resource management.
4. the Andes.

49. The word, harbor, as used in the selection, most nearly means

1. pier.
2. injure.
3. shelter.
4. classify.

**GO ON TO NEXT PAGE**

**TEST THREE, PASSAGE EIGHT**

Dr. Phil McGraw talked his way onto a spot as a therapist on *Oprah*. Thanks to his appearances every Tuesday, viewership of Oprah is 24 percent higher for that day than the rest of the week. Now in 2002 he is the hottest talk-show commodity to come along since Oprah herself.

Dr. Phil is famous for his blunt, take-no-prisoners style of therapy: "People are used to being coddled," he says. "It's so much easier to tell people what they want to hear instead of what they need to hear." Although he has a Ph.D. in clinical psychology, McGraw has a way of offering advice that sounds like something you might hear from a good ole Texas boy, which McGraw, 51, just happens to be.

McGraw has a sort of X-ray vision when it comes to analyzing people's problems. He sometimes sounds more like a trial lawyer than a therapist in the way he interrogates people, digging deeper into their lives until they almost confess the answer to their problems. It's not always pretty to watch. McGraw tends to see the world in black and white—his favorite catch phrase is "you either get it or you don't"—and he doesn't have a lot of patience for people who don't get it, who refuse to take a hard look at their own lives.

Americans have long had a fascination with self-help experts, from Ben Franklin's Poor Richard ("Early to bed . . .") to the positive thinking of Norman Vincent Peale. But in the last few decades, gurus like Marianne Williamson have turned self-help from a stick into a crutch, with the emphasis on "codependency" and the dreaded "find your inner child"—ideas built on blaming someone else for your troubles. Maybe McGraw's tough take on personal

**TEST THREE, PASSAGE NINE**

responsibility is what people are demanding now.        -Peyser, pp. 50-52

50. According to the article, the characteristic that distinguishes Dr. Phil is

1. that he has a Ph.D. in psychology.
2. that he tells people what they want to hear.
3. his no-nonsense way of talking.
4. that he appeared first on *Oprah*.

51. The author implies that Dr. Phil

1. refuses to take a hard look at his own life.
2. does not have a lot of patience.
3. has long been a guru.
4. only works on Tuesdays.

52. The author's attitude toward Marianne Williamson is one of

1. admiration.
2. impartiality.
3. enthusiasm.
4. disrespect.

53. The purpose of paragraph two is to

1. describe Dr. Phil.
2. relate that Dr. Phil is a guru.
3. contrast Dr. Phil's style with Oprah's style.
4. define psychotherapy.

54. We can infer from the last paragraph
that

1. Norman Vincent Peale has a psychology
      degree.
2. having a crutch is not such a bad idea.
3. blaming someone else for your troubles will
      help in the healing process.
4. the public is tired of the self-help
      approach of the last few decades.

# SIMULATED EXAM FOUR

Perhaps like me you once believed sea-horses existed only in the imagination. In mythology, they guided Neptune's chariot, and sailors once tattooed them on each other to prevent drowning. Their relatively small size and unique body composition render them barely able to swim—and the only fish capable of holding your hand. Their stillness and grace cast them in the starring role in the world's first wildlife film made in Italy in the 1890s.

Despite previous taxonomic classifications as insects and amphibians, they are fish.  Like most fish they have gills for breathing, a swim bladder for buoyancy, two pectoral fins for balance, and dorsal fins that flutter as much as 35 times per second. They lack teeth, a stomach, and a caudal fin for speed. Although beautiful, seahorses are the Frankensteins of the underwater world, seemingly made up of parts from several animals.  As their name suggests, they possess the head of a horse, on top of which they wear a crown, as unique as a human fingerprint. Their snout and body armor resemble an aardvark's. They come in many shades and combinations of color. As chameleons, coloration can change to blend in with the environment.

The most fascinating aspect of seahorse behavior is child birth.  During mating, couples are monogamous. (It is not known if they mate for life, however.) Like most fish, the male parent assumes prenatal care duties.  But male seahorses actually carry and birth babies. The number of offspring varies from five to over one thousand. Following a gestation period, the father experiences labor. Contractions begin before sunrise when tides are highest (maximizing foraging opportunities for the newborns).

At birth, babies' heads are disproportion-ately larger than their bodies, making them look even stranger than adult seahorses. They emerge hungry, yet fully formed and self-sufficient.

-Dames, internet

1. We can infer from the passage that

1. seahorses prevent drowning.
2. seahorses are excellent swimmers.
3. the author believes seahorses are unintelligent creatures.
4. sailors believed seahorses brought good luck.

2. It is suggested in the passage that scientists

1. have always regarded seahorses as amphibians.
2. have always regarded seahorses as insects.
3. have changed their classification of seahorses over the years.
4. do not regard seahorses as worthy of study.

3. Seahorses are not like fish because seahorses

1. reproduce differently.
2. have gills.
3. have a swim bladder.
4. flutter their fins more times per second.

4. The author uses the metaphor, "seahorses are the Frankensteins of the underwater world," because seahorses

1. are frightening creatures.
2. are not beautiful.
3. are composed of features from several different animals.
4. have a large head like Frankenstein.


5. It is stated in the passage that seahorses

1. have very sharp teeth.
2. have a crown like an aardvark.
3. swim faster than fish.
4. are chameleon-like.


6. The male seahorse

1. does not assume prenatal care duties.
2. has a head which is larger than the female.
3. goes through labor and births the babies.
4. cares for babies after they are born.


**GO ON TO NEXT PAGE**


**TEST FOUR, PASSAGE ONE**

"I'm really stunned," said John, a new college graduate just in his second month of work with a major corporation. He had just had a meeting with his boss. "In the staff meeting last week, I talked about a new technique I learned in school that could be helpful. Now my boss tells me I'm too cocky; that my attitude is irritating others, and that I need to be more of a team player. Where did I go wrong?"

Every year thousands of college students work hard at planning their careers, honing their interview skills, and preparing for their job searches. Many will find good jobs and start work with high enthusiasm—only to be disillusioned.

Starting to work in an organization is a critically important time that requires you to use special strategies to be successful. You need to recognize that the first year on a new job is a transition stage. Few graduates realize that it takes time to earn the rights of a full-fledged professional.

Much of your early career success will be charted by the impressions you make on the people you work with in the early months on the job. Research suggests that how you approach your first year will have a major impact on your future salary, advancement, job satisfaction, and ability to move within the organization.

The key is to come into the organization with enough savvy to have appropriate expectations and attitudes, to know how to establish yourself, and to figure out what you need to do to earn respect.

Your challenge is to use strategies to help you establish your reputation as a bright, capable, and valuable employee: 1) slow down; 2) learn the company culture;

3) manage a good impression; 4) manage your expectations; 5) become a savvy "subordinate."          -Holton, pp. 73-6

7. In the context of paragraph three, full-fledged most nearly means

1. respected.
2. perfect.
3. full-time.
4. thoughtful.

8. The main idea of the selection is that

1. every year thousands of students find jobs.
2. college graduates are always disappointed with their first work experience.
3. starting to work in an organization is an easy transition from college.
4. college graduates are usually not aware of what the first work experience entails.

9. The article suggests that John's situation is

1. unusual.
2. typical.
3. absurd.
4. shocking.

**TEST FOUR, PASSAGE TWO**

10. According to the selection, research indicates that

1. the first year on a job is a permanent stage in a career.
2. many college graduates quit the first company they work for.
3. the first year of work will impact your future salary.
4. slowing down will guarantee a raise.

11. <u>Disillusioned,</u> as used in the second paragraph, most nearly means

1. ignored.
2. fired.
3. ridiculed.
4. disappointed.

12. The discussion which follows this passage probably

1. presents testimonials of successful college graduates.
2. expounds upon John's future employment opportunities.
3. discusses the second year in a new job.
4. expands on the useful strategies mentioned.

**GO ON TO NEXT PAGE**

**TEST FOUR, PASSAGE TWO**

Similar to the trigger mechanism of landslides, snow avalanches start mainly because of some mechanical disturbance. A frequent cause is the fall of a snow cornice, an elongated shelf-like slab of snow that forms on the downwind side of a mountain peak. Under the pull of its ever-increasing weight, it will first bend downward and eventually break off and trigger an avalanche on the slope below.

Several factors may start an avalanche: rock and icefalls, unstable cornices, sonic booms, a tree falling over in a storm, or a snowpack fracturing. A number of avalanches, especially the slab avalanches, are initiated by skiers. It is estimated that, in the European Alps, about 80 percent of all avalanche victims are skiers.

The danger of avalanches can be reduced by educating people so that they can understand the causes and the nature of this mountain phenomenon. This is especially important for novice skiers and climbers. Also, many technical measures can be taken to reduce avalanche risks: construction of retaining walls; placing of protective gallery tunnels over hazardous highways or railroad sections; and leaving protective stands of forest above villages.

In addition to these techniques, it is also a constructive practice to trigger avalanches before their potential for harm becomes too great by "shooting down" threatening snow masses with explosives.                    -Ebert, pp. 49-52

13. The reader can infer from the passage that

1. landslides are not as dangerous as avalanches.
2. snow cornices are not a major cause of avalanches.
3. a fallen tree is never a hazard.
4. technical measures are successful in preventing avalanches.

14. The paragraph which comes before this passage most probably discussed

1. snow cornices.
2. the worst avalanche in history.
3. the causes of landslides.
4. mechanical disturbances.

15. About 80 percent of all avalanche victims are

1. novice skiers.
2. professional climbers.
3. passengers in railroad cars coming out of tunnels.
4. skiers.

16. The word constructive, as used in the last paragraph, means

1. beneficial.
2. building.
3. conceptual.
4. dangerous.

**TEST FOUR, PASSAGE THREE**

17. This passage was probably found in an article about

1. rock-climbing.
2. natural disasters.
3. sports.
4. European travel.

18. According to the passage, the danger of avalanches can best be reduced by

1. limiting the number of skiers.
2. restricting railroad and highway traffic.
3. deforestation.
4. educating the public.

**GO ON TO NEXT PAGE**

Somewhere en route from dirt-poor
Mississippi schoolgirl to TV news anchor
to talk-show empress to therapist for an
anxious nation, Oprah Winfrey became
a businesswoman. It's a title she doesn't
like much. "I don't think of myself as a
business woman. The only time I think
about it is while I'm being interviewed,
like now."

Sitting in an overstuffed armchair in her
office in Harpo Inc.'s Chicago headquarters,
her two cocker spaniels lying at her feet,
the chairman swears that if she is a businesswoman, it's in spite of herself. She happily
admits that she cannot read a balance sheet.
She has no corporate role models. She's
declined invitations from AT&T, Ralph
Lauren and Intel to sit on their corporate
boards. And she's so wary of investing her
own money in the stock market that she
once hoarded $50 million in cash, calling
it her personal "bag-lady fund."

Winfrey is kidding herself. Despite her
protestations, she is at the helm of a mighty
successful business. *The Oprah Show* is
clearly the core of her business, contributing
the lion's share of revenues (some $300
million last year) to Harpo. It airs in 107
countries and has held its No. 1 spot in U.S.
daytime talk for 16 years despite challenges
from at least 50 rivals. Her two-year-old
magazine, *O, The Oprah Magazine*, is the
most successful startup ever in the industry.
Last year it raked in more than $140 million
in revenues.

Forced to listen to these accomplishments,
Oprah tucks her loafered feet into the cushion
of her big chair and fesses up. "Yeah,"

she acknowledges, "I guess I am a
business woman."        -Sellers, pp. 50-51


19. It can be inferred that Oprah

1. has a fondness for dogs.
2. can not read well.
3. was not a successful TV anchor.
4. sits on several corporate boards.


20. When asked about her success as a
businesswoman, Oprah responds

1. enthusiastically.
2. reluctantly.
3. angrily.
4. nonchalantly.


21. According to the article, Oprah is
from

1. an upper class Chicago family.
2. a middle-class family of New York
      City.
3. a blue-collar family.
4. a lower-class Mississippi family.


22. The phrase, the lion's share, most
nearly means

1. small amounts.
2. a few dollars.
3. the largest part.
4. $300 million.


**TEST FOUR, PASSAGE FOUR**

23.  The author portrays Oprah as

1.  not very intelligent.
2.  stingy.
3.  a bag lady.
4.  humble.


24.  *O, The Oprah Magazine* is considered
unique because it

1.  raked in more than $140 million in 2001.
2.  mimics *The Oprah Show*.
3.  is the most successful startup ever in the
        industry.
4. is published in 107 countries.


**GO ON TO NEXT PAGE**

It has been customary in this country to make a sharp distinction between governmental and non-governmental administration. In the popular imagination, governmental administration is "bureaucratic"; private administration is "business-like"; governmental administration is political; private administration is nonpolitical; governmental administration is characterized by "red-tape"; private administration is not.

In actual administration there is often a greater difference between small and large organizations than there is between public and private ones. For example, the differences in administrative problems between a hospital with 1,000 beds and one with 50 beds will be far greater than the differences that result from the fact that one hospital is privately owned and the other publicly owned.

Actually, large-scale public and private organizations have many more similarities than they have differences. In fact, many of the same skills are required in public and private administration. A statistician might transfer from a large insurance company to the Bureau of Labor Statistics in Washington and find his tasks almost identical. He possesses skills that can be used by a great many organizations, public or private. Similarly, a doctor performing an appendectomy will use the same technique whether he is employed in an Army hospital or in private practice. Dwight Eisenhower left the Army to become president of Columbia University. Two more different organizations would be hard to imagine. Yet it is likely that the administrative

problems of the two organizations were sufficiently similar so that Eisenhower had little difficulty in making the adjustment.                    -Peterson, et. al. p. 153

25. In paragraph one, the authors make their point through

1. example.
2. contrast.
3. narration.
4. persuasion.

26. According to the selection, governmental administration is characterized by all of the following *except*

1. politics.
2. red-tape.
3. business.
4. bureaucracy.

27. According to the passage, administrative problems occur most frequently because of

1. size.
2. type of ownership.
3. personnel.
4. paper work.

28. According to the selection, General Dwight Eisenhower was president of

1. the United States.
2. a governmental organization.
3. a university.
4. a business corporation.

**TEST FOUR, PASSAGE FIVE**

29. The example of the statistician is used to

1. illustrate the vast differences between governmental and nongovernmental organizations.
2. show the similarities between governmental and nongovernmental organizations.
3. contrast the statistician's situation with that of General Dwight Eisenhower.
4. reveal the difficulty of transferring from a private company to a government position.


30. In paragraph three, the author utilizes

1. definition and description.
2. argumentation and persuasion.
3. statistics and contrast.
4. examples and comparison.


**GO ON TO NEXT PAGE**


**TEST FOUR, PASSAGE FIVE**

We wouldn't let toxic waste pile up around us, so why do we tolerate toxic language, day in and day out—especially when it makes us miserable? According to Dr. Elgin, it's not because we possess any character flaws; there are three primary reasons for our strange tolerance, and they have little to do with our character. They are the result of our *culture*, the environment of beliefs that we grew up with and share with the other members of our society:

First, since we were small children we have heard the myth, "sticks and stones will break my bones, but words will never harm me!" But everyone knows words do hurt us.   So, the message is loud and clear:  If you feel pain as a result of other people's words, something is wrong with *you*, not the person <u>spouting</u> abusive words.

Second, like fish who are unaware of the water they swim in, we tend to have little awareness of our language environment. The idea that language can be wholesome and pure–or contaminated and toxic–rarely occurs to us.  We take our language environment for granted and notice it only when something goes dramatically wrong.

Last, we believe that much of our physical environment is almost completely beyond our control as individuals. When we do become aware of our language environment (because it has become uncomfortable), we tend to assume that we're helpless to do anything about it.                    -Elgin, pp. xv-6

(*Note*: Elgin suggests that we recognize patterns of verbal abuse in our lives and take action against them.)

31.  <u>Spouting</u>, as used in the second paragraph, most nearly means

1.  pouring over.
2.  whispering.
3.  spitting out.
4.  intoxicating.

32.  Dr. Elgin is most probably a(n)

1.  doctor interested in psychology.
2.  anthropologist interested in psychology.
3.  journalist interested in psychology.
4.  linguist interested in psychology.

33.  The tone of the passage is

1.  emotional.
2.  nostalgic.
3.  informative.
4.  passionate.

34.  The author uses the phrase "sticks and stones will break my bones, but words will never harm me," to emphasize how we are affected by

1.  belief systems.
2.  children.
3.  nursery rhymes.
4.  toxins.

**TEST FOUR, PASSAGE SIX**

35.  Dr. Elgin states that we tolerate toxic language because

1.  we have basic character flaws.
2.  we believe they can control their physical environment.
3.  others are more aggressive than we are.
4.  culture dictates behavior.

36.  The main idea of paragraph three is that

1.  fish are unaware of the water in which they swim.
2.  we are unaware of our language environment.
3.  language is wholesome and pure.
4.  we are aware of toxic language but do nothing about it.

**GO ON TO NEXT PAGE**

**TEST FOUR, PASSAGE SIX**

"Life begins," I thought, as I waved goodbye to my parents and pulled away from the curb in my reliable old Valiant stuffed with the belongings I'd packed for my first year at college. I felt strong, independent, ready for anything. Singing to myself above the radio's music, I sped north across the freeways of Los Angeles. Just before dusk, my descent through the hills brought me a shimmering view of San Francisco Bay. My excitement grew as I neared the Berkeley campus.

After finding my dormitory, I unpacked and gazed out the window at the Golden Gate Bridge sparkling in the darkness. Five minutes later I was walking along Telegraph Avenue, looking in shop windows, breathing the fresh northern California air, savoring the smells drifting out of tiny cafes. The next morning immediately after breakfast, I walked down to Harmon Gymnasium, where I'd be training six days a week, four sweaty hours each day, pursuing my dreams of becoming a champion.

Two days passed, and I was already drowning in a sea of people, papers, and class schedules. Soon the months blended together, passing and changing softly, like the mild California seasons. In my classes I survived; in the gym, I thrived. By the end of my first two years I had flown to Germany, France, and England, representing the U.S. Gymnastics Federation. My trophies were piling up in the corner of my room, my picture appeared in the *Daily Californian* with such regularity that people began to recognize me. Women smiled at me.

However, in the early autumn of my junior year, something dark and intangible began to take shape. By then I'd moved out of the dorm and was living alone in a small studio. During this time I felt a growing melancholy, even in the midst of all my achievements.

-Millman, pp. 15-16

37. The main idea of the third paragraph is that the writer

1. is a below average student.
2. often appears in the newspaper.
3. is achieving in his gymnastic endeavors.
4. is able to attract a lot of women.

38. In the opening paragraph, the narrator's feelings can best be described as those of

1. depression.
2. reluctance.
3. anticipation.
4. indifference.

39. The reader can infer from the last paragraph that the narrator

1. is going to have a difficult time ahead.
2. will soon experience a nervous breakdown.
3. has a problem with women.
4. is happy with his life.

**TEST FOUR, PASSAGE SEVEN**

40.  <u>Drowning in a sea of people, papers, and class schedules</u> connotes that the writer feels

1.  satisfied with his situation.
2.  overwhelmed by his situation.
3.  apathetic about his situation.
4.  overjoyed with his situation.


41.  According to the passage, the narrator believed his life begins when

1.  he starts winning trophies.
2.  women become interested in him.
3.  he leaves home.
4.  he commences training at Harmon Gym.


42.  The writer conveys his point through the use of

1.  narration.
2.  persuasion.
3.  explanation.
4.  reporting.


**GO ON TO NEXT PAGE**


**TEST FOUR, PASSAGE SEVEN**

The immediate aftermath to the Versailles Treaty of World War I was economic and social chaos for Germany. Deprived of the economic resources of many of their territories and saddled with exorbitant war debts, Germany nearly collapsed under the weight of worsening inflationary spirals.

Circumstances such as these produced radical, extremist groups of all types– communists, anarchists, monarchists. One such group was the German Workers Party, a fervent nationalist and patriotic party which aimed to compete with the Communists for support among the masses in Munich. Worried about the possible dangerous nature of this organization, the political department of the district army assigned an army reservist, Adolph Hitler, to check on it.

The thirty year-old Hitler was an Austrian, son of a minor customs' official and a servant girl. In 1913 he moved to Munich where he became an ardent supporter of his newly adopted country. The next year, Hitler enlisted in an infantry regiment, served at the front, and earned the Iron Cross. He suffered a leg wound and near the end of the war was gassed. His survival convinced him that he had been spared for some special mission in his life.

Hitler found that the group he had been sent to observe and report on intrigued him. Interested in the aims and goals of the organization, he accepted an invitation to attend a meeting. Two days later he joined the small group. Revealing a gift, both for propaganda and organization, Hitler soon became the leader of the Party. He subsequently changed the name to National Socialist German Workers Party, or Nazi.                                -Layton, p. 2

43. According to the passage, Germany was unable to maintain economic stability because

1. the Versailles Treaty was unfair.
2. Germany had participated in WWI.
3. Germany had always been on the verge of collapse.
4. the treaty deprived Germany of economic resources.

44. The phrase such as these refers to

1. war debts and deprivation of resources.
2. communists, anarchists, and monarchists.
3. radical groups.
4. German workers.

45. The author states that Hitler

1. was raised in Munich.
2. never fought on the front lines of a war.
3. was not German.
4. considered himself one of the masses.

46. Hitler investigated the German Workers Party because

1. they were communists.
2. the party was considered a threat to the German government.
3. he wanted to join the party.
4. he lived in Munich.

**TEST FOUR, PASSAGE EIGHT**

47. The paragraph that came before this selection probably discussed

1. economic and social chaos in Germany.
2. radical extremist groups like the German
   Workers Party.
3. Adolph Hitler's war crimes.
4. the Versailles Treaty.

48. Based on the passage, the Nazi party can be described best as a

1. nationalist organization.
2. German organization.
3. communist organization.
4. military organization.

**GO ON TO NEXT PAGE**

The Roman Catholic Church in all its history has granted but two women the title of doctor. One of these remarkable women was Catherine of Siena. History bears evidence of her travels across country and her power to attract an audience. Catherine was the center of a group drawn from many levels of society and varied religious traditions, and they regarded her as teacher and spiritual guide.

Catherine, born in 1347, was the twenty-fourth of twenty-five children. What we know of her childhood is limited, but it is clear that she was a strikingly pleasant youngster, imaginative and idealistic in her devotion. The stubborn independence that was to be a hallmark of most of her life showed itself early. What emerges of her life was a passion for the truth. Her confessor, Raymond, tells us she was only seven years old when she vowed her virginity to God; fifteen when she cut off her hair in defiance of efforts to make her marry; eighteen when she received the Dominican habit. Somewhere, somehow in that silence she learned to read.

In 1370, at the age of 23, Catherine's mystical experiences intensified. She wrote of her "mystical death"—four hours during which she experienced ecstatic union with God while her body seemed lifeless to all observers. After that she lived an austere life, devoid of adequate food and sleep.

In 1380, a written summons came from the Pope, and Catherine set out for Rome—the last journey she was to make.

**TEST FOUR, PASSAGE NINE**

Working hard for the Pope, meeting with cardinals, and counseling her disciples took its toll. Soon after her arrival, Catherine could no longer eat or even swallow water. On February 25 she lost the use of her legs. She died on April 29. She was thirty-three years old.

-Noffke, pp. 1-7

49. It is implied that Catherine felt allegiance to

1. the Pope.
2. Raymond.
3. Siena.
4. the Protestant faith.

50. According to the passage, Catherine

1. had a limited childhood.
2. was the first woman Catholic priest.
3. had a long, productive life.
4. came from a large family.

51. The author's attitude toward Catherine is one of

1. pity.
2. admiration.
3. nostalgia.
4. indifference.

52. The reader can infer that Catherine cut off her hair

1. when she joined the Dominican order.
2. to enhance her looks.
3. to make herself less desirable to the opposite sex.
4. because she had always been a tomboy.

53. <u>Austere,</u> as used in the selection, most nearly means

1. useless.
2. independent.
3. strict.
4. luxurious.

54. It is suggested that

1. religious leaders considered Catherine unstable.
2. Catherine had tremendous influence on religious leaders.
3. the Pope thought Catherine's mystical experiences were faked.
4. the religious leaders were surprised Catherine died at such a young age.

# SIMULATED EXAM FIVE

Any person who has lived through a hurricane will immediately recall the roar of the winds, the debris hurtling through the air, the splintering of glass panes, the <u>ominous</u> groaning and cracking of the rafters under the force of the storm. Yet, wind may be the least destructive aspect as far as damage and loss of life are concerned.

Storm surges are considered to be the most dangerous aspect of these storms. About nine out of ten hurricane deaths result from drowning in surge flooding. The case studies of Galveston, Texas (1900), with 6,000 fatalities, and that of the Ganges Delta, Bangladesh (1970), with more than 300,000 deaths, illustrate this point. The bulge of water, corresponding in size to the eye of the hurricane, may be from 40 to 100 miles wide. One of the highest storm surges in the United States occurred in connection with Hurricane Camille (1969). It measured 24.2 feet in an area of Mississippi and resulted in more than 140 deaths.

Hurricanes may produce mountainous ocean waves. Most narratives of hurricane disasters deal with their impact on land, on communities, and on land-based installations. Yet, powerful hurricanes have wreaked havoc with ships all over the world. Both wave action and wind pressure can doom ships. On September 26, 1954, the Japanese ship *Toyo Maru* capsized in a typhoon with a loss of 794 people, and on September 22, 1957, the West German merchant marine training ship *Pamir* sank in a violent hurricane in the North Atlantic with only five out of 86 crew members surviving. Hurricane winds of 73 to 82 mph may build waves in excess of 60 feet. The largest ocean wave, with a height of 112 feet, was seen in February 1935 by the crew of the United States Navy tanker *Ramapo*.

-Ebert, pp. 101-103

1. The most dangerous aspect of a hurricane

1. is high winds.
2. is flying debris.
3. may be the eye of the hurricane.
4. is surge flooding.

2. In the second paragraph, the author makes his point through the use of

1. persuasion.
2. examples.
3. contrast.
4. comparison.

3. The purpose of paragraph one is to

1. define "hurricane."
2. sympathize with hurricane victims.
3. describe the effects of hurricanes.
4. frighten the reader.

4. <u>Ominous</u>, as used in the first paragraph, most nearly means

1. cautious.
2. threatening.
3. silent.
4. destructive.

5. The largest ocean wave was seen by

1. Americans.
2. Japanese.
3. Germans.
4. Indians.

**TEST FIVE, PASSAGE ONE**

6. It is implied that most individuals

1. know the details of hurricane behavior.
2. have been in a hurricane.
3. mourn the deaths caused by Hurricane Camille.
4. are unfamiliar with the havoc wreaked on ships by hurricanes.

**GO ON TO NEXT PAGE**

**TEST FIVE, PASSAGE ONE**

During the Cold War, the Soviet Union established several hundred research institutes that were dedicated to the research, development, and production of weapons of mass destruction.   Although precise figures are not available, science center officials estimate that at the time of the Soviet Union's collapse, from 30,000 to 75,000 highly trained senior weapons scientists worked at these institutes. These figures do not include the thousands of less experienced junior scientists and technicians who also worked in these institutes. After the collapse of the Soviet Union in 1991, many of these scientists suffered significant cuts in pay and lost their government-supported work.  By early 1992, the United States and other countries were concerned that senior weapons scientists struggling to support their families could be tempted to sell their expertise to terrorists or countries of concern such as Iraq, Iran, and North Korea.

To address this threat, the United States (along with the European Union, Japan, and Russia) signed an agreement creating the International Science and Technology Center in Moscow.  A year later, the United States, Sweden, Canada, and Ukraine created a center in Ukraine.  The United States has appropriated $227 million to support the two multilateral science centers in Russia and Ukraine that pay scientists of the former Soviet Union who once developed nuclear, chemical, and biological weapons and missile systems.  By employing scientists through science centers, the U.S. seeks to reduce the risk of weapons <u>proliferation</u> associated with underemployed, highly trained personnel.

Accordingly, the program has employed thousands of weapons scientists in a variety of research areas, including projects aimed at developing new anticancer drugs, improving nuclear safety, and enhancing environmental cleanup techniques.        -GAO, pp. 1-3

7. The word, <u>proliferation</u>, most nearly means

1. destruction.
2. expectations.
3. reduction.
4. expansion.

8. The U.S. employed Soviet scientists in the early 1990s because

1. the United States felt threatened.
2. the scientists offered to sell their expertise.
3. the United States officials felt sorry for the scientists.
4. the Soviet Union was poor.

9. The reader can assume that during the Cold War era the Soviet Union

1. couldn't afford to pay their senior scientists.
2. was collaborating with Iraq, Iran, and North Korea.
3. hired renegade scientists.
4. paid its senior weapons scientists well.

10.  The point of the passage is to

1.  persuade the reader that the U.S. is
        winning the Cold War.
2.  inform the reader of the weapons threat
        after the Cold War.
3.  give a testimonial of a top U.S. official.
4.  have the reader sympathize with the
        Soviet scientists.


11.  The author would probably agree that

1.  the U.S. should never have hired the
        Soviet scientists.
2.  during the Cold War, development of
        weapons was at a standstill.
3.  it was necessary for the U.S. to hire the
        Soviet scientists.
4.  the U.S. and other countries pressured
        the Soviet scientists to work for
        them.


12.  An estimated 30,000 to 75,000 senior
weapons scientists were out of work

1.  during the Cold War.
2.  at the time of the Soviet Union's
        collapse.
3.  before 1991.
4.  in the late 1990s.


**TEST FIVE, PASSAGE TWO**                          **GO ON TO NEXT PAGE**

When President Roosevelt decided in 1940 to move the United States Pacific fleet from California to act as a deterrent to Japanese aggressive action, there were few choices other than Pearl Harbor, but Pearl Harbor was far from an ideal base. Located about 3000 miles from the mainland, its distance made for logistical problems. In addition, it had to be entered through a narrow channel, two miles long and a quarter mile wide. Any ship sunk here could stop the fleet's passage into or out of its mooring place. The harbor itself was also restricted in size and because it was so shallow it could barely accommodate large vessels. A congested harbor meant that maneuvering was difficult and in order to provide more space, the torpedo nets around the ships were usually left down. Most all of the base could be seen from the surrounding hills, thus allowing enemy spies to relay accurate information about Pearl Harbor's defenses. The Japanese commander, Yamamoto, knew that there were no barrage balloons to stop low-flying planes at Pearl Harbor and that there was no torpedo netting around the ships. Admiral Richardson, Commander of the Pacific fleet in 1940, had indeed opposed stationing it in Hawaii, recommending its return to the safer haven of California. But for diplomatic reasons, Roosevelt decided against his advice.

-Layton, p. 111

**TEST FIVE, PASSAGE THREE**

13. President Roosevelt moved the U.S. Pacific fleet

1. because he thought Pearl Harbor was safer.
2. since Pearl Harbor was restricted in size.
3. because it was surrounded by hills.
4. for diplomatic reasons.

14. The reader can assume that torpedo netting and barrage balloons

1. are only used during war time.
2. are usually used around fleets.
3. do not deter torpedoes nor low-flying aircraft.
4. were not employed by the United States due to expense.

15. According to the passage, Pearl Harbor was not a good location for a fleet. Of the following, which is *not* mentioned as a disadvantage?

1. It was too close to Japan.
2. It was shallow.
3. It had to be entered through a narrow channel.
4. It was too far from the mainland.

16. It is suggested that Yamamoto knew Pearl Harbor could be easily attacked because

1. he was told by a diplomat.
2. there were traitors in the U.S. Navy.
3. information was relayed and intercepted by the Japanese.
4. he most likely had spies in the hills around Pearl Harbor.

17. In this selection, the author's attitude toward Roosevelt is such that he

1. exposes the president for making a tragic mistake.
2. esteems the president for his bravery during the Pearl Harbor attack.
3. describes the president as a great war time strategist.
4. argues for the president's diplomatic actions.

18. The person who argued against Roosevelt's decision was

1. a crew member of the Pacific fleet.
2. Yamamoto.
3. an admiral in the U. S. Navy.
4. a California politician.

**GO ON TO NEXT PAGE**

**TEST FIVE, PASSAGE THREE**

Katherine went out through a gate into the brilliant sunshine of the street.  Something pricked her hand, and she looked down at the Queen's brooch. The inscription on it read: *Foi vainquera*, "Faith Conquers."

"Hah!" she thought. "Faith had conquered nothing!" There were no miracles. She let the brooch drop into the filth of the gutter.

A man passing behind Katherine saw the brooch drop, picked it up, and lumbered after her.

Looking closely at her face, his heart filled with tenderness.  Because he had suffered greatly himself, he guessed something of what must have happened. He put the brooch in his pocket and followed Katherine at a distance.  People crossed themselves as he walked by them, but some reached out and touched him for luck–for he was a hunchback.

Katherine walked until she came to the market square where there were benches jammed with other pilgrims who had visited the shrine and were now celebrating.

Pain throbbed in her head; black swimming weakness crushed her.  She slumped down on a bench and shut her eyes.

Then it happened.  Voices from the direction of the pilgrims: "The Duke has renounced his mistress–shipped her off, maybe to one of his northern dungeons." A woman giggled then: "It's well known he was tired of her anyway and has found someone else, wicked lecher that he is."

Katherine bolted from the bench, running towards the river until it widened into a mill pond.  The hunchback hurried after her.  Here on the grassy bank she stopped.  Katherine advanced to the edge of the pond.  She gazed down into the dark brown depths. She clasped hands against her breasts and stood swaying on the brink.

She felt a grip on her arm, and a deep, gentle voice whispered,  "No, my sister. That is not the way."

-Seton, pp. 516-8

19.  The reader can infer that

1.  Katherine was going to commit suicide.
2.  the hunchback would fall in love with Katherine.
3.  Katherine's miracle happened.
4.  Katherine knew the other pilgrims.

20.  The underlined word, <u>renounced</u>, as used in the passage most nearly means

1.  made up with.
2.  cast off.
3.  killed.
4.  paid off.

21.  It is suggested that Katherine's relationship with the Duke had been

1.  a business arrangement.
2.  frivolous.
3.  romantic in nature.
4.  a cordial one.

22.  The passage implies that Katherine had been

1.  on vacation.
2.  to visit relatives.
3.  strolling by the mill pond.
4.  on a pilgrimage.

23. The people wanted to touch the
hunchback because they

1. felt sorry for him.
2. had never seen someone like him before.
3. wanted to get the brooch away
        from him.
4. thought he was blessed.

24. In the paragraphs one and two, the
author uses the brooch to bring out
Katherine's

1. disillusionment.
2. trust.
3. disgust.
4. faith.

**GO ON TO NEXT PAGE**

**TEST FIVE, PASSAGE FOUR**

Andrew Jackson was born in the backwoods of North Carolina in 1767. He was a bright boy, quick to fight and to profane. At thirteen he fought in the Revolution and was taken prisoner. A British officer demanded Andy clean his boots, and when Andy refused the officer drew his sword. Jackson never lost the scar or his hatred of the British.

After the war, Jackson moved west to Tennessee and became public prosecutor. He boarded at a widow's house and met the attractive and unhappily married daughter, Rachael. When Rachael's husband began divorce proceedings, the two ran off and got married. Later, they found out they had been married before Rachael's divorce had been finalized. Jackson fought several duels with those who made <u>snide</u> comments about his wife.

In 1802 the Tennessee militia elected Jackson their commander. In 1815 he thrashed the British in the Battle of New Orleans. When the war was over, he retired to the Hermitage, but Indian attacks from Florida prompted President Monroe to call on Jackson. Jackson was overenthusiastic. He captured St. Marks and Pensacola, kicked out the Spanish governor, and hanged two British citizens whom he accused of aiding the Indians. Although controversial, his threat convinced the Spanish to yield Florida.

By 1824 Jackson's friends had drafted him as a candidate for the White House, but the House of Representatives chose John Q. Adams as President in a questionable deal. A fighting mad Jackson began to organize for the 1828 election and built a new party, the "Democrats."

The election was a victory for Jackson as the "champion of the common man" but it was also a smear campaign. He and Rachael were attacked in public as "immoral." Before Jackson was inaugurated, Rachael died–in part, it is said, because she could not stand the strain.

-Solberg, p. 64

25. All of the following is true about Andrew Jackson's life until age 15 *except* that he

1. was intelligent.
2. loved to fight.
3. was a soldier.
4. was from the North.

26. It can be inferred that the biggest factor making Jackson's actions in Florida controversial was that he

1. exiled the Spanish governor.
2. hanged two British citizens.
3. routed the Indians.
4. was apathetic.

27. The passage suggests that Jackson's hatred for the British stemmed from

1. a British politician making comments about his wife.
2. being a public prosecutor.
3. the Tennessee militia experience.
4. a childhood encounter with a British officer.

**TEST FIVE, PASSAGE FIVE**

28. The word, <u>snide</u>, as used in the passage most nearly means

1. public.
2. complimentary.
3. contemptuous.
4. interesting.

29. According to the passage, Andrew Jackson started

1. the Democratic party.
2. the idea of the common man.
3. the first smear campaign.
4. the Revolution.

30. The author, throughout the discussion, uses

1. definition.
2. statistics.
3. time order.
4. comparison.

**GO ON TO NEXT PAGE**

History tells us that some individuals bear on their hands, feet, or brow the marks of the stigmata. These marks seem bloody and supposedly appear on individuals empathetic to Christ's sufferings. The existence of stigmata is so well established historically that they are no longer disputed by unbelievers.

No cases are known prior to the thirteenth century. The first mentioned is St. Francis of Assisi. His stigmata were beheld by his brethren as well as a number of contemporary historians. Dr. Imbert counts 321 stigmatics (41 men) and believes that others would be found by consulting the libraries of Germany, Spain, and Italy. Some of the women include St. Margaret (1247-1297); St. Clare (1268-1308), and St. Catherine (1347-1380).

St. Margaret of Cortona, when seventeen, did not begin her life particularly empathetic to Christ's sufferings. She fled the home of her father and stepmother with her lover. For nine years she lived with him in his castle near Montepulciano, and a son was born to them. She often asked her lover to marry her; he as often promised to do so, but never did. Even during this period of her life, Margaret was compassionate towards the poor and helped them. She also sought out quiet places where she would dream of a life given to virtue and the love of God. She was at last set free from her unsettled life by the tragic death of her lover, who was murdered while on a journey.

Margaret then began her new life, subsisting upon bread and herbs. She lived in strict poverty, following the example of St. Francis. But while living on alms, she gave her services freely to others. She founded a hospital and repaired the church of St. Basil. There her body remains enshrined to this day in a silver shrine over the high altar.

-New Advent, Internet

31. The phrase, subsisting upon, in the last paragraph most nearly means

1. creating for.
2. being under.
3. cooking up.
4. living on.

32. In paragraph three, the author gets his point across through

1. sarcasm.
2. contrast.
3. example.
4. analytical reasoning.

33. The author conveys his ideas in paragraph two through

1. information and dates.
2. emotion and persuasion.
3. comparison and contrast.
4. narration and rhetoric.

34. It is suggested that stigmatics are

1. saints.
2. mostly women.
3. mostly men.
4. only Italians.

**TEST FIVE, PASSAGE SIX**

35.  The first known stigmatic was

1.  Dr. Imbert.
2.  St. Clare.
3.  St. Francis.
4.  St. Margaret.


36.  The reader can infer that

1.  no one believes in stigmata.
2.  only the blessed believe in stigmata.
3.  stigmatics have existed from the dawn
        of time.
4.  very few have questioned the existence
        of stigmata.


**GO ON TO NEXT PAGE**

**TEST FIVE, PASSAGE SIX**

When Tolkien began writing *The Hobbit* in the 1930s, he was unaware that he was essentially defining a genre. Tolkien was not the first author to write what would eventually be labeled as "fantasy," but his synthesis of elements (mythology, stories of larger-than-life heroism, the supernatural, and fairy tales) was unique. Nor had anything on the scale or scope of *The Lord of the Rings* (abbreviated *TLR*) previously been seen—not even the tales of King Arthur were as well developed.

In the late 1990s, New Zealand-based director Peter Jackson had a project on the drawing board: a three-film adaptation of *TLR*. Finally, because of Jackson, 2001 has seen the belated emergence of this fantasy as a legitimate cinematic genre. He has used it to re-invent fantasy for the cinema in the same way that the novel provided the blueprint for the written word.

This astounding movie accomplishes what no other fantasy film has been able to do: to transport viewers to an entirely different reality, immerse them in it, and maroon them there for nearly three hours. *TLR* brings Middle Earth to glorious life.

*TLR* devotees will be delighted to learn that the motion picture adaptation is as faithful as one could imagine possible. Jackson and his screen writers do an excellent job condensing more than five hundred pages of text into a script that never feels choppy, uneven, or rushed. Like all great movies of adventure, this one is characterized by tremendous action scenes punctuated by moments of rest and reflection. Along the way, there is triumph, sorrow, and a little philosophical depth.

*TLR* emphasizes two themes: the importance of brotherhood and the need for true strength that comes from within.

-Berardinelli, Internet

37. In paragraph one, the author's purpose is to

1. discredit the author of *The Hobbit*.
2. list works of fantasy.
3. show how the legend of King Arthur was created.
4. praise Tolkien.

38. Peter Jackson's influence on the genre of fantasy has been

1. little.
2. great.
3. somewhat important.
4. negative.

39. It is suggested that Peter Jackson most probably

1. is a new director.
2. was born in the late 1930s.
3. is an admirer of Tolkien.
4. will direct the *Legend of King Arthur* next.

40. The movie, *The Lord of the Rings*, is basically a(n)

1. adventure.
2. romance.
3. drama.
4. fairy tale.

**TEST FIVE, PASSAGE SEVEN**

41.  The author implies that the movie is unique because it

1.  is a legitimate cinematic genre.
2.  was written in the 1930s.
3.  contains the element of the supernatural.
4.  transports the viewer to a different reality.


42.  Overall, the author's attitude toward the movie is that of

1.  sympathy.
2.  indifference.
3.  admiration.
4.  sarcasm.


**GO ON TO NEXT PAGE**

**TEST FIVE, PASSAGE SEVEN**

With nothing more than a narrow board on wheels, the sidewalk surfers of early times had a straightforward mission: start at the top of a hill and ride down. The first type of skateboards were actually more like scooters. These contraptions, which date back to the early 1900s, featured roller skate wheels attached to a two-by-four. Often the wood had a milk crate nailed to it with handles sticking out for control. The goals of someone who utilized these boards were not to fall off and to avoid collisions.

Toward the late 1950s, surfing became increasingly popular and people began to tie surfing together with cruising on a board. By 1959, the first Roller Derby Skateboard was for sale. Clay wheels entered the picture and sidewalk surfing began to take root.

By the time the 1960s rolled around, skate boarding had gained an impressive following among the surf crowd. In fact, Stevenson's company, Makaha, designed the first professional boards in 1953, and he appointed a team to promote the product.

While most skaters took to the street or sidewalk, some brave souls decided to ride empty swimming pools. By 1965, international contests, movies, and a magazine (*The Quarterly Skateboarder*) elevated the sport to enormous heights. Over fifty million boards were sold within a three-year period.

The first denouncement of skateboarding came during the mid 1960s mainly because the public was upset by what it thought was reckless riding. The culprit was not the surfer, but rather the manufacturer. Although companies developed better quality wheels, clay wheels were the cheapest to manufacture. However, clay wheels did not grip the road well and skaters fell everywhere. After a few fatal accidents, cities banned skateboards in response to health and safety concerns. Over the next eight years, skateboarding remained fairly underground.

-Brooke, Internet

43. The earliest skateboards were like

1. surfboards.
2. scooters.
3. milk crates.
4. the first Derby Skateboard.

44. It is implied that skateboarding remained underground because

1. it was illegal.
2. it was not safe.
3. the public established vigilante groups to stop it.
4. manufacturers no longer produced skateboards.

45. The overriding attitude of the writer toward skateboarding is one of

1. confusion.
2. concern.
3. irritation.
4. support.

**TEST FIVE, PASSAGE EIGHT**

46. Clay wheels were manufactured

1. during the early 1900s.
2. after 1965.
3. in 1959.
4. in the mid 1960s.


47. Denouncement, as used in the third
paragraph, is best defined as

1. reward.
2. acclaim.
3. arrest.
4. criticism.


48. The purpose of the passage is to

1. criticize skateboard enthusiasts.
2. expose the dangers of skateboarding.
3. discuss the early history of skateboarding.
4. praise Makaha for its pioneering
        approach to skateboarding.


**GO ON TO NEXT PAGE**


**TEST FIVE, PASSAGE EIGHT**

Have you ever tried to find information on visiting a specific country overseas? The U.S. Department of State's "Consular Information Sheet" gives detailed information and warnings about each country. The following is information found on the country of China. Please note that the description is but a sampling of what you can find on the website.

"The People's Republic of China was established on October 1, 1949, with Beijing as its capital city. With well over 1.3 billion citizens, China is the world's most populous country. Political power remains centralized in the Chinese Communist Party.

A valid passport and visa are required to enter China. Americans arriving without valid papers are subject to a fine and immediate deportation. Travelers should not rely on Chinese host organizations claiming to be able to arrange a visa upon arrival.

*Warnings*: Americans who rent apartments with gas appliances should be aware that in some areas, natural gas is not scented to warn occupants of gas leaks. In addition, heaters may not always be well vented which allows excess carbon monoxide to build up in living spaces. Due to recent fatal accidents involving American citizens, travelers are advised to ensure all gas appliances are properly vented or bring carbon monoxide detectors with them.

Traffic conditions are generally safe if occupants wear seatbelts (if the vehicles are equipped with seatbelts). Most traffic injuries involve pedestrians who are involved in collisions or who encounter unexpected road hazards (e.g., unmarked open manholes). Americans who wish to ride bicycles in China are urged to wear safety helmets meeting U.S. standards.

Driving etiquette in China is developing. As a result, traffic is often chaotic, and the right-of-way is often ignored. Travelers should note that cars and buses in the wrong lanes frequently hit pedestrians on sidewalks."

-U.S. Department of State, Internet

49. The main idea of the first paragraph is that

1. Americans usually do not visit China.
2. information on countries can be found on the Department of State's website.
3. most Americans have not been overseas.
4. government websites give warnings about countries overseas.

50. Overall, the author disseminates information by

1. contrasting the United States and China.
2. narrating the experiences of Americans in China.
3. persuading the reader to go to China.
4. using China as an example.

51. The purpose of the passage is to

1. inform.
2. entertain.
3. compare.
4. narrate.

**TEST FIVE, PASSAGE NINE**

52. We can infer from the selection that to date the Chinese

1. have few accidents.
2. hit foreigners on purpose.
3. are not very good drivers.
4. are required to take driver's education
    courses.

53. In the context of the last paragraph, <u>etiquette</u> can best be defined as

1. regulations.
2. dainty manners.
3. habits.
4. expectations.

54. The reader can deduce that a build-up of carbon monoxide can be

1. harmless.
2. negligent.
3. safe.
4. fatal.

# SIMULATED EXAM SIX

In later years it became common for historians to <u>lament</u> the fact that the West, after Adolph Hitler came to power, never stood up to his aggressions until it was too late to do anything about them. Less often considered, however, is the question of what made Hitler possible in the first place. What conditions prevailed in Germany that put the German people in such a frame of mind that they ultimately accepted someone like Hitler?

After World War I, the treaty was such that the Germans were forced to evacuate all territories invaded by her and surrender military equipment including warships and submarines. The terms of the treaty were harsh enough to "brand in the minds of the German people, a desire for revenge," as Hitler was to later phrase it.

Under the military clauses, Germany was to reduce her army to 100,000 men, and the General Staff was to be dissolved. She was not to maintain a navy in excess of six battleships, six light cruisers, twelve destroyers and twelve torpedo boats. She was neither to manufacture nor possess military aircraft, heavy artillery, or poison gas.

The most grating of all provisions of the treaty was the so-called "guilt clause" by which Germany was forced to accept the responsibility for causing all loss and damage for World War I. She was required to pay 20,000,000,000 gold marks by May 1921. In addition, she was to deliver coal and timber to France, livestock to Belgium, and ships to Britain. These demands were beyond Germany's capacity, and this guilt clause was to <u>rankle</u> the German minds for years to come and to create a fertile ground for a nationalist voice in Adolph Hitler.

-Layton, pp. 1-2

**TEST SIX, PASSAGE ONE**

1. The main idea of the passage is presented in which of the following questions?

1. Why was Hitler not assassinated?
2. What made Hitler's rule possible?
3. Why did the Allies not stand up to Hitler until it was too late?
4. Why did Germany have to pay for the loss and damage she caused?

2. The author makes his point in paragraphs three and four through the use of

1. a listing of the terms of the treaty.
2. examples of military aircraft.
3. a definition of the term "guilt clause."
4. a description of Germany.

3. The style of writing is

1. scientific.
2. informal.
3. persuasive.
4. academic.

4. The reader can infer that the author

1. researched reasons for Germany's acceptance of Hitler's ideas.
2. is angry that the West did not stop Hitler sooner.
3. is sympathetic to the German war mongers.
4. is of German descent.

5. The word, <u>lament</u>, in the first sentence
most likely means

1. extol.
2. print.
3. regret.
4. ignore.


6. The word, <u>rankle</u>, in the last sentence
is synonymous with the phrase

1. "take from."
2. "eat away at."
3. "broaden."
4. "physically destroy."


**GO ON TO NEXT PAGE**

**TEST SIX, PASSAGE ONE**

Throughout history, within the Afro-American community in America, there has always been some form of verbal "play" involving rhymes: signifying, testifying, school yard rhymes, and double Dutch jump rope rhymes, to name a few.

Modern day rap music finds its immediate roots in the city of New York. Characterized by slang and the recitation of popular phrases, an early form of rap was dubbed over early 1970s reggae music. For example, it was fashionable for DJs to acknowledge people who were at a party. These early raps featured someone shouting over the instrumental break: 'Yo this is Kool Here in the joint-ski saying my mellow-ski Marky D is in the house.' This would usually evoke a response from the crowd, who began to call out their own names and slogans. At that time, rap was not yet known as "rap" but was called "emceeing."

Rap is popular among today's youth for the same reasons it was a draw in the early days. First, rap caught on because it offered young party goers a chance to freely express themselves. Second, it was an art form accessible to anyone. No expensive resources were needed to rhyme. Further, rap allowed one to accurately and efficiently inject her personality. If you were laid back, you could rap at a slow pace. If you were hyperactive, you could rap faster. No two people rapped the same, even when reciting the same rhyme. Fourth, rap became popular because it offered unlimited challenges. There were no set rules. One could make up a rap about

the man in the moon or how good the DJ was—as long as it was original. Finally, the fact that the praises a rapper received from peers were on par with any other hero (sports star, tough guy) was a definite attraction to the art.

-D'Cook, Internet

7. We can infer that many DJs in the 1970s

1. were early rappers.
2. signified and testified.
3. were not reggae enthusiasts.
4. were antisocial.

8. The author's purpose is to

1. entertain.
2. persuade.
3. argue.
4. inform.

9. Overall, in paragraph three, the author

1. gives reasons why rap became popular.
2. tries to persuade the reader to appreciate rap.
3. contrasts rap to other types of verbal play.
4. offers examples of rap music.

10. The phrase <u>verbal play</u>, as used in paragraph one, most nearly means

1. the creation of rap.
2. the telling of jokes.
3. the manipulation of language.
4. oral questioning.

11. During the early 1970s,

1. "rap" was dubbed "instrumental breaks."
2. rappers never attended parties; they preferred clubs.
3. rap was not accessible to everyone.
4. "rap" was called "emceeing."

12. The main idea of paragraph three is that

1. rap gives everyone a chance to freely express themselves.
2. there are many reasons why rap was and is so popular.
3. no two people rap the same.
4. hyperactive people can rap faster.

13. The writer's tone is

1. sympathetic.
2. sarcastic.
3. impartial.
4. defensive.

The general presumption in the U.S. is that speech is free; the burden of proof is upon those who wish to restrict it. What restrictions are justified? This question has been posed at the national level by both Congress and the Supreme Court.

There are four kinds of speech that governments have often tried to restrict: 1) speech that undermines officially supported religious opinions; 2) speech that tends to damage the reputation of other people; 3) speech that threatens to disrupt public order or undermine the government; and 4) speech considered obscene.

In the first area, because the founding principles of American government are based on freedom, freedom of religious speech under the First Amendment is accepted. Americans have generally agreed that there is no public injury if their neighbors say there are twenty gods or no God.

In the second area, <u>libel</u> laws that penalize speech endangering the reputation of other individuals have been enacted. To sue for libel, ordinary private individuals must show that statements made against them are false and injurious and that the author was negligent in making them. When it comes to public officials, however, the Supreme Court has made it harder to win. In *New York Times v Sullivan* (1964), the Court decided that a public official must prove not only that the statements made against him were false but that the news agency that made them acted with reckless disregard of

the truth. This same standard now applies to persons who have become prominent in the news, such as Monica Lewinsky. This standard provides great latitude to news agencies in dealing with public affairs, but is detrimental to individuals who are unfairly named.

But it has been in the last areas—restricting criticism of the government and controlling obscene speech—that disagreements have been greatest.

-Ceaser, p. 490

14. The paragraph that would follow this selection most probably would focus on

1. standards for news agencies.
2. restricting criticism of the government.
3. tabloids and gossip columns.
4. Monica Lewinsky.

15. The reader can assume that the issue of restricting speech

1. has long been an issue at the national level.
2. has recently been rejected.
3. is exaggerated.
4. is not a crucial issue in the United States

16. The purpose of the selection is to discuss

1. libel and obscene language.
2. speech that criticizes government and religious speech.
3. religious speech and obscene language.
4. libel and freedom of religious speech.

**TEST SIX, PASSAGE THREE**

17. The word, <u>libel</u>, as used in the passage most nearly means

1. true statements that injure reputations.
2. obscene language that endangers individuals.
3. false and negligent statements which damage reputations.
4. legal language used in the *New York Times v Sullivan* case.

18. Overall, the author gets his point across through

1. classification.
2. contrast.
3. argumentation.
4. narration.

19. This article probably appeared in a(n)

1. professional journal on politics.
2. *Time* magazine.
3. law book.
4. American Government textbook.

**GO ON TO NEXT PAGE**

**TEST SIX, PASSAGE THREE**

Eldrick Woods was born December 30, 1975 in Long Beach, California. Standing at the height of 6'2", he is of African and Thai descent. Eldrick attended high school in Anaheim and then attended college at Stanford University in Palo Alto, California. During his years at Stanford University, Eldrick majored in Economics. There, he also played golf. He was affectionately nicknamed "Urkel" by his team mates, but his favorite nickname came from his father. It's the same nickname of a South Vietnamese combat buddy, Nguyen Phong, who saved his father's life in the Vietnam War. So Eldrick Woods became "Tiger" Woods.

Tiger had some great years playing for the Stanford Cardinal Varsity Golf Team. He was first in 1996 in the following: NCAA Championships, the Honors Course, Pac-10 Championships, The Cougar Classic, The Brawl, and the SW Intercollegiate.

Since his college days, Tiger has become a well known <u>presence</u> on the professional golf circuits. Close to his mother, Tiger carries the handmade club head cover his mother stitched for him. The words "Love from Mom" are embroidered on the cover in the Thai language. In addition, because of his mother's beliefs, Tiger always wears the color red on the final day of the tournament: according to his mother, red signifies luck and power. The color must work because *Sports Illustrated*

named him "Sportsman of the Year" not only in 1996 but also in 2000!

-Arthur

20. Which of the following is true about the last sentence in paragraph one?

1. It disgusts the reader.
2. It is a bit unexpected.
3. It instills pride.
4. It gives a feeling of detachment.

21. According to the article, Eldrick Woods is famous because

1. he played golf at Stanford University.
2. his mother is Thai.
3. he wears red at tournaments.
4. he is a professional golfer.

22. It is implied that Tiger Woods

1. is in constant contact with his mother.
2. always wanted to be an economist.
3. was frustrated playing college golf.
4. was not very intelligent.

23. Eldrick's nickname, Tiger, came from

1. his mother.
2. college teammates.
3. the Thai language.
4. his father.

24. The word <u>presence,</u> as underlined,
most nearly means


1. attendance.
2. college golfer.
3. personality.
4. college student.


**GO ON TO NEXT PAGE**

Recent results published in the journal *Nature* used DNA testing to support the theory that Thomas Jefferson fathered his slave, Sally Hemming's, last child. This testing generated media attention, and Jefferson's ideals as a political thinker and his relationships with his slaves were re-examined. But, lost in the process was the significance that DNA testing has the ability to prove, or disprove, an ancestry.

The ingenious method of proof compares claimed black descendants with known white descendants. Jefferson's Y-chromosome would not be diluted by the passage of generations. Rather, to each offspring it is either passed intact (if the offspring is a boy), or not passed at all (to a girl). Hence, if Jefferson had a son from his white wife, who had a son, . . .who had a son alive today, then from that patrilineal descendant the Y-chromosome traits are available just as from Jefferson himself. Then, assuming that among the descendants of Sally Hemming who may be alive today and may be descended from Jefferson, there are some who are patrilineal, they should also have some of the same Jeffersonian traits on the Y-chromosome.

Sound too easy? Some still don't believe DNA test results. One theory is that Jefferson didn't father Hemming's children, but his nephew did. If the nephew was Jefferson's brother's child, then he too would share the infamous Jeffersonian Y-chromosome.

Whatever the case, it is a method that has <u>profound</u> implications for the genealogy of the future. Not only will we prove descent, we may also find ourselves disproving what the paper trail claims is true. Many of our cherished family traditions and history may hold some surprises.

-ancestry.com & DNA-view, internet

25. The main topic of the article is

1. Thomas Jefferson.
2. descendants of Sally Hemming.
3. the Y-chromosome.
4. DNA testing.

26. Proof of ancestry in this instance basically traces the Y-chromosome of

1. white females.
2. African-American females.
3. male descendants.
4. nephews.

27. The author illustrates his point through

1. definition.
2. example.
3. comparison.
4. persuasion.

28. It is suggested that the marvel of DNA testing was overlooked because

1. more attention was given to Jefferson and Hemming's relationship.
2. Sally Hemming had children.
3. the story was published in *Nature*, an insignificant journal.
4. the method used was so ordinary.


29. The purpose of paragraph three is to

1. reaffirm the accepted theory.
2. confuse the reader.
3. inform the reader that Jefferson had a brother.
4. reveal that others are trying to discredit the accepted theory.


30. The word, <u>profound</u>, in the last paragraph is best defined as

1. insignificant.
2. major.
3. objective.
4. neglectful.

31. The author would probably agree that this kind of testing

1. can only help those interested in finding their roots.
2. Sally Hemming bore all of Jefferson's children.
3. is totally unsubstantiated.
4. may destroy some longstanding ideas and traditions, publicly and privately.

In my opinion, every member of the Mormon Church owes it to himself to become familiar with the story of Mark Hofmann and his dealings with the church, especially since the implicatons are so damaging. Being a dealer in historical documents, he had earned an honest reputation as a man skilled in this field. Unfortunately, to stave off debt, he decided to forge some documents and sell them.

It is common knowledge that all its sensitive documents relating to Mormon Church history are hidden away in the "Church Archives" and "the First Presidency's vault." Only select historians in the church's employ are ever granted access. In light of this secrecy, Hofmann strongly suspected that church leadership was willing to suppress any historical document which tended to reflect negatively on the church. Hence, he began "finding" negative documents (which were in actuality his own forgeries).

Part of Hofmann's scheme was to leak news of his "discovery" of these negative documents. He had two reasons for doing this: one was to inflate their prices; the other was to force the church to admit its history as opposed to white washing it. According to Hofmann, he was merely trying to "help the history of the Mormon Church along" by crafting the missing pieces of a puzzle which, according to his intensive study of Mormon history, were there all along but had been purposefully ignored.

-Throckmorton, p. 565

32. We can infer that Mark Hofmann invented documents that

1. were then hidden in the church archives.
2. damaged high officials in the church.
3. negatively reflected on basic Mormon beliefs.
4. reaffirmed the traditions of the Mormon Church.

33. The reader can assume that the elders of the Mormon Church thought that the documents they bought

1. were damaging.
2. were fakes and no one would pay attention to them.
3. had been missing for some time from the vault.
4. were not crucial to the archival inventory.

34. The author suggests that the Mormon leaders

1. will probably sue Hofmann.
2. want to protect the church.
3. are not interested in historical topics.
4. spend a lot of time researching Mormon history.

35. Hofmann "leaked" discovery of the documents mainly to

1. keep from going to prison.
2. hurt Hinckley's reputation.
3. ensure his own notoriety.
4. inflate their price.

36.  As used in the context of the passage, the word <u>suppress</u> may be defined as

1. forge.
2. print.
3. hide.
4. reveal.

37.  The author's style of writing is

1. scientific.
2. entertaining.
3. informal.
4. informational.

**GO ON TO NEXT PAGE**

**TEST SIX, PASSAGE SIX**

About 2000 B.C., new invaders moved into Mesopotamia. Some were Semitic peoples known as the Amorites. The Amorites founded their capitol city of Babylon (the world's first metropolis) about 1900 B.C. The greatest king of the Amorites was Hammurabi, who ruled from 1792 to 1750 B.C. By far the most remarkable of the Hammurabi records is his code of laws; Hammurabi <u>promulgated</u> a law code based on earlier Sumerian codes. He is the earliest-known example of a ruler proclaiming publicly to his people an entire body of laws so that all men might know what was required of them. The code was carved upon a black stone monument, eight feet high, and clearly intended to be in public view. This noted stone was found in the year 1901 in the Persian mountains.

The Code of Hammurabi categorized criminal behavior based on social class. If a nobleman committed a murder of a peasant, the punishment for the crime was treated more leniently than if a peasant murdered a nobleman. The code reflected the principle of an eye for an eye, or <u>retribution</u>. For example, if a man builds a house badly, and it falls and kills the owner, the builder is to be slain. If the owner's son was killed, then the builder's son is slain. These grim retaliatory punishments took no note of excuses or explanations, but only of the facts—with "one striking exception." An accused person was allowed to cast himself into "the river," the Euphrates. Apparently the art of swimming was unknown, for if the

**TEST SIX, PASSAGE SEVEN**

current bore him to the shore alive he was declared innocent. If he drowned, he was guilty.

-Kehoe, p. 24 & Horne, Internet

38. The word, <u>promulgated</u>, as used in the passage most nearly means

1. destroyed.
2. reversed.
3. enacted.
4. coded.

39. Babylon was

1. in Sumer.
2. founded within the Persian mountains.
3. a small village of Amorites.
4. in Mesopotamia.

40. Hammurabi is most famous because he

1. was the first to have retaliatory law.
2. publicly proclaimed the law.
3. carved the black stone.
4. categorized criminal behavior based on social class.

41. According to the passage, the concept of <u>retribution</u> can be described as

1. "the sins of the fathers are visited on their sons."
2. "death to all that commit a crime."
3. "innocent until proven guilty."
4. "an eye for an eye."

42.  The author probably agrees that the
"one striking exception" (last
paragraph)

1.  was an order given by the judge.
2.  could not be considered real justice.
3.  was designed to protect the guilty.
4.  is progressive in its concept.

**GO ON TO NEXT PAGE**

The term "club drugs" is a general term used for certain illicit substances, primarily synthetic, that are usually found at nightclubs and raves. The substance most often used as a club drug is MDMA or ecstasy. To some, club drugs seem harmless. In reality, these substances can cause serious physical and psychological problems—even death. Because club drugs are illegal and are often produced in un-sanitary laboratories, it is impossible for the user to know exactly what he or she is taking. The quality and potency of these substances can vary significantly from batch to batch. Often, the raves where these drugs are used are pro-moted as alcohol-free events; therefore, parents are not often aware that raves may actually be havens for the illicit sale and abuse of club drugs.

The 2001 National Household Survey on Drug Abuse indicates that more than 8 million people have used ecstasy at least once during their lifetime. There are serious dangers associated with the use of club drugs:

1. MDMA can cause a user's blood pressure and heart rate to increase to dangerous levels, and can lead to heart or kidney failure. It can cause severe hyperthermia from the combination of the drug's stimulant effect with the often hot, crowded atmosphere of a rave.

2. MDMA users may also suffer from long-term brain injury. Research has shown that MDMA can cause damage to the parts of the brain that are critical to thought and memory.

The number of ecstasy emergencies reported to the Drug Abuse Warning Network increased 94.5% from 2,850 in 1999 to 5,542 in 2001.

-NCJRS, internet

43. Another name for MDMA, as underlined, is

1. illegal substance.
2. rave.
3. club drug.
4. ecstasy.

44. The style of this passage is

1. personal.
2. informal.
3. academic.
4. sarcastic.

45. The author would probably agree that club drugs are

1. harmless.
2. injurious.
3. not prevalent.
4. useful in some circumstances.

46. The topic of the second paragraph is

1. the dangers of club drugs.
2. the benefits of club drugs.
3. long-term brain injuries.
4. the Drug Abuse Warning Network.

**TEST SIX, PASSAGE EIGHT**

47. According to the passage, it is difficult to know exactly what a user is taking because

1. the drugs are produced in unsanitary labs.
2. it is difficult to see anything in the dark atmosphere of a club.
3. the drugs are usually mixed with alcohol.
4. no physical change can be measured.

48. It is implied that ecstasy can cause all of the following *except*

1. heart attacks.
2. strokes.
3. amnesia.
4. cancer.

**GO ON TO NEXT PAGE**

As soon as the men joined them in the drawing room Celia jumped up crying, "Let's do something! It's Saturday night. I know, let's dance! We'll go to Richard's music room."

"Splendid!" cried Igor, twirling gracefully on his toes and waving his beautiful white hands.

Everyone looked at Richard, who removed his unfathomable gaze from his wife and said, "'Music room' is a bit grand for the old schoolroom on the second story. I do happen to have a stereo there, and a collection of records which appeal to me."

His decisive tone piqued Myra, who cried, "Let's go invade the schoolroom. He so obviously doesn't want us to!"

Richard reddened. A furious refusal nearly burst out, but he controlled himself, and said, with a shrug, "Your lurid hopes will be disappointed. I lock it simply to keep out house maids who disturb everything."

This was not quite true. Richard locked the door because he had locked it since he was twelve, and the abandoned schoolroom represented the only privacy from his stepmother. It was situated in a remote part of the house next to the servants' quarters. He had gone there seldom since his marriage, and then only when Celia had been shopping in Lewes, or up to London for the day. He had not known that she knew the room existed, and he resented her idiotic wish to expose it to all these people as much as he resented her extraordinary behavior since the return

from Ighthom Mote. Yet, he was aware of her as he had not been in months— aware that she was alluring, desirable.

Richard silently led the party upstairs into the south wing. He cautiously unlocked the huge, wooden door.

-Seton, pp. 60-62

49. We can infer that Celia suggests going to the music room because she

1. suspects Richard of something.
2. really wants to dance.
3. wants to impress her guests.
4. has never been inside the music room.

50. The reader can assume that the relationship between Richard and Celia is that of

1. a teacher and student.
2. close relatives.
3. spouses.
4. friends.

51. Richard's attitude toward his stepmother can best be described as

1. compassion.
2. detachment.
3. awe.
4. melancholy.

52.  In the context of the passage, the word, lurid, most nearly means

1. gracious.
2. complex.
3. cheerful.
4. sensationalistic.

53.  The author's purpose in the last paragraph is to give the reader a sense of

1. the ridiculous.
2. frustration.
3. suspense.
4. optimism.

54.  The author gets her point across through

1. persuasion.
2. narration.
3. comparison.
4. argumentation.

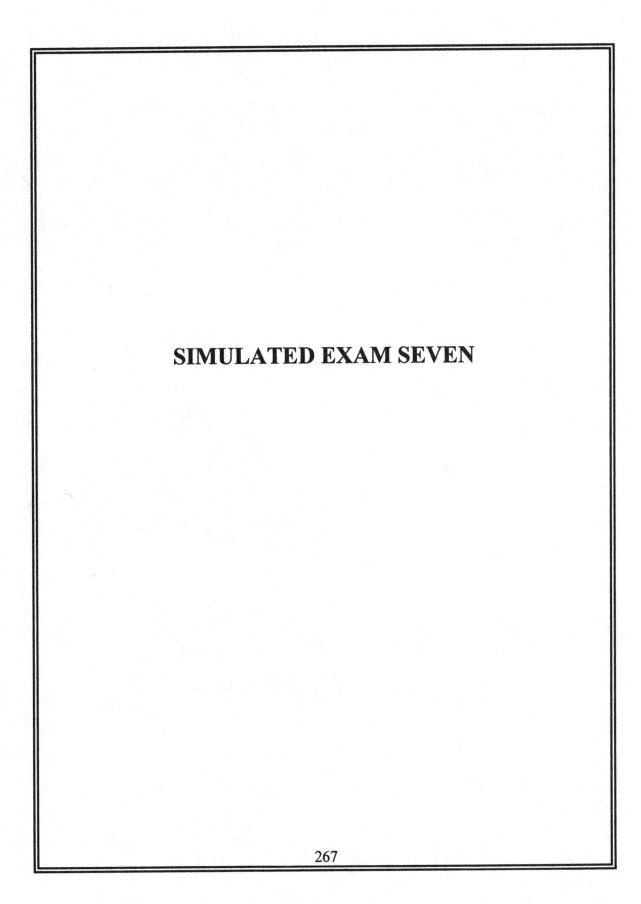

# SIMULATED EXAM SEVEN

When we let ourselves be defined by our worst moments instead of our best ones, we learn to think of ourselves as people who never get it right.

I can remember from my growing-up years occasions of feeling shame: giving wrong answers, forgetting my lines in a play, tripping over myself in a game. What I find remarkable is not that those things happened, but that decades later, after a life rich in achievements, I can still remember them—and they still have the power to hurt.

One would expect world-class athletes to demand perfection of themselves in every play. But studies have shown that athletes who obsess over their mistakes do much worse than athletes who say, "the next [play] will be better." I can think of out-standing athletes whose careers were ruined because they could not get over having made one mistake at a crucial moment. In 1986, an out-standing major league relief pitcher, Donnie Moore of the California Angels, needed one more "out" to put his team into the World Series. Instead he gave up a home run that cost his team the game. A few years later, Donnie Moore tragically took his own life.

In contrast, I can think of others who overcame that sort of failure. A few years ago, a nineteen-year-old college basketball player, Chris Webber, made a mental mistake in a national champion-ship game, calling a time out when his team had already used up all of its time-outs: he lost possession of the ball in the last seconds of a close game. But Webber refused to let that one play define him, knowing himself well enough to believe that he could be an outstanding player even if not a perfect one. A year later, he was Rookie of the Year.                -Kushner, pp. 37-38

1. The excerpt is written from the point of view of

1. an athlete.
2. Donnie Moore.
3. Rookie of the Year.
4. the writer.

2. A central focus of the passage is that

1. one would expect world-class athletes to demand perfection of them-selves.
2. Donnie Moore committed suicide because he cost his team the World Series.
3. seeing our worst moments as our defining moments teaches us we are people who never get it right.
4. a person should feel ashamed when making mistakes.

3. The author would probably agree that

1. someone could have kept Donnie Moore from harming himself.
2. positive thinking enhances self-esteem.
3. people should remind themselves often of their worst moments so they can improve themselves.
4. most athletes have mental problems.

**TEST SEVEN, PASSAGE ONE**

4. The author's purpose is to

1. persuade individuals to remember their achievements rather than their failures.
2. describe athletes who have made major mistakes.
3. narrate the story of Chris Webber's success.
4. contrast world-class athletes with ordinary persons.

5. The author's style is

1. formal.
2. scholarly.
3. informal.
4. scientific.

6. The main purpose of the second paragraph is to

1. illustrate a point through personal experience.
2. describe the author's childhood.
3. entertain the reader with a personal story.
4. expose the writer as a clumsy athlete.

**GO ON TO NEXT PAGE**

**TEST SEVEN, PASSAGE ONE**

The small child ran out of the hide-covered lean-to toward the rocky beach. It didn't occur to her to look back. Nothing in her experience ever gave her reason to doubt that the shelter and those within it would be there when she returned.

She splashed into the river; she dived into the cold water and came up sputtering. She had learned to swim before she learned to walk and, at five, was at ease in the water. The girl played for a while, swimming back and forth, then let the current float her down stream. Where the river widened and bubbled over rocks, she stood up and waded to shore, then walked back to the beach and began sorting pebbles. She had just put a stone on top of a pile when the earth began to tremble.

The child looked with surprise as the stone rolled down of its own accord, and stared in wonder at the small pyramid of pebbles shaking. Only then did she become aware she was shaking too. The small river, which moments before had flowed smoothly, was roiling with choppy waves that splashed over its banks as the rocking stream bed moved at cross purposes to the current, dredging mud up from the bottom. Beyond, stately trees lurched grotesquely.

As the girl started toward the hide-covered shelter, she felt a low rumble rise to a terrifying roar. A sour stench of wetness and rot issued from a crack opening in the ground, like the reek of morning breath from a yawning earth.

She stared uncomprehendingly. The lean-to, perched on the far edge of the abyss, tilted, as half the solid ground beneath it pulled away. It teetered undecidedly, then collapsed and disappeared into the deep hole, taking its hide cover and all it contained with it.

-Auel, pp. 1-2

7. The author conveys her point through

1. analytical reasoning.
2. persuasive rhetoric.
3. contrast and comparison.
4. narrative description.

8. Roiling, as used in the third paragraph, is best defined as

1. settled.
2. stirred up.
3. glassy.
4. rolling.

9. The reader can conclude that

1. everyone in the lean-to escaped.
2. the girl had relatives who lived down the river.
3. no one in the clan was injured.
4. the girl's parents were killed.

**TEST SEVEN, PASSAGE TWO**

10. <u>Like the reek of morning breath
from a yawning earth</u> is an example of

1. figurative language.
2. narration.
3. analysis.
4. irony.

11. The first two paragraphs portray
the girl as

1. worried.
2. carefree.
3. in shock.
4. doubtful.

12. We can infer that the girl
experienced

1. a thunderstorm.
2. hurricane-like weather.
3. an earthquake.
4. tidal flooding.

**GO ON TO NEXT PAGE**

**TEST SEVEN, PASSAGE TWO**

In July 1941 Japan gave France an ultimatum and demanded the right to send troops into Indochina (now called Vietnam). The French government knuckled under, and Japanese soldiers went ashore and occupied both Saigon and Da Nang. These locations were essential for any future operations in Southeast Asia. President Roosevelt reacted to the Japanese troop movements by placing an embargo on all oil shipments to Japan. He had already embargoed shipments of other vital materials such as scrap iron to Japan. In addition, all trade with Japan was cut off, and all Japanese assets in the United States were frozen. Great Britain and the Netherlands soon followed the lead of the United States.

The effects of the American actions, particularly the oil embargo, were immediate for Japan. She had no domestic supply of oil, although she had stored enough to last for two years. Denying her the opportunity of replenishing it would be a severe blow to her expansionist plans, indeed to her very survival. Japanese leaders also feared that being deprived of U.S. dollars would lead to Japanese economic bankruptcy within two years.

Roosevelt and Secretary of State Hull made it clear that the embargoes would be lifted only if: 1. Japan got out of Indochina; 2. Japan got out of China; and 3. Japan renounced the Tri-Partite Pact with Germany and Italy. These were demands to which Japan would not consent. To back down from her newly won possessions would mean to

lose face, and in the samurai mentality that would be equivalent to the disgrace of surrender.                    -Layton, p. 109

13. It can be inferred that Roosevelt placed embargoes on Japan

1. because Japan threatened France.
2. the U.S. could not afford to give Japan more scrap iron.
3. in an attempt to stop her expansionist plans.
4. to make Japan lose face in the eyes of the international community.

14. If Japan were deprived of U.S. dollars

1. Japan would go bankrupt within two years.
2. it would help the Japanese economy.
3. Japan would substitute French francs.
4. there would be no change in Japan's economic structure.

15. Ultimatum, as used in the passage, may be defined as

1. request.
2. excuse.
3. a sum of money.
4. last-chance.

**TEST SEVEN, PASSAGE THREE**

16.  The main idea of paragraph two is
that Japan

1.  Japan stored enough oil to last two
        years.
2.  Japan depended on products from
        America to survive.
3.  Japanese leaders feared the U.S.
        leaders.
4.  Japan had no oil of her own.


17.  Japan wanted to occupy Vietnam
because

1.  their cultures were alike in so many
        ways.
2.  they did not want Great Britain to
        occupy Vietnam first.
3.  they wanted to provoke Roosevelt
        into declaring war.
4.  Vietnam was essential for operating
        in southeast Asia.


18.  The main idea of the last paragraph
is that

1.  Roosevelt forced Japan out of
        Indochina.
2.  under the circumstances, Japan would
        not surrender.
3.  Japan was in a pact with Germany
        and Italy.
4.  Roosevelt was ridiculous to demand
        anything of Japan.

The greatest tool of all–indeed, the greatest gift of all–is the human body and the immense intelligence that directs it. The human body has to be nature's finest creation. It is unmatched in power, capacity, and adaptability. The intelligence inherent in our bodies is so vast that it is positively staggering.

The human heart beats about one hundred thousand times every twenty-four hours. Consider the fact that the heart and its pumping system, which scientists have attempted to duplicate without success, pumps blood through over ninety-six thousand miles of blood vessels. This is an equivalent of sixty-three hundred gallons per day: that is almost one hundred fifteen million gallons in only fifty years. This pumping system has the capability of working nonstop for decades without skipping a beat.

Consider the heat this machine must generate in accomplishing these functions, yet it maintains a constant temperature of around 98.6 degrees. The biggest organ of the body, the skin, is made up of over four million pores that are constantly acting as the cooling system for this machine. Perfect balance is always maintained, and if it were off by only a small faction, the balance would be destroyed.

-Diamond, pp. 19-20

19. The author's attitude toward the human body is one of

1. objectivity.
2. tremendous respect.
3. love and caring.
4. condescension.

20. The purpose of the selection is to

1. narrate.
2. entertain.
3. argue.
4. educate.

21. According to the passage, the human heart

1. has not been duplicated successfully.
2. pumps an equivalent of sixty-three hundred gallons of blood in only 50 years.
3. must skip a beat every so often to function.
4. is a very fragile organ.

22. The article states that the body's cooling system functions through the

1. skin.
2. heart.
3. circulatory system.
4. brain.

23. The style of writing employed is

1. nostalgic.
2. academic.
3. subjective.
4. suspenseful.

**TEST SEVEN, PASSAGE FOUR**

24.  The author is probably a(n)

1.  statistician.
2.  journalist interested in medicine.
3.  heart surgeon.
4.  expert in health matters.

**GO ON TO NEXT PAGE**

**TEST SEVEN, PASSAGE FOUR**

It can be said that most persons shy away from discussions of mysticism (a belief incorporating the idea that knowledge of spiritual truths is possible through meditation). Perhaps they believe it goes against other existing religions. But mysticism has thrived from the beginning of time.

As Epstein explains, "from the earliest times the practice of Jewish mysticism, called Kabbalah, has been shrouded in secret. Fearful of persecution from within and without the Jewish community, the masters and wise men buried an already elite tradition even deeper. The complicated diagrams and mystic texts were often deliberately distorted in order to confuse the common person. The tradition was itself passed down orally from master to disciple, thus insuring its integrity, on the one hand, and providing personal guidance and instruction to the novice, on the other.

Kabbalah is first and foremost a mystical practice, but it is also fully dependent on, and integrated with, Judaism as a whole. Trying to practice kabbalistic meditation without understanding its foundation in the Torah would be like trying to fly without wings: one cannot even begin to live the mystical life as a Jew without a knowledge of the first five books of the Bible.

Contrary to most other spiritual disciplines which urge the disciple to get away from it all, to retire to a quiet place in the country and meditate, the Jewish mystic is urged to start living in the midst of worldly activity in a new way. He begins with the advice of the wise men who urge him to 'eat bread with salt, drink water moderately, sleep on the ground, lead a close life, and study hard.'

The Kabbalah has flourished—sometimes darkly and sometimes brilliantly—for over five thousand years. Often so incorporated into the everyday life of the Jews that it has gone unnoticed, mysticism once again appears to be enjoying a popular resurgence."

                                        -Epstein, pp. xvi-xviii

25. We can infer that the Torah is most likely

1. the Kabbalah.
2. like most New Age texts.
3. the first five books of the Bible.
4. impossible to read.

26. Novice, as used in the second paragraph, is a referent for

1. the common person.
2. Kabbalah.
3. master.
4. disciple.

27. According to the passage, most spiritual disciples of the Kabbalah are encouraged to

1. remove themselves from society.
2. live in the midst of society.
3. become monks.
4. experience a life in the country-
       side.

**TEST SEVEN, PASSAGE FIVE**

28.  <u>Like trying to fly without wings</u>
implies that one cannot understand
the Kabbalah without

1.  a knowledge of the Torah.
2.  being extremely religious.
3.  attending church services.
4.  being a disciple.


29.  The phrase, <u>shrouded in</u>, as used in
the first sentence most nearly
means

1.  highlighted into.
2.  covered in.
3.  protected from.
4.  disclose to.


30.  The selection states that one reason
the Kabbalah was kept a secret was

1.  fear of outsiders.
2.  overzealous insiders.
3.  fear of persecution.
4.  corrupt masters who desired more
        power.


**GO ON TO NEXT PAGE**


**TEST SEVEN, PASSAGE FIVE**

John Walsh is widely recognized as a tireless advocate for victim's rights and missing children and host of the nation's number-one crime-fighting show, *America's Most Wanted* (*AMW*). The public, though, may be unaware of the reason why this man is so impassioned about his work.

In the summer of 1981, Walsh was a partner in a management company in Florida. He was living the American dream. He and his wife, Reve, had a beautiful six-year-old son, Adam, the joy of their lives. They never thought that crime could touch them. But their dream was shattered on July 27, 1981, when Adam was abducted and later found dead. Walsh recalls: "When Adam was abducted, there was no system in place for tracking information or leads about abducted children. Law enforcement agencies were not trained or equipped to investigate missing children cases, and even fewer had ever experienced the murder of a child. Many agencies—including the FBI—were reluctant to get involved."

Because of their ordeal, the Walshes decided to turn their grief into positive energy. Battling bureaucratic resistance and legislative nightmares, they pushed the passage of the Missing Children's Assistance Act of 1984. The bill founded the National Center for Missing and Exploited Children.

Then came *America's Most Wanted*. John's comment about the success of the show is to the point: "I am sometimes amazed when I think how *AMW* led to its 500th arrest in 1997. The public's response to *AMW* proves that people care, that they want to make a difference, and that they are willing to get involved. They are helping to take vicious criminals off our streets."

John Walsh has been honored by every American president since Ronald Reagan. Also, law enforcement officials around the nation have praised his efforts: in 1988 he was named the "U.S. Marshals' Man of the Year."

-Keppler & Laney, Internet

31. The purpose of the first paragraph is to

1. present *America's Most Wanted* as an example of a crime-fighting show.
2. give a testimony from John Walsh.
3. show the popularity of *America's Most Wanted*.
4. introduce John Walsh.

32. Before Adam's death, John

1. was in law enforcement.
2. managed a company in Florida.
3. was hosting *America's Most Wanted*.
4. advocated for missing children's rights.

33. The main point of the last paragraph is that John Walsh

1. met President Ronald Reagan.
2. has been in law enforcement since
        1988.
3. has been honored for his work.
4. was named "Man of the Year."

34. It is suggested that before 1981,
law enforcement

1. was not used to dealing with missing
        children in an effective way.
2. could easily track leads about
        abducted children.
3. lobbied for the Missing Children's
        Act.
4. could not care less about missing
        children.

35. It is implied that *America's Most
Wanted*

1. never got good television ratings.
2. was a way John could get revenge.
3. proved that the public did not want
        to get involved.
4. was a total success for many years.

36. The phrase, impassioned about, as
used in the first paragraph most nearly
means

1. imprisoned by.
2. impersonal toward.
3. passionate toward.
4. unemotional about.

**TEST SEVEN, PASSAGE SIX**

**GO ON TO NEXT PAGE**

The first major problem in legal research is searching through tons of <u>chaff</u> for the few tiny kernels of useful information. And the legal records are vast indeed. In the U.S. alone, law has been supplemented and amended for over two hundred years. It has been generated by Congress, state legislatures, and even city councils. It has also been created by legal court decisions at the federal, state, and local levels. In addition, legally binding decrees may be declared by presidents, governors, and mayors; there are literally millions of laws and court opinions available in the legal record.

As if this were not enough, American courts often recognize the laws of Great Britain. The laws of merry old England can be useful, providing both information and legal precedent (especially in regard to varying interpretations of law which the American colonies inherited from the British Empire). And to a certain extent, the laws of Spain and France have on occasion been found relevant as well, particularly in the southwestern United States and in Louisiana. Anything may be useful in legal research.

For example, in the highly controversial case of *Roe v. Wade*, in which the Supreme Court found that women have rights to an abortion procedure under certain circumstances, the research net was cast very widely indeed. If one reads the official court opinion in that case, it is surprising that the legal record included references to ancient Babylonian laws, the laws of classical Greece, the laws of the Roman Empire, the Medieval Christian Church—and of course the laws of England and colonial America. What the court found in its review of this extensive legal record of actual cases and controversies (covering over two thousand years of lawmaking) was that abortion law is peculiarly subject to current public opinion: it is never resolved, just recycled.

-Peterson, et al, pp. 55-56

37. The main idea of paragraph one is that

1. the legal record has been amended for over 200 years.
2. Congress has generated the laws in the United States.
3. there are millions of laws available in the legal record.
4. only presidents, governors, and mayors can declare a legally binding decree.

38. Based on historical law, abortion

1. is not a matter for legal research.
2. must be deemed illegal.
3. will always be controversial.
4. has been resolved.

39. Spanish law has most likely been utilized in

1. New Mexico.
2. Louisiana.
3. the Supreme Court.
4. the American colonies.

40. Chaff, as used in the first sentence, can best be defined as

1. useful information.
2. extraneous information.
3. garbage.
4. seedlings.

41. In *Roe v. Wade*, the Supreme Court found that

1. abortion is illegal.
2. abortions have been performed since the times of classical Greece.
3. abortion is legal under certain circumstances.
4. the question of the right to abortion had already been resolved.

42. If one reads the official court opinion in the case of *Roe v. Wade*, he or she might be surprised to learn that

1. legal research entailed reaching back thousands of years.
2. the federal government enacted laws.
3. *Roe v. Wade* concerned abortion rights.
4. ancient civilizations had sophisticated laws.

**GO ON TO NEXT PAGE**

**TEST SEVEN, PASSAGE SEVEN**

It is midnight. Off the right wing of the plane the moon floods a vast field of clouds with light, like cobblestones. Inside the plane it is dark except for a few dim lights and the exit signs. The stewardess moves quietly up the aisle, taking a blanket to someone. The man and woman next to me are apparently asleep. They have been quiet for a long time. I try to fit my legs into the cramped space allotted, but they are too long. The seat is too narrow. The pillow is too small to cradle my head comfortably. In spite of the deep thrum of the engines, smooth and regular, I can't sleep.

The woman beside me moves, obviously trying to find her purse. The man stirs. Neither says anything. I can see the outline of the man; he leans forward and hands the woman her purse.

Only the most ordinary of gestures, meaning almost nothing, I suppose, to them. But for me, sitting there by the window looking out again at the cold stars, it speaks of a whole world that is lost to me now—man and a woman together, his hand stretched toward her to help.

I am traveling alone. I remember another hand—bit bigger than that one, with fingers strong for carpentry, dexterous for drawing.

I lean my forehead against the glass and a great heaving tide pours over me, drowns me—as it has done a hundred times in the past year. But I try to remember that there are so many much worse off than I. How blessed I have been. Yet, in the most unpremeditated ways, in the oddest places and for the

most absurd reasons, as I'm going about my business, generally calm, even cheerful, that sudden tide sweeps in.

-Elliot, pp. 11-12

43. Overall, in the first paragraph, the author makes her point through

1. describing her environment.
2. defining her situation.
3. persuading the reader to be apathetic.
4. arguing her point of view.

44. The author writes of the man and woman to illustrate

1. that they have been married a long time.
2. their condemnation of each other.
3. their togetherness.
4. that not much has meaning in their lives.

45. The writer's overall feeling toward the couple is one of

1. resentment.
2. irritation.
3. excitement.
4. envy.

46. The reader can conclude that the narrator

1. had been married briefly.
2. lost her partner in a tragic accident.
3. had lived with a man.
4. is divorced.

47. <u>A great heaving tide pours over me</u>
connotes that the woman is

1. filled with happiness.
2. overwhelmed with loneliness.
3. experiencing a blessing.
4. drowning.

48. The overall style of writing is

1. emotional.
2. opinionated.
3. sarcastic.
4. romantic.

**GO ON TO NEXT PAGE**

**TEST SEVEN, PASSAGE EIGHT**

Although I was an American, newly arrived in Japan, my indoctrination began like that of any newcomer to the Japanese firm of Sony. I was escorted into an enormously long, open room, filled with desks and workers, and I was offered a seat next to one of them.

Saito-san sat down at the desk and said, "Congratulations, you are now a Sony trainee." He beamed. I smiled back, not sure how to respond.

For any new Japanese employee, you are expected to give yourself over to the group, to be molded to think "the Sony way." In return, the company bestows security, benefits, and even identity. From that first moment the line is drawn between yourself, within the company, and all those outside it.

Saito-san recounted a brief history of the company, explained its product lines, and handed me a book, *The Sony Story*. Rules and regulations followed, and I was issued a Sony uniform—a gray vest with detachable sleeves. The vest was comfortable, and I remembered suddenly that no one stands out wearing gray.

Saito-san then produced a rotary wheel with ten cards on it. They were my location cards, he explained, and they were to be set to indicate my where-abouts whenever I left my desk. If I was away from my desk for more than thirty minutes without properly setting my location card, my name would be announced over the public-address system and the infraction noted in my record.

Returning to my room, I set about unpacking. My two large suitcases were filled with clothes for all climates. And I had packed both suits and sports jackets, not sure which would be appropriate for wear at the office. Now, with my all-purpose gray vest, I realized I needn't have bothered.

-Katzenstein, pp. 8-12

49. The style of writing is meant to be

1. humorous.
2. idealistic.
3. formal.
4. factual.

50. The young man has just

1. joined a Japanese company in the United States.
2. become a Sony employee and resides in Japan.
3. written a book, *The Sony Story*.
4. had his name announced over the company's loudspeaker.

51. It is implied that a Japanese company

1. expects an employee to socialize with employees of similar companies.
2. dress as they like, as long as it is nondescript.
3. forms an employee's identity.
4. expects strange behavior from a foreigner.

**TEST SEVEN, PASSAGE NINE**

52. The word, <u>recounted</u>, most nearly
means

1. had written.
2. recovered.
3. numbered.
4. related.


53. We can infer that the Japanese

1. treat foreign employees differently.
2. are not strict about company rules.
3. do not like to stand out.
4. think "the Sony Way" only during
        office hours.


54. The narrator makes a comment
about the number of suits he brought
because

1. his suitcases were extremely heavy.
2. he did not bring enough of them.
3. he would have to have them cleaned
        weekly.
4. his company-issued, gray vest was
        obviously all he needed for work.

# SIMULATED EXAM EIGHT

Each year over one million people experience drug-related poisoning in the U.S.—10% of those cases resulting in death. In fact, drug overdose is a leading cause of fatal poisoning. What can we do if we are confronted with a case of poisoning?

In an emergency, call your emergency contact immediately; they will want to know what drug was taken and how much. Try to determine the age and weight of the victim and any chronic medical problems and medications s/he takes regularly.

After making your call, remove anything that might interfere with the person's breathing. A victim not getting enough oxygen will turn blue (the tongue or the skin under the fingernails changes color first). If this happens, lay the victim on his or her back, open the collar, place one hand under the neck and lift the victim's jaw so that it juts outward. This will open the airway between the mouth and lungs as wide as possible.

The best way to deal with a poisoning is to prepare for it. Do the following now: First, have the number for your local poison control center on hand, near the phone. If there is no poison control center in your locale, post the hospital emergency number. Second, decide which center or hospital you will go to and how you will get there. Third, buy ipecac syrup from your pharmacy and read the directions. Fourth, learn to give mouth-to-mouth resuscitation (perform *only* if the victim is not breathing).

To avoid poisoning incidents, keep medications in a locked place. Do not store them in containers that previously held food, and do not remove the labels from bottles. Do not take your medicine in a dimly lit room. Last, discard medications when you no longer need them by flushing them down the toilet.

-Silverman, pp. xi-xiii

1. According to the passage, the best possible way to deal with a poisoning is to

1. make the call.
2. know the victim's age and weight.
3. prepare for it.
4. discard medications when you no longer need them.

2. We can infer that about how many people die from drug-related poisoning each year?

1. 100,000
2. 10,000
3. 1,000
4. 100

3. In the context of the fourth paragraph, on hand most nearly means

1. posted throughout the house.
2. at a distance.
3. nearby.
4. in your hand.

4. The tone of the excerpt is

1. passionate.
2. chatty.
3. enthusiastic.
4. matter-of-fact.


5. It is stated that you can know the victim is not getting enough oxygen

1. when the collar is tight.
2. when his or her jaw just outward.
3. when his or her tongue turns blue.
4. if s/he has chronic medical problems.


6. The main purpose of the first paragraph is to

1. introduce the idea of preparing for a case of poisoning.
2. give the testimonial of a victim of poisoning.
3. set an argumentative tone so the reader will re-read the passage.
4. inspire the reader to join a support group.

Hamilton's *Report on a National Bank* drove another wedge between the two developing agricultural and manufacturing classes in the United States. The first Bank of the United States was chartered because of this report. The bank was a profit-making venture, and the Treasury declared the currency of the bank as the legal tender. The bank was financed by shareholders who purchased eighty percent of the bank stock. The remaining twenty per cent was provided by the federal government.

The bank specialized in short-term com mercial loans. The bank also opposed west ward expansion, preferring instead consolidation and growth in the manufacturing regions. Because of Hamilton, Congress raised the price of western land from $1 per acre to $2 an acre in 1796. The doubling of the prices hurt small farmers and land speculators. The one-hundred percent increase for government land stalled agricultural expansion.

The Bank of the United States was not only responsible for the doubled land prices, it also eschewed agricultural loans but favored loans to manufacturing endeavors. The loans for manufacturers were shorter term unlike the agricultural loans that had been spread out over several years. The agricultural class resented this because they were a numerically larger class than the manufacturers, and they were paying to maintain the Bank of the United States through taxes. Also

because of government laws, the farmers had trouble selling their crops abroad due to high tariffs.

Even though the farmers were contributing a percentage of money for the Bank of the United States, they did not receive dividends as did private investors. In essence, not only were they denied farm loans, they were also denied dividends.           -Duke, p. 44

7. The Bank of the United States was owned by

1. the Treasury Department.
2. shareholders and the federal
         government.
3. Congress.
4. Hamilton.

8. In order to discourage westward expansion

1. Congress lowered land prices.
2. Hamilton closed the national bank.
3. the national bank made short-term
         loans to farmers.
4. land prices were doubled.

9. The focus of the second paragraph is that

1. the national bank gave short-term
         commercial loans.
2. Congress helped land speculators.
3. agricultural expansion was purpose-
         fully stalled.
4. Congress preferred westward
         expansion.

**TEST EIGHT, PASSAGE TWO**

10. <u>Eschewed</u>, as underlined, means

1. avoided.
2. favored.
3. gave.
4. doubled.


11. The author's writing is

1. scientific.
2. nostalgic.
3. persuasive.
4. academic.


12. In regard to establishing a
National Bank, it is implied that

1. Hamilton was at odds with
       Congress.
2. Congress backed Hamilton.
3. Hamilton was not esteemed by the
       manufacturing class.
4. Congress had the best interest of the
       farmers in mind.


**GO ON TO NEXT PAGE**


**TEST EIGHT, PASSAGE TWO**

Television images haunt us: stunted, bony bodies. This is hunger <u>in its acute form</u>, the kind no one could miss. What is hunger? Is it the physical depletion of those suffering chronic undernutrition?

Yes, but hunger is more. We became convinced that as long as we conceive of hunger only in physical measures, we will never understand it.

A friend of ours, Dr. Clements, writes of a family whose son and daughter had died: "Both were lost in the years when the parents chose to pay their mortgage rather than keep the money to feed their children. Each year, the choice was always the same. If they paid, their children's lives were endangered. If they didn't, their land could be repossessed."

Being hungry thus means *anguish*— the anguish of impossible choices.

In Nicaragua, we met Amanda Espinoza who never had enough to feed her family. She watched five of her children die before the age of one. To Amanda, being hungry means watching people you love die. It is *grief.*

Throughout the world, the poor are made to blame themselves for their poverty. Walking into a home in the rural Phillippines, the first words we heard were an apology for the poverty of the dwelling. Being hungry also means living in *humiliation.*

In Guatemala in 1978, we met two highland peasants who were teaching their neighbors how to reduce erosion. The peasants were pushed onto steep slopes by wealthy landowners monopolizing the valley land. Two years later we learned that one of the highlanders had been forced into hiding, the other had been killed. Their "crime" was teaching their neighbors better farming techniques. The plantation owners felt threatened by any change that makes the poor less dependent on low-paying jobs on their plantations. Thus, a fourth dimension of hunger is *fear*.

-Lappe & Collins, pp. 2-4

13. Overall, the authors get their point across through

1. testimonials.
2. analysis.
3. description.
4. contrast.

14. This selection discusses all of the following as characteristics of hunger except

1. fear.
2. grief.
3. chronic undernutrition.
4. apathy.

15. The tone of the passage is

1. neutral.
2. depressing.
3. cynical.
4. hopeful.

**TEST EIGHT, PASSAGE THREE**

16.  The parents that Dr. Clements
writes about used their money to pay
for

1.  food for their children.
2.  their house.
3.  medical attention for themselves.
4.  tools to farm the land.


17.  In its acute form, as used in
paragraph one, most nearly means

1.  "in its best light."
2.  "in an ordinary state."
3.  "at its worst."
4.  "taking shape."


18.  It is suggested in the last paragraph
that the highland peasants of Guatemala

1.  will be killed if caught teaching
              better farming techniques.
2.  will soon be aided by the wealthy
              landowners.
3.  will be able to improve their
              conditions.
4.  may soon move into the valley.


**GO ON TO NEXT PAGE**


**TEST EIGHT, PASSAGE THREE**

During the night the snow stopped. Only a light covering was on the ground next morning when Dr. Munsterberg walked to North Main Street. He turned right at the corner, stopping at the red brick building next to the bookstore. A sign pointed the way upstairs to "Mr. Cayce's Studio." With much effort, the doctor trudged up the steps. He opened the door and entered a small reception room. In a few minutes a young lady entered with a patient. The two went into a small adjoining room, seating themselves at a table near a couch.

"And here is the young man himself," Munsterberg said as the door again opened. The young man smiled and shook hands. "Are you going to lie on that couch?" the older gentleman asked.

"Yes. I'll bring a chair in for you."

"My seat here is very comfortable. I can see the couch, [take notes], and hear what you say."

The young man went into the adjoining room. Sitting on the side of the couch he unfastened his cuff links and loosened his shoelaces. Then he swung his legs up, lay flat on his back, closed his eyes, and folded his hands on his abdomen.

Dr. Munsterberg watched the young man. His respiration deepened gradually. After that he seemed to be asleep. The woman spoke to the sleeping man, "You have your patient before you. You will go over the body carefully, telling us what may be done to correct anything which is wrong. You will speak distinctly."

For several minutes there was silence. Then the young man began to mumble in a voice that sounded faraway and haunting, as if he were speaking from a dream. Suddenly he cleared his throat and spoke forcibly. "Yes, we have the patient," he said. "There is a great deal of trouble within the body."                                   -Sugrue, pp 28-30

19. From the selection the reader can infer that Dr. Munsterberg is a(n)

1. medical doctor.
2. astrologer.
3. psychic.
4. observer.

20. As used in the passage, the young man probably refers to

1. Dr. Munsterberg.
2. Mr. Cayce.
3. the patient.
4. the doctor.

21. Dr. Munsterberg's attitude toward the young man is

1. sympathetic.
2. pleasant.
3. critical.
4. mocking.

**TEST EIGHT, PASSAGE FOUR**

22. As used in paragraph one, the word <u>trudged</u> most nearly means

1. ambled.
2. leapt.
3. ran.
4. plodded.


23. The woman in the story is most likely

1. an assistant to the young man.
2. Dr. Munsterberg's friend.
3. the patient's mother.
4. the young man's wife.


24. In the next to the last paragraph, it is implied that the young man is

1. preparing to operate on his patient.
2. psychotic.
3. in a state of hypnosis.
4. asleep.


**GO ON TO NEXT PAGE**

Human beings appear to be happy just so long as they have a future to which they can look forward—whether it be a "good time" tomorrow or an everlasting life beyond the grave. When this "good time" arrives, however, it is difficult to enjoy it to the full without some promise of more to come.  If happiness always depends on something expected in the future, we are chasing a will-o'-the-wisp that ever eludes our grasp.

There is the feeling that we live in a time of unusual insecurity.  In the past hundred years so many long-established traditions have broken down–traditions of family and social life, of government, of the economic order, and of religious belief.  As the years go by, there seem to be fewer and fewer rocks to which we can hold, fewer things which we can regard as absolutely right and true, and fixed for all time.

To some this is a welcome release from the restraints of moral dogma. To others it is a dangerous breach with reason and sanity, tending to plunge human life into  chaos. To most, though, the immediate sense of release has given a brief exhilaration, to be followed by deep anxiety.

As a matter of fact, our age is no more insecure than any other. Poverty, disease, war, change, and death are nothing new.  In the best of times "security" has never been more than temporary.                  -Watts, pp. 14-15

25.  Will-o'-the-wisp that ever eludes our grasp can best be interpreted as

1.  "our destiny."
2.  "something we can never have."
3.  "our own tails."
4.  "dreams that have already come to pass."

26.  In the second paragraph, the writer sets a tone of

1.  excitement.
2.  compassion.
3.  desperation.
4.  bitterness.

27.  In paragraph one, it is implied that most human beings

1.  have a "good time."
2.  cannot be happy without a vision of the future.
3.  need to work on being right more often.
4.  have obtained the security they need.

28.  From the passage, we can conclude that a state of insecurity will likely generate

1.  anxiety.
2.  faith.
3.  truth.
4.  freedom.

29. The author states that the state of insecurity

1. is unique to the present generation.
2. is unacceptable to all people.
3. has existed for many generations.
4. may have a calming effect.


30. The word dogma, as used in the passage, most nearly means

1. questions.
2. freedom.
3. chaos.
4. rules.

**GO ON TO NEXT PAGE**

**TEST EIGHT, PASSAGE FIVE**

The appreciation of the unique values of folk art, the art of children, and that of primitive people is one of the peculiar achievements of our age. There are many reasons for this, but the most important is that modern man, living in a complex and highly industrialized urban society, finds in these arts a freshness and simplicity which is lacking in the self-conscious and sophisticated art of our time. Men like Paul Gauguin, who settled in Tahiti, and Robert Louis Stevenson, who spent his last years in Samoa, were symptomatic of this trend, which resulted in a new interest in primitive civilizations and their arts. In the same way, Paul Klee, by trying to portray the world with the naive spontaneity of a child, opened the way for the consideration of children's art as a serious form of artistic expression.

The interest in and the systematic study of folk art is yet another aspect of the same trend. The city-dweller, sick of his decadent world, discovers in the art of simple, rural people a directness of vision and honesty of purpose. These primitive arts are to him both spiritually refreshing and artistically appealing. It is for this reason that folk art today is enjoying such great popularity.

Folk art is not, as some have suggested, merely an unsophisticated reflection of the culture of cities. It is a creation of the ordinary people of small towns and villages, especially those who are cut off from the main stream of urban civilization. Folk art has a tradition which remains unchanged over generations so that it is impossible to date it with accuracy.

Furthermore, since this craft art encompasses the actual lives of the people, it is a part of the life of the community: this art form has an appeal which modern art often lacks.

-Munsterberg, pp. 19-20

31. It is implied that one characteristic of folk art, children's art, and primitive art have in common is

1. complexity.
2. naive sophistication.
3. simplicity.
4. unique peculiarities.

32. In the first paragraph, the author makes use of

1. listing terms.
2. persuasive techniques.
3. comparison and contrast.
4. presenting examples.

33. The passage states that folk art is

1. a reflection of the cities.
2. always changing.
3. less appealing than modern art.
4. a creation of ordinary, rural folk.

**TEST EIGHT, PASSAGE SIX**

34. <u>This</u>, as underlined, refers to

1. folk art.
2. appreciation.
3. age.
4. that.

35. The reader can infer that Robert Louis Stevenson was interested in

1. the simple life.
2. urban society.
3. children's art.
4. self-conscious art.

36. In the last paragraph, the author makes his point through

1. narration.
2. definition.
3. cause-effect.
4. example.

**GO ON TO NEXT PAGE**

**TEST EIGHT, PASSAGE SIX**

Many young people are wearing decorative contact lenses they have bought at flea markets, convenience stores, beach shops, video stores, costume shops, and/or off the Internet.

Marketing of these lenses is particularly heavy during party seasons. Whether the purpose is to change the color of their eyes or produce special effects for Halloween, cosmetic lenses have gained in popularity. Some lenses are even made to add a design to the iris (e.g., a professional sports team insignia), or to impart a nonhuman appearance to the eye (e.g., eyes of cats, snake, or wolves). Looking to movie and rock stars as their role models, teens buy the decorative lenses to match their clothing—or their mood.

Eye experts are concerned because many teenagers do not bother to consult an eye care professional. Recently, the Food and Drug Administration (FDA) issued a warning about decorative contact lenses that are being distributed directly to consumers without a prescription. The FDA has cautioned against using them if they have not been fitted by a qualified eye care professional. The warning has come after the FDA became aware of eye-related injuries. These products can cause corneal ulcers, which can progress rapidly, leading to internal ocular infection if left untreated. Uncontrolled infection can lead to corneal scarring and vision impairment. In extreme cases, this condition

can result in blindness and eye loss.

Because of the safety concerns these decorative lenses present, the FDA is taking a number of actions. In addition to communicating with the public and health care community, it has issued an "import alert" instructing personnel of the U.S. Customs Service to detain and seize all cosmetic lens shipments at the ports of entry.

-FDA website & Preidt, Internet

37. Which of the following does the author primarily use to support his view?

1. comparison.
2. persuasion.
3. personal experience.
4. definition.

38. The author would probably agree that

1. no one should wear decorative lenses due to the inherent dangers.
2. there is too much attention given to decorative lenses; they are harmless.
3. individuals should do what makes them feel good about themselves, regardless of the FDA warnings.
4. wearers of decorative lenses should be required to consult an eye care professional.

**TEST EIGHT, PASSAGE SEVEN**

39. <u>Consumers,</u> as underlined in the second paragraph refers to

1. eye experts.
2. contact lenses.
3. the FDA personnel.
4. teenagers.


40. In the second paragraph, the meaning of the word <u>ocular</u> alludes to

1. an organism.
2. the brain.
3. the eye.
4. an ulcer.


41. It is stated in the passage that the FDA is taking all the following steps except

1. detaining health care personnel.
2. educating the public.
3. seizing shipments of the lenses.
4. talking with health care
        professionals.


42. In the last paragraph, the author illustrates his point by

1. contrast.
2. narration.
3. cause-effect.
4. example.

The philosophical basis for animal protection using the concept of "rights" is not, as many believe, a recent phenomenon. One of the classic books on the subject was published in 1892 by the great humanitarian Henry Salt. Just who was Henry Salt? Perhaps this brief extract from his most noted book may serve for an introduction to one of the least-known but most outstanding champions of animals' rights. A scholar, and then a master, at Eton, Salt was a friend of Gandhi. A vegetarian and pacifist, he was civilized and witty but chose a life of great simplicity.

In Salt's writings, he questioned: "if men have rights, have animals their rights also?" He then goes on to say: "From the earliest times there have been thinkers who answered 'yes' to this question. The Buddhist and Pythagorean canons included the saying 'not to kill or injure any innocent animals.' However, it was not until the eighteenth century, the Age of Enlightenment of which Voltaire and Rousseau were the spokesmen, that the rights of animals obtained more deliberate recognition.

To Jeremy Bentham in particular belongs the high honor of first asserting the rights of animals with authority and persistence. 'The legislator,' he wrote, 'ought to interdict everything which may serve to lead to cruelty. The spectacles of gladiators no doubt contributed to give the Romans that ferocity which

they displayed in their civil wars. A people accustomed to despise human life in their games could not be expected to respect it amid the fury of their passions. It is proper for the same reason to forbid every kind of cruelty toward animals, whether by way of amusement, or to gratify gluttony. Why should the law refuse its protection to any sensitive being? The time will come when humanity will extend its mantle over everything which breathes.' "

-Ronan, Internet

43. Jeremy Bentham's belief about gladiator behavior could be summarized as

1. "an eye for an eye."
2. "no one is above the law."
3. "it is impossible to live in harmony
          with earth's creatures."
4. "cruelty begets cruelty."

44. The writer makes his point in the second paragraph by

1. name dropping.
2. using Salt's own words.
3. mentioning Buddhist principles.
4. giving his own testimony.

45. The concept of animal rights obtained deliberate recognition

1. during the eighteenth century.
2. at the height of gladiatorial combat.
3. recently.
4. in 1892.

**TEST EIGHT, PASSAGE EIGHT**

46. The author's attitude toward
animal rights is one of

1. skepticism.
2. condemnation.
3. support.
4. indifference.


47. Canons, as used in the second
paragraph most nearly means

1. weaponry.
2. laws.
3. dictations.
4. rights.


48. The phrase any sensitive being
alludes
to

1. everything which breathes.
2. human beings who are sensitive.
3. gladiators who were injured.
4. Romans.


**GO ON TO NEXT PAGE**


**TEST EIGHT, PASSAGE EIGHT**

When Chicken Little of children's storybook fame was hit on the head by an acorn that fell from a tree, he immediately jumped to the conclusion that the sky was falling. And he went forth to spread the alarm. Chicken Little, though, can't manage to do much more about this supposed catastrophe he faces than run around screaming.

This is the sort of behavior known as catastrophizing: the mind leaps to believe the worst. Disaster appears to lie just around the corner. Psychologist Albert Ellis calls it "awfulizing," because the individuals involved imagine a consequence so awful that they will not be able to endure it. We all know that on some occasions the mind seems to leap automatically toward pessimism rather than optimism.

Sometimes the end result of the Chicken Little syndrome is not just missing a turn but failing to look for one. A common tendency of those who believe that disaster is unavoidable is to simply give up—to make no effort to resolve the problem. After all, if you have concluded that there is nothing you can do, then it follows you will probably do nothing.

Unfortunately, this tendency promotes self-fulfilling prophecies. For example, Masako turned down a friend's invitation to a party because she was sure she would be ignored, rejected, and humiliated. Masako makes sure she "stays safe." One aspect of this situation to think through, though, is this: It is certain that Masako will not meet anyone interesting if she stays home. In her attempt to eliminate supposed negative feelings—in not taking a risk—Masako also eliminates the possibility of having a good time.

-Freeman & DeWolf, pp. 20-23

49. The author uses Chicken Little to illustrate

1. delusional behavior.
2. optimism.
3. catastrophizing.
4. realism.

50. The main idea of the passage is that

1. the end result of the Chicken Little syndrome is happiness.
2. by not taking risks, people miss opportunities.
3. catastrophizing is normal behavior.
4. people need to fix all their problems without seeking help.

51. The word pessimism relates most closely to

1. awfulizing.
2. leaping.
3. optimizing.
4. consequences.

**TEST EIGHT, PASSAGE NINE**

52. In Masako's case, she wants to

1. get out and experience life.
2. reject someone before she is
        rejected.
3. avoid being hurt.
4. go to the party.


53. <u>Catastrophizing</u>, as underlined in the second paragraph, most nearly means

1. behaving in a dignified way.
2. thinking positively.
3. feeling depressed.
4. imagining the worst.


54. Overall, the author uses which pattern of organization?

1. listing.
2. examples.
3. reporting.
4. storytelling.

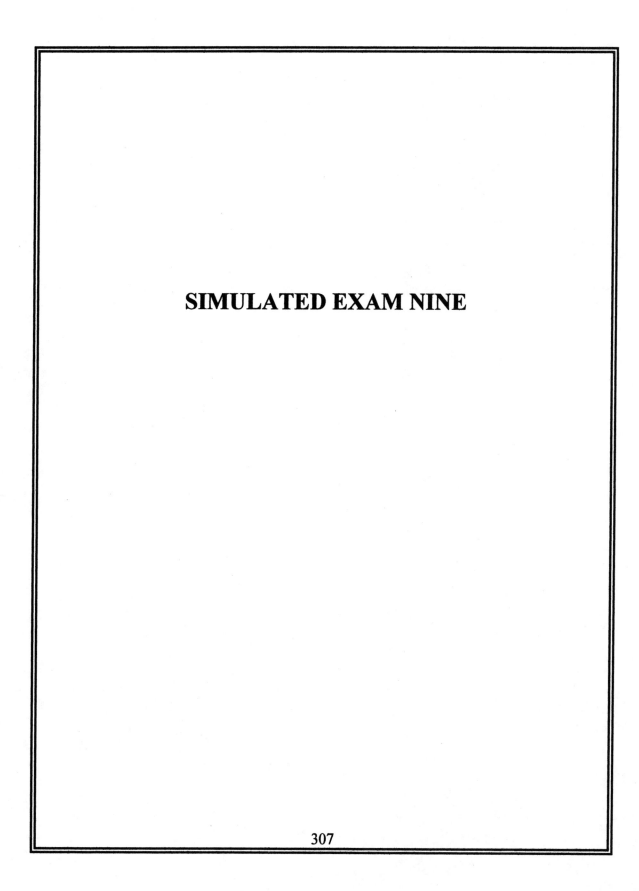

# SIMULATED EXAM NINE

Why do we make the choices we make? What behavioral choices are we making that directly influence our health-related fitness? Most of us have tried to make a long-term change in our lifestyles. The most common behaviors we want to change are: use of tobacco, alcohol consumption, stress management, and physical activity.

Over time, however, we find ourselves noncompliant and return back to our old, bad habits and ways. Unfortunately, as a result of this process, we quickly learn that behavior change doesn't happen simply because we want it to.

When attempting to achieve a positive lifestyle and optimal health and fitness, all of us will have to fight unique personal battles. What makes the task even more difficult is that (many times) motivation for change in American culture most likely involves goals such as looking better, being more popular, or improving at a sport, rather than being concerned about what is going to happen when we get older. It would be nice if everyone practiced primary prevention and avoided all illness, disease and injury. That, however, is not the case. Ultimately, many of us choose to use tobacco, pay little or no attention to dietary needs, fail to remain active throughout life, engage in risky sexual behavior, and inappropriately use alcohol and illicit drugs.

The good news is that we can change. Some of us may change due to external sources, such as the social pressure to stop smoking. Others may change by increasing their awareness of the risks associated with behaviors by reading books, attending classes, or by just experiencing life.

-Adams, pp. 37-40

1. The main relationship discussed in paragraph one is that between

1. a positive lifestyle and alcohol and illicit drug consumption.
2. change and the ease of overcoming personal battles.
3. behavioral choices and health-related fitness.
4. physical activity and looking better.

2. Noncompliant, as used in paragraph two, most nearly means

1. compassionate.
2. more motivated.
3. flexible.
4. uncooperative.

3. In the last sentence, the author

1. describes types of social pressure.
2. offers suggestions for change.
3. contrasts motivation and external forces.
4. states the impossibility for behavioral change.

4. A behavior not mentioned as one we commonly want to change is

1. verbal abuse.
2. stress management.
3. the consumption of alcohol.
4. physical activity.

5.  It is suggested that for most Americans the desire for change is based on

1.  long-term needs.
2.  more immediate goals.
3.  parental approval.
4.  preventing illness, disease, and
        injury.

6.  The overall style of writing is

1.  humorous but informative.
2.  sarcastic and indifferent.
3.  informal but academic.
4.  formal and scientific.

**GO ON TO NEXT PAGE**

**TEST NINE, PASSAGE ONE**

In a home video made when she was ten, Cayenne was <u>wiry and scrappy</u>, all sixty-eight pounds of her focused on the ball as she ran down the soccer field. Her red ponytail bobbed, her face shone with sweat as she ducked in and around the other players, always hustling. When she scored a goal, she held her arms over her head in a moment of self-congratulation.

Her parents loved her willingness to take on the universe. One day she dressed up like a belly dancer, the next like an astronaut. She liked adults and babies, boys and girls, dogs and sparrows.

When outraged, she took on the world. She got a black eye from fighting with a boy who said that girls couldn't play soccer. Because she was good at standing up for herself and concerned with justice, her teachers predicted she'd go to law school.

In elementary school Cayenne didn't fret much about her appearance. She weighed in once a year at the doctor's office and was pleased with gains in her height and weight chart. She wore jeans and T-shirts unless forced to dress up. Her mother had to beg her to go shopping and remind her to brush her hair.

At twelve, Cayenne matured. As her body grew rapidly, it became awkward and unpredictable. She gained weight, and she got acne. She was nervous the first day of junior high because she'd heard rumors that seventh-graders' heads were stuffed in the toilets.

Fortunately this didn't happen, but she came home upset that some boys teased her and that the girls wore makeup and expensive clothes.

A few months after school began, Cayenne grew quieter and less energetic. For the first time she needed to be coaxed into doing things with the family.

-Pipher, pp. 29-30

7. The author's purpose is to

1. expose Cayenne's parents as being too idealistic.
2. illustrate that girls mature faster than boys.
3. show a change in Cayenne from girlhood to adolescence.
4. pronounce that girls are just as capable as boys at sports.

8. <u>Wiry and scrappy</u> connotes that Cayenne was

1. thin.
2. feisty.
3. dirty.
4. slow.

9. It is suggested that Cayenne liked all of the following except

1. injustice.
2. boys.
3. tomboys.
4. freedom.

10.  Her teachers predicted Cayenne
would become a lawyer because she

1.  was good at standing up for
        herself.
2.  did not fret about her appearance,
        only whether things were fair.
3.  liked everyone.
4.  was mature for her age.


11.  It is implied that Cayenne grew
quieter because

1.  she was nervous about the first day
        at school.
2.  the teachers in junior high school
        were more difficult.
3.  her parents became extremely strict
        with her when she entered
        junior high school.
4.  her body was changing.


12.  What Cayenne's parents most
loved about her was

1.  that she loved to dress up.
2.  her love of sports.
3.  her willingness to take on the
        universe.
4.  that she took care of all stray
        creatures.


**GO ON TO NEXT PAGE**


**TEST NINE, PASSAGE TWO**

A former socialist, Benito Mussolini broke with the Socialist Party because of its opposition to World War I. Mussolini then joined the Italian army in 1915 and fought on the Alpine front, rising to the rank of sergeant.

Even though Italy had been on the victor's side in World War I, she came out of that conflict seriously divided and disillusioned. Lured into the conflict on the Allied side by promises of territorial gains, Italy had been denied the fruits of victory at the peace table. In addition, she was beset with serious economic problems. The war had cost 138 billion lire, double the country's total expenditures between 1861 and 1913. This in turn generated inflation, unemployment, strikes, <u>pillaging of</u> food shops, and street battles among the conflicting extremist groups.

After the war, it was among the veteran soldiers that the most serious discontent arose. Mussolini joined one of the disgruntled groups. He outlined his plan to organize a combat group to uphold the material claims of the veterans, to oppose the imperialism of "any countries damaging to Italy," and to fight all those who did not support candidates favorable to the veterans. Mussolini's first attempt to get elected to the Italian Parliament in 1919 was not very successful. However, utilizing strong-arm tactics and force, the Fascists grew in strength and within one year boasted some 320,000 enrolled members of the party. By

May, 1921, thirty-five Fascists, including Mussolini, were in the Italian Parliament. Threatened by the Fascist party, King Victor Emmanuel III turned over the reins of government to Mussolini. Mussolini became the youngest Premier in Italy's history.                              -Layton, pp. 4-5

13. It is stated that Italy was conflicted after WWI because she

1. lost the war.
2. was lured into the war by the Allies.
3. was not awarded promised territories.
4. there was no strong leader in the government sector.

14. The second paragraph focuses on

1. Mussolini.
2. Italy.
3. World War I.
4. the Allied side.

15. <u>Pillaging of</u>, as underlined, most nearly means

1. stealing from.
2. stocking up.
3. trading in.
4. rebuilding of.

**TEST NINE, PASSAGE THREE**

16.  According to the selection, Mussolini broke with the Socialist party because

1.  the Party was composed of war mongers.
2.  the party was disintegrating.
3.  he was promoted by the Italian army.
4.  the party opposed going to war.


17.  Mussolini's political platform was based on

1.  establishing combat groups.
2.  international diplomacy.
3.  support for veterans.
4.  promoting peace.


18.  The reader can infer that Mussolini became Premier

1.  through force.
2.  because he was elected.
3.  because he was a noted Fascist.
4.  through his close relationship to the King.


**GO ON TO NEXT PAGE**

**TEST NINE, PASSAGE THREE**

The greater part of the Middle Ages was a time of widespread ignorance and superstition. Many of our fairy tales have come down to us from the time when most people truly believed in supernatural beings. It was an imaginative age, and people fancied that there were all sorts of strange creatures in existence: hobgoblins, pixies, trolls, giants. To them, witches were people who rode through the air on broomsticks. This belief led to much persecution during the Middle Ages, and many harmless women accused of being witches were tortured or put to death.

The people of the Middle Ages knew little about nature. Various plants were thought to have remarkable powers, according to the shape of their leaves. Wood sorrel, being shaped like a heart, was supposed to be a remedy for heart ailments; liverwort, resembling the form of the liver, was for liver complaints.

There were men called alchemists who tried to pry into the secrets of nature. They were seeking to discover what was called "the philosopher's stone." This magic substance, it was thought, could be dissolved and the liquid made from it would turn any common metal, like copper or iron, into gold. A tiny drop of it taken as medicine would prolong life indefinitely. Secretly the alchemists worked in dark underground laboratories cluttered with furnaces and odd-shaped bottles filled with medicines.

For centuries the alchemists pursued their search for the philosopher's stone.

They never found it, but in their experiments they stumbled upon much useful knowledge about various substances, which were of value to later scientists. Without knowing it, they laid the foundation for our modern science of chemistry.

-Hartman, pp. 281-4

19. The word prolong, underlined in the third paragraph, most nearly means

1. decrease.
2. extend.
3. obliterate.
4. expound.

20. The underlined word, them, (first paragraph) refers to

1. creatures.
2. supernatural beings.
3. people.
4. witches.

21. According to the passage, people of the Middle Ages based the usefulness of some plants on their

1. shape.
2. size.
3. taste.
4. secret ingredients.

**TEST NINE, PASSAGE FOUR**

22. It is suggested in the selection that alchemists were

1. magicians.
2. blacksmiths.
3. performing illegal experiments.
4. precursors to present-day chemists.

23. The word <u>persecution</u> (first paragraph) most nearly means

1. unjustified cruelty.
2. fatal accidents.
3. fair assessment.
4. uncalled for ridicule.

24. Based on the information given, the writer believes that the period of the Middle Ages was an age of

1. ignorance.
2. academic excellence.
3. bliss.
4. scientific revelation.

**GO ON TO NEXT PAGE**

**TEST NINE, PASSAGE FOUR**

You would have to live on Pluto to not know about the phenomenal popularity of *Who Wants to be a Millionaire, The Bachelor, Survivor* and other reality-based shows now populating the network television landscape. *Survivor* currently ranks as the most-watched summer primetime series in modern TV history. What's going on here? The executive producer of *Millionaire* may have put his finger on things, saying his show's success has almost nothing to do with striking it rich, and almost everything to do with the fact that it features ordinary Americans.

He's certainly onto something, but the reality-driven networks are actually playing catch-up to their traditional advertising <u>brethren</u>, who for years have tapped the potential of ordinary Americans. Our company has been fortunate to work with agencies on powerful real people advertising, such as one for Kodak, where a proud papa reflects on his about-to-be married son; and for Philip Morris, where kids talk about why they don't smoke, and how to be cool without lighting up.

What makes this real people advertising so believable, and in my mind so enduring, is the power to convey simple truths through everyday experience. We connect with the honesty of someone who has "lived it"; we naturally identify with their problems —cheer for their triumphs—and often buy the products that have made a difference in their lives. What advertisers have raised to an art form (what reality shows have only recently come to appreciate) is that we Americans like watching and rooting for people on television who are much like us. It's everyman—or woman—as television hero.

-Gartenberg, Internet

25. The author's style is

1. chatty.
2. sarcastic.
3. academic.
4. humorous.

26. The author's attitude toward traditional advertising is

1. mocking.
2. complimentary.
3. empathetic.
4. critical.

27. According to one executive producer, reality TV is popular because

1. the public has the opportunity to become millionaires.
2. it reveals that stars are real people too.
3. it features ordinary Americans.
4. people can watch and forget their own troubles.

28. The author uses the phrase "You would have to live on Pluto" to emphasize

1. how unfamiliar the public is with reality TV.
2. the prevalence of reality TV.
3. the lengths people will go to in order to participate in reality-based TV.
4. how far fetched reality TV is.


29. In the context of the second paragraph, <u>brethren</u> most nearly means

1. brothers.
2. preachers.
3. partners.
4. counterparts.


30. Which of the following utilized "the ordinary American" first?

1. reality TV.
2. *Who Wants to be a Millionaire.*
3. traditional advertisers.
4. executive producers of network television.


**GO ON TO NEXT PAGE**


**TEST NINE, PASSAGE FIVE**

Roger Wakefield stood in the center of the room, feeling surrounded. He thought the feeling largely justified, insofar as he *was* surrounded: by heavy Victorian-style furniture. And the books —my, the books!

The study where he stood was lined on three sides by bookshelves, every one crammed past bursting point. Paper back mystery novels lay in bright, tatty piles, next to thousands upon thousands of pamphlets, leaflets, and handsewn manuscripts. A similar situation prevailed in the rest of the house. In eighty odd years, the Reverend Reginald Wakefield had never thrown anything away.

Roger repressed the urge to run out of the front door, leap into his car, and head back to Oxford, abandoning the home and its contents to the mercy of weather and vandals. Be calm, he told himself, inhaling deeply. You can deal with this. The books are the easy part; nothing more than a matter of sorting through them and then calling someone to come and haul them away. Granted, they'll need a large truck, but it can be done. Clothes—no problem. Goodwill charity gets the lot. Although he didn't know what Goodwill was going to do with black serge suits, circa 1948, but perhaps the deserving poor weren't all that picky. He began to breathe a little easier. He had taken a month's leave from the History Department at Oxford in order to clear up the Reverend's affairs. Perhaps that would be enough, after all.

The doorbell rang, startling Roger. The door of the house had a tendency to stick in damp weather, which meant that it was stuck most of the time. Roger freed it with a rending screech, to find a woman on the doorstep.

"Can I help you?"

-Gabaldon, pp. 3-5

31. From the reading, we can deduce that a relative of Roger Wakefield

1. moved.
2. died.
3. abandoned his house.
4. was selling his home.

32. It is implied that Roger wanted to run out the front door because

1. the house was haunted.
2. the woman scared him.
3. he felt overwhelmed with responsibility.
4. he was due in Oxford.

33. Reginald Wakefield was a

1. book dealer.
2. Victorian antiques dealer.
3. history professor.
4. preacher.

**TEST NINE, PASSAGE SIX**

34. Which of the following does the author primarily use in writing the passage?

1. narration
2. contrast
3. persuasion
4. definition

35. Roger thought that giving the clothes to Goodwill might be problematic because

1. the poor were picky.
2. the clothes were mostly old, black suits.
3. Goodwill would not pick up.
4. he should really burn them.

36. Based on the last sentence, the reader knows that Roger

1. did not know the woman at the door.
2. had been waiting for the woman at the door.
3. would soon begin a romantic relationship with the woman at the door.
4. slammed the door in the woman's face.

We remained in Germany for five years, and as I grew from a child to a woman, I was aware of great restlessness and dissatisfaction with life. It is hard to be exiled from one's own country; we all felt it deeply, my parents most of all, but they seemed to take refuge in religion.

If my father had previously leaned heavily towards Protestantism, he was, at the end of his time in Germany, one of its strongest adherents.

"There is one thing," he used to say to us, for naturally we saw more of him than we ever did in England when he was always at Court, "the people's dissatisfaction with the Catholic Queen will turn them to Elizabeth, because Elizabeth is Protestant and in line for the throne. But meanwhile the great fear is that the current Queen will have a child to inherit the throne."

We prayed for the Queen's infertility, and I found it ironic that she was praying equally hard to have a child. My sisters were shocked by my thoughts. My father used to say: "Lettice, you will have to guard your tongue."

That was the last thing I wanted to do because my comments amused me. They were a characteristic—which set me apart from other girls and made me more attractive.

Terrible news came to us from England of the bitter persecution of Protestants. Cranmer and Latimer were burned at the stake with three hundred other victims, and it was said that the smoke of the Smithfield Fires was like a black pall hanging over London.

-Holt, pp. 13-14; 15

37. Within the context of the last paragraph, the phrase guard your tongue most likely means

1. never speak of it again.
2. think before you speak.
3. always say what is on your mind.
4. do not speak unless spoken to.

38. The phrase refuge in most nearly means

1. communion with.
2. advantage of.
3. comfort in.
4. offense at.

39. The narrator found it ironic that the Queen was praying to have a baby because

1. her family was praying that the Queen would not have a baby.
2. the Queen was too old to have a baby.
3. no one in Germany wanted the Queen to have a baby.
4. the Queen did not need an heir; she already had three sons.

40. The main point of the fifth paragraph is to illustrate that Lettice

1. has low self-esteem.
2. is not at all attractive.
3. is shy and reticent.
4. thinks highly of herself.


41. The reader can infer that the family was living in Germany because

1. Lettice offended the Queen of
       England.
2. they were Protestants, and the
       Queen wanted Catholics at her
       Court.
3. the father killed someone in
       England.
4. the sisters were engaged to German
       royalty.


42. Overall, the passage basically utilizes

1. description.
2. narration.
3. persuasion.
4. cause-effect.


**GO ON TO NEXT PAGE**


**TEST NINE, PASSAGE SEVEN**

A few years ago, while I was helping a friend <u>renovate</u> her apartment, I asked a passing carpenter for advice about my next task—removing an old floor. He said casually, "Get yourself a cat's paw; it'll be ripped up in an hour." So, armed with this specific professional guidance, I <u>strode boldly</u> into the hardware store and asked for a cat's paw, even though I had never seen or heard of one before. "Cat's paw? Cat's paw?" The clerk reacted sarcastically, and rolling his eyes he completely demolished my assertive frame of mind. I mentioned almost apologetically that I wanted to rip up some old floorboards.

After much gesticulating, the clerk, relieved, proceeded to sell me a pry bar. It turned out he was wrong. About a week later I finally finished ripping up the floor, cursing the new tool and wondering why the carpenter had suggested it. I found out that the cat's paw and the pry bar are distinctly different tools.

Whether you are an apartment dweller or someone helping your parents, you no doubt have often entered a home center full of fear prior to making a small purchase. This uneasiness generally stems from two facts: first, people rarely know the correct name of even the most everyday item, which often leaves the customer with an unusable and unreturnable purchase. Second, store clerks may often be unavailable or unknowledgeable.

Probably the most frustrating thing is that after you ask a clerk for an item, the clerk will come back at you with a barrage of questions: "Well, what are you using it for?" "What size do you want?" "You want top-of-line or cheap?" "Silicone or acrylic?" "Galvanized or plain?" If you haven't thought these questions through, this can be pretty demoralizing, embarrassing, and intimidating. I know.

-Philbin & Ettlinger, pp. xiii-xiv

43. The phrase strode <u>boldly</u> most nearly means that the narrator walked

1. quickly.
2. colorfully.
3. confidently.
4. professionally.

44. The clerk's reaction to the narrator's initial question was

1. rude.
2. respectful.
3. apologetic.
4. sympathetic.

45. The author believes that most people

1. are relieved that clerks are so knowledgeable.
2. know what a cat's paw is.
3. spend many hours browsing the local home center.
4. have little confidence when it comes to purchasing tools.

**TEST NINE, PASSAGE EIGHT**

46. According to the passage, the most frustrating aspect of buying an item in a hardware store is

1. not knowing the name of the tool.
2. having to gesticulate.
3. that the item is unreturnable.
4. the barrage of questions from the clerk.

47. The word <u>renovate,</u> as used in the first sentence, is best defined as

1. renegotiate.
2. move into.
3. remodel.
4. purchase.

48. The writers of this selection address their readers in a manner that is

1. distant.
2. familiar.
3. sarcastic.
4. intimate.

**GO ON TO NEXT PAGE**

**TEST NINE, PASSAGE EIGHT**

Years after giving birth, I became a mother against my will because I saw that my daughter needed me to become one. What I really would have preferred was to remain a writer who dabbled in motherhood. That felt more comfortable, more safe. But Molly would not permit it. She needed a mother, not a dabbler. And because I love her more than I love myself, I became what she needed me to be. I do attempt to focus on her needs above my own. And I know in my heart (as I know I will die) that Molly is more important than my writing. Any child is. That's why motherhood is so difficult for writing women. Its demands are so compelling, so clearly important and also so profoundly satisfying.

You give up yourself, and finally you don't even mind. You become your child's guide to life at the expense of that swollen ego you thought so immutable. I wouldn't have missed this for anything. It humbled my ego and stretched my soul. It awakened me to eternity. It made me know my own humanity, my own mortality, my own limits. It gave me whatever crumbs of wisdom I possess today.

What do I wish for Molly? The same. Work she loves and a child to lead her to herself.

-Jong, pp. 35-36

**TEST NINE, PASSAGE NINE**

49. The author would probably agree that

1. most children need too much attention.
2. to be a better mother, women should serve their own needs first.
3. children are more important than careers.
4. no child is more important than a career.

50. Its, as underlined in the last sentence of the first paragraph, refers to

1. writing.
2. motherhood.
3. heart.
4. child.

51. The writer suggests that she was not a good mother

1. since her daughter's birth.
2. until she was a writer.
3. during her pregnancy.
4. the first years after her daughter was born.

52. The author's attitude toward motherhood can be summed up in which of the following sentences?

1. "I wouldn't have missed this for anything."
2. "I am a dabbler, not a mother."
3. "I have no will to become a mother."
4. "I know in my heart that my writing is clearly more important than children."

53. The writer states that the reason
she became a mother was because

1. she felt lonely.
2. she was not successful at writing.
3. its demands were so compelling.
4. her daughter needed her.


54. The selection is written from the
point of view of

1. the child.
2. Molly.
3. the author.
4. a single mother.

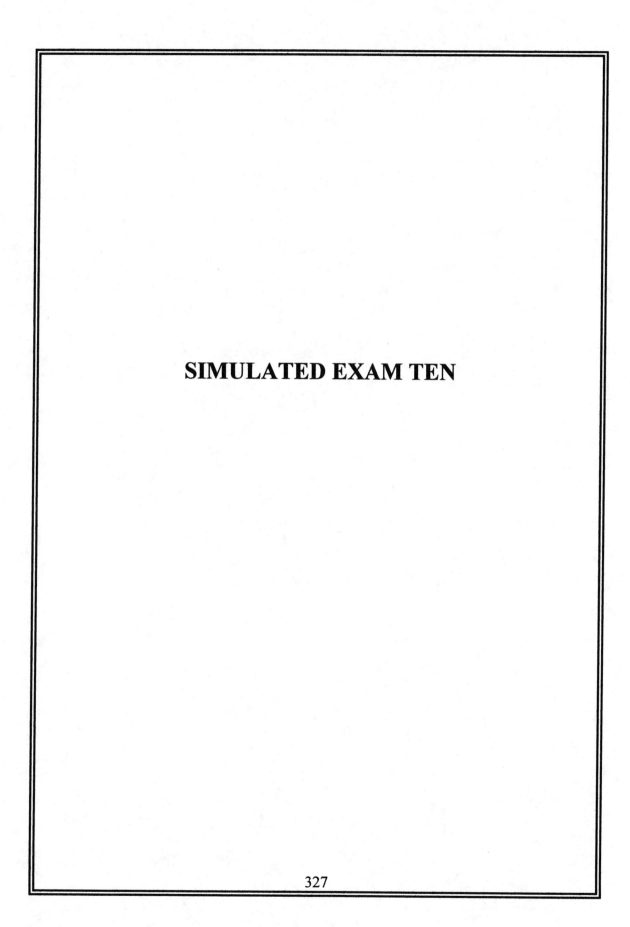

# SIMULATED EXAM TEN

The first attempt at connecting the various economic centers was in full bloom by 1790. The first massive road-building undertaking was the turnpike system and plank roads. The roads were financed by a combination of government and private investment. The government provided land, money, and engineering reports (completed by the U.S. Army Corps of Engineers) for the projects.

Private companies provided a portion of the money, built and maintained the roads, and then charged tolls to the individuals using the systems. The precedent of combining the federal government's resources and private investment for transportation infrastructure was firmly established from the turnpike system.

But as industry expanded, a more efficient method was needed to transport the goods the United States produced. The response to the economic boom from 1800 to 1807 was to utilize the numerous rivers in the United States. Introduction of the steam boats in 1807 made river transportation more efficient and cheaper, especially on the Mississippi River.

Prior to steam power, however, rafts were constructed and loaded with goods. The raft was floated down river and the goods sold at a Southern destination. Because it was impossible to pole a raft upstream, once the rafts reached their destination, they were disassembled and sold for lumber.

In contrast to rafts, the steam-powered boats allowed the shipper to not only take advantage of the downstream river currents, but to load the boats for an upstream voyage as well. Steamboats carried cargo back up the river as well as down and increased profits by traveling with a load of goods or passengers on the return trip. Shipping costs were also reduced because the steamboats could carry larger quantities of goods than rafts and offered discounted prices for volume shipping. It is easy to see how steamboats revolutionized shipping within the United States.                    -Duke, p. 56

1. According to the passage, the U.S. enjoyed an economic boom

1. in 1790.
2. before 1860.
3. in the early 1800's.
4. after 1815.

2. Who provided engineers for the turnpike system?

1. private companies
2. the U.S. Army
3. the state governments
4. industry

3. The turnpike system and plank road systems were unique in that

1. private companies built and maintained the roads.
2. no one had ever driven on plank roads.
3. the federal government charged tolls for the use of the roads.
4. the federal government and the private sector worked together.

4. In paragraph four, the author gets
his point across through

1.  time order.
2.  description.
3.  narration.
4.  contrast.


5.  As stated in the selection, which of the
following revolutionized shipping?

1.  plank roads.
2.  the turnpike system.
3.  steamboats.
4.  the use of rafts.


6.  <u>Pole</u>, as used in the last paragraph, most
likely means

1.  a long, slender piece of wood.
2.  navigate.
3.  barge.
4.  a type of oar.


**GO ON TO NEXT PAGE**


**TEST TEN, PASSAGE ONE**

Administrators at Alfred University instituted a survey of hazing among college athletes. The survey was released in 1999, and revealed that 42 percent of college athletes first experienced hazing in high school. Concerned about those figures, the university instituted a new survey exploring hazing among high school students.

This second report "Initiation Rites in American High Schools: A National Survey" was based on a survey of more than 1,500 high school juniors and seniors. The results, according to Dr. N. Pollard, were alarming.

Nearly half the students who responded to the survey reported being victims of hazing. Some were thrown into bodies of water, including toilets. Students were forced to act as personal servants or embarrass themselves publicly—to skip school, to tattoo, to pierce, or to shave themselves or one another.

Overall, 43 percent of the students surveyed reported being subjected to humiliating activities. Twenty-three percent reported hazing that involved substance abuse. The report states: "Based on...the best estimate available, we project that more than 1.5 million high school students in the U.S. are subjected to some form of hazing each year."

Pollard explains that particularly for athletes, participation in sports is a primary means of socialization. Suddenly, after years of involvement in youth sports, they are expected to do something humiliating in order to be part of a team. For a young person, choosing not to participate

in team sports is a horrible alternative. To give up sports is to give up identity. For them, to be humiliated is a better alternative than to be isolated and ostracized. We believe that most adults are unaware of the extent of hazing because it is not publicized; hazing by its very nature is private and secret, and victims are often ashamed. Students don't know who to tell or how to tell.

-Starr, Internet

7. The best headline for paragraph two would be

1. "Initiation Rites Performed in High Schools."
2. "Results of Study on H.S. Hazing Alarming."
3. "More Than 1,500 Students Participate in Study"
4. "Dr. N. Pollard is Alarmed."

8. From the information in paragraphs three and four, we can assume that many students

1. were psychologically traumatized by the hazing.
2. dropped out of the hazing rites.
3. enjoyed the rituals.
4. were injured during the rituals.

9. According to the selection, parents

1. approve of hazing.
2. participated in hazing when they were younger.
3. want their children to be accepted and encourage hazing rites.
4. are unaware of the extent of hazing.

**TEST TEN, PASSAGE TWO**

10.  It is implied that hazing has become

1.  an event parents want to support
        in the future.
2.  unacceptable by students.
3.  acknowledged as a ritual connected to
        sports.
4.  a way to get revenge.


11.  The word ostracized underlined
in the next to last paragraph most nearly
means

1.  beaten.
2.  excluded.
3.  identified.
4.  accepted.


12.  What percent of high school
students reported being hazed?

1.  nearly one-third.
2.  one and a half.
3.  about fifty.
4.  twenty-three.


**GO ON TO NEXT PAGE**


**TEST TEN, PASSAGE TWO**

A few centuries ago, the land on which Atlanta stands was the exclusive domain of Creek Indians. The Chattahoochee River was the ancient boundary between the Creeks and Cherokees, with the latter residing northwest of the river. Actually, the earliest non-Indian settlement in what are now the city limits of Atlanta was erected in 1814 at the Indian village of Standing Peach Tree; it was called Fort Gilmer. Also known as Fort Peachtree, it was one in a loose chain of forts designed to protect the frontier. Dismantled after the War of 1812, the site of the fort is now owned by the city and is partly occupied by the River Pumping Station of the Atlanta Water Works.

Most of the Atlanta area's settlers farmed. They arrived during the early 1820s, from Northeast Georgia—Franklin, Elbert, Madison, and other counties. Others, but in fewer numbers, came in from the Carolinas and Virginia. Most acquired at least one land lot, a square of ground containing 202 ½ acres. A number of the pioneers, whose lands lay along the major creeks, Peachtree, Nancy, Snap Finger, established water-powered saw and grist mills. The roads leading to the mills, in many instances, took the name of the mill owner. Thus, we have Moore's Mill, Tilly Mill, Henderson Mill, Howell Mill, and Randall Mill Roads.

As early mills gave names to roads, so did pioneer ferries. During the early 1830s, as the former Cherokee Indian country northwest of the Chattahoochee River was opened (Cobb County was created in 1832, and Marietta laid out in 1833), travel increased across the river. A number of ferries were established for there were no bridges in the early days. The roads leading to the ferries took the names of their proprietors. So it is that we have Johnson's Ferry, Powers' Ferry, Pace's Ferry, and numerous others.

-Garrett, pp. 9-10

13. We can deduce that in the 1600's Atlanta was inhabited by

1. soldiers.
2. settlers from northeast Georgia.
3. the Creek Indian nation.
4. Native Americans of varying tribes.

14. The settlement of Atlanta began as a(n)

1. an English village.
2. fort.
3. river town.
4. river pumping station.

15. The word latter, as underlined, refers to

1. Cherokees.
2. the Chattahoochee.
3. Atlanta.
4. the Creek nation.

16. The reader can conclude that the
earliest non-Indian settlers in the
Atlanta area were

1. ferry toll workers.
2. soldiers.
3. mill owners.
4. farmers.

17. The roads leading to the mills in the
area were named after

1. ferry proprietors.
2. the Creeks.
3. early pioneer farmers.
4. the mill owners.

18. It is stated that travel increased
across the Chattahoochee River because

1. the Cherokees disappeared.
2. Cobb County was created.
3. bridges were constructed.
4. water-powered saw mills were
flourishing.

**GO ON TO NEXT PAGE**

**TEST TEN, PASSAGE THREE**

In his tenth year, the young Earl of Essex was sent to Trinity College, Cambridge, where in 1581, at the age of fourteen, he received the degree of Master of Arts. The youth loved hunting and all the sports of manhood, but he loved reading too. He could write correctly in Latin and beautifully in English; he might have been a scholar, had he not been so spirited a nobleman.

As he grew up, his double nature seemed to be reflected in his physical complexion. The blood flew through his veins in vigorous vitality; he ran and tilted with the sprightliest; and then suddenly health would ebb away from him, and the pale boy would lie for hours in his chamber, obscurely melancholy.

When he was eighteen he was sent with an army to the Netherlands, and was appointed General of the Horse. The post was less responsible than picturesque, and Essex performed its functions perfectly. He returned unscathed to England, unlike others who had been injured. He forthwith began an assiduous attendance at Court.

Queen Elizabeth I, who had known him from his childhood, liked him well. The rising influence of Walter Raleigh was no competition; there was soon no reason to push Essex forward. It was plain to all—the handsome, charming youth, with his open manner, his boyish spirits, his words and looks of adora-tion, his tall figure, his exquisite hands and auburn hair had fascinated Elizabeth. The new star, rising with extraordinary swiftness, was suddenly seen to be shining alone in the firma-ment. The Queen and the Earl were never apart. She was fifty-three, and he was not yet twenty.

-Strachey, pp. 8-9

19. It is suggested in the passage that

1. Elizabeth and Essex were lovers.
2. Essex had an Oedipus complex.
3. Essex was only attracted to older women.
4. Elizabeth and Essex had a close relationship.

20. Essex's double nature refers to his

1. vitality and his melancholy.
2. Master of Arts and being a scholar.
3. love for older and younger women.
4. being a pale boy and a Latin scholar.

21. The new star (last paragraph refers to

1. Elizabeth's new astrologer.
2. Elizabeth.
3. Walter Raleigh.
4. The Earl of Essex.

22. Paragraph one is intended to

1. expose Essex's deceitful nature.
2. ridicule Essex for his love of reading.
3. reveal Essex as an unusually talented child.
4. condemn Essex for not becoming a scholar.

23. Essex's position as General of the Horse was

1. stressful.
2. picturesque.
3. uncalled for.
4. stripped from him.

24. Unscathed, found in the third paragraph most nearly means

1. exuberant.
2. maimed.
3. unharmed.
4. with honors.

**GO ON TO NEXT PAGE**

**TEST TEN, PASSAGE FOUR**

The peaks of the Snow Mountains, on bright mornings, part the dense clouds and soar into the skies of Oceania. Beneath the clouds, like a world submerged, lie the dark rocks which form the great island of New Guinea. On a high flank in the central highlands lies a sudden valley—the Baliem. This valley was discovered from the air in 1938, but no white man came to live there until 1954, when a government post was established on the abandoned lands. Dutch patrols have now explored much of the valley, which supports more than forty thousand people; they also explored the last large blank on the most recent maps—a region of perhaps thirty square miles under the northeast wall.

This remote corner is controlled by those tribes of the Dani-speaking peoples known as the Kurelu. Because the southern Kurelu were entirely untouched by civilization, their culture was chosen for study by the Harvard-Peabody Expedition of 1961. The expedition, sponsored in part by the government of the Netherlands, entered the Baliem at the end of March and remained until September. Its purpose was to live among the people as unobtrusively as possible and to film and record their wars, rituals, and daily life with a minimum of interference, in order that a true picture of a Stone Age culture— one of the few in which both war and agriculture are important—might be preserved. The Kurelu offered a unique chance, perhaps the last, to describe a lost culture in the terrible beauty of its pure estate.                                       -Matthiessen, pp. ix-xii

25. The reader can deduce that the Baliem is *most* unique in that

1. it was explored by Dutch patrols.
2. the valley was chosen for study by Harvard.
3. Baliem valley supports more than forty thousand people.
4. no white man lived there until 1954.

26. The main idea of the first paragraph is supported through

1. description.
2. statistics.
3. cause-effect.
4. examples.

27. In the context of the second paragraph, the best description for the phrase entirely untouched by civilization is

1. underdeveloped.
2. nonindustrial.
3. stone-age.
4. ignorant.

28. According to passage, the Harvard study was supported by the government of

1. New Guinea.
2. the Netherlands.
3. the United States.
4. Kurelu.

29. The word <u>unobtrusively</u> most nearly means

1. openly.
2. defiantly.
3. honestly.
4. quietly.

30. The reason the members of the expedition wanted to record the Kurelu was to

1. capture a true picture of the Stone Age culture.
2. ensure the researchers' fame and fortune.
3. educate the Kurelu.
4. advance the cause of the Dani-speaking people.

**GO ON TO NEXT PAGE**

**TEST TEN, PASSAGE FIVE**

In the Declaration of Independence nothing is said about ensuring economic equality. Nor was the distribution of wealth an important issue in the American Revolution. Still, the practice of the equality of rights should have eliminated (in America) the kinds of economic inequalities found in Europe based on class privileges.

Some of the founding fathers believed that equal rights would promote economic mobility and lead to a greater degree of monetary equality among all of American society. In the mind of Alexander Hamilton however there was never any doubt that within such a system, there would be the rich and the poor.

A concern for economic inequality has been a constant issue in American politics over time. Disputes about the distribution of wealth were common in the nineteenth century. A major contention was that policies of the federal government produced a wealthy class. For some, the economic system (if left to its own devices) would produce an acceptable allocation of wealth in society; it was government interference that created great inequalities.

In the twentieth century, those concerned with economic inequality emphasized a different argument. They contended that in a modern economy, government must take positive steps to correct the system. According to President Roosevelt, "political rights have proved inadequate to assure us equality . . . true, individual freedom cannot exist without economic security and independence."

Roosevelt's statement laid the foundation for what is known as "the welfare state." The welfare state is a general name given to the idea that government, by positive programs, should provide citizens with a certain level of welfare and economic security. Economic equality may not be achievable, but closing the gap between rich and poor in some sense is.

-Ceaser, p. 13

31. In the nineteenth century, a major contention was that, in regard to economic issues, the government

1. must step in and take action.
2. should stay out of the way.
3. should give money directly to the poor.
4. should institute a welfare state.

32. The reader can infer that, unlike Europeans, most Americans

1. did not encourage class distinctions.
2. believed Europe had no equal rights.
3. did not want an organized economic system like Europe.
4. admired the economic equality in Europe.

33. The mention of opinions about the economy in the nineteenth and twentieth centuries is used to show

1. persuasion.
2. comparison.
3. sarcasm.
4. contrast.


34. The "founder" of the welfare state was

1. a founding father.
2. a European.
3. Roosevelt.
4. Hamilton.


35. Roosevelt's statement as underlined in the passage means

1. Americans have freedom but not security.
2. Americans have money but not freedom.
3. to have political rights, Americans must have money.
4. to be truly free, Americans must have enough money to feel secure.


36. The author's attitude toward the welfare state is

1. negatively biased.
2. extremely skeptical.
3. somewhat favorable.
4. totally indifferent.

**TEST TEN, PASSAGE SIX**

**GO ON TO NEXT PAGE**

Obsessive love knows no gender. Both men and women can become obsessed, and both men and women can be targets. Jim and Gloria's story is a classic case of obsessive love. Jim's suffocating behavior and unwillingness to accept that Gloria did not want to be in a relationship with him anymore was, in different ways, destroying both of their lives. Intellectually, Jim knew he had to give up on Gloria, but emotionally, he could not.

I told Jim that I understood how alone, confused, and out of control he felt. Most obsessors feel this way yet they often have nowhere to turn for support. Their friends and family can't understand why they don't just "forget about" their lover and get on with their lives.

By the same token, I knew that Gloria must be plagued by questions of her own. Shouldn't she have known early on that something was wrong? Was she unwittingly feeding Jim's obsession? Why couldn't she get him to take her seriously? While I sympathized with Jim's pain, I also felt a lot of compassion for Gloria. Targets of obsessive love are often forgotten victims.

Obsessive love is characterized by the following: 1) the obsessor must have a painful, all-consuming preoccupation with a real or wished-for lover; 2) the obsessor must have an insatiable longing either to possess or to be possessed by the target of their obsession; 3) the target must have rejected them or must be unavailable in some way, either physically or emotionally; and 4) the target's unavailability or rejection must drive the obsessor to behave in self-defeating ways. Anyone can be an obsessor.

Likewise, there are no rules about what kinds of people get singled out as targets. Some targets encourage their obsessive lover, others bluntly refuse all contact. Some targets initially share their lover's passion, others reject it out of hand.

-Forward & Buck, pp. 4-7

37. This selection is written from the point of view of

1. Jim.
2. Gloria.
3. a counselor.
4. an obsessor.

38. It is implied that targets of an obsessor

1. are playing hard to get.
2. are compassionate.
3. unknowingly feed the obsessor.
4. are most likely married.

39. The authors get their point across in paragraph one through

1. narration.
2. cause-effect.
3. description.
4. example.

40. According to the passage, who are obsessors?

1. anyone.
2. everyone.
3. men only.
4. women only.

41. Which of the following is not true of obsessors?

1. They behave in self-defeating ways.
2. They rejected the target of their obsession at one point .
3. They are consumed by the target of their obsession.
4. They may want to possess the target of their obsession.

42. <u>By the same token</u> can be substituted with which of the following words/phrases?

1. Contrarily,
2. In a like manner,
3. Meanwhile,
4. Then,

**GO ON TO THE NEXT PAGE**

**TEST TEN, PASSAGE SEVEN**

There is an increasing force pulling live plants into our environment today. The increased demands of discount outlets and home centers, as well as nurseries, have forced the mass growing of house plants. With this development comes scientific knowledge—and stronger strains. Today you can buy green livestock more resistant to disease. The content of each pot or tub has better shape, texture, leaf color, and limberness. And there are more varieties to choose from.

Of course you can live without greening up, ecologists excepted, but why should you? With a modest amount of helpful information and a fertile imagination you can develop "grow power" in your personal paradise, be it mobile home or mansion. Admittedly, it's not easy going for nonbelievers, but an old proverb from Kenya says that seeing for yourself is different from being told. When you watch a plant thrive on the magic combination of personal interaction, adequate light, temperature, moisture and a happy location, you will learn what a living, growing thing can do for you—how it can feed your soul.

House plants do their bit for ecology, too. They consume the carbon dioxide you exhale and hand back life-giving oxygen. There's also a good chance that some of the rare plants which will grow inside may be destined for extinction, just like the wildlife. Swiss-based studies indicate ten percent of the known species are headed for extinction.

Luther Burbank, the geneticist in Santa Rosa, looked at plants in the desert and reasoned that every one was spiny, bitter, or poisonous because of years of fighting for survival in a threatening environment.

Why not consider adopting a house plant; but, remember, it's a two-way street.                    -Baylis, pp. 4-6

43. The author uses the Kenyan proverb to describe

1. "seeing is believing."
2. "nonbelievers will never believe."
3. "being told is the best way to learn."
4. "magic is what works best."

44. We can infer that the major benefit of taking care of a house plant is that houseplants

1. consume carbon dioxide.
2. feed one's soul.
3. excrete protective poisons.
4. exhale oxygen.

45. Green livestock, as underlined in the first paragraph, refers to

1. cattle.
2. "grow power."
3. houseplants.
4. our environment.

46. In regard to house plants, all of the following are mentioned as scientific improvements except

1. texture.
2. shape.
3. variety.
4. size.

47. In which country were studies on the extinction of plant species completed?

1. Switzerland.
2. Kenya.
3. the United States.
4. Africa.

48. In the context of the first sentence of paragraph two, the phrase ecologists excepted figuratively means that ecologists

1. can live without plants.
2. want society to live without plants.
3. can not live without plants.
4. want society to live with plants.

**GO ON TO THE NEXT PAGE**

**TEST TEN, PASSAGE EIGHT**

Those who teach film rarely have time to discuss writing about film. Most instructors are busy presenting films and books about those films, and the usual presumption they are forced to make is that students know how to put what they see and think into a comprehensible written form. As common as that presumption may be, it is less reliable today than ever before.

One way to avoid this problem is to rely on examinations that elicit short answers. Yet, as useful and as necessary as this method is, especially with large lecture courses in film history, it sidesteps several beneficial demands that the critical essay makes, demands that lead to real differences in the quality of a student's thinking.

An essay forces a student to use special skills: to generate and focus original ideas; to organize, sustain, and support those ideas until they are fully developed; to fine-tune perceptions by revising the language used to describe them; to employ proper grammar and syntax as part of a convincing presentation of an argument; and to make use of the opinions of others through intelligent research.

Writing about films is one of the most sophisticated ways to respond to them. To elicit scope, originality, and rigor in a student's thinking, an instructor, I believe, needs to guide that student through the mechanics of the essay form.

-Corrigan, p. 13

49. The word sophisticated, as used in the last paragraph, most nearly means

1. highly developed.
2. classy.
3. mature.
4. naive.

50. According to the selection most instructors presume that

1. students do not know how to write.
2. students are not interested in writing about film.
3. their students know how to write.
4. it is too difficult a task for students to write critical essays.

51. Overall, the author illustrates his point by using

1. description and narration.
2. definition and example.
3. comparison and contrast.
4. opinion and persuasion.

52. The author would probably agree that

1. most students are good writers.
2. all teachers should give some guidance in the writing process.
3. teachers should only give multiple-choice exams.
4. many instructors across the curriculum do not know how to write.

**TEST TEN, PASSAGE NINE**

53. Writing forces a student to use specific skills such as

1. memorization.
2. pronunciation.
3. generation of original ideas.
4. plagiarism.

54. It is suggested that instructors of large classes in film history

1. do not give essay exams.
2. only give essay exams.
3. do not like the format of short answer exams.
4. show films as part of the exam.

# PROGRESS CHART FOR SIMULATED EXAMS

*Instructions.* Place a dot ( • ) in cell that represents your grade on each test. Then draw a line from dot-to-dot to visualize your progress.

| | Diagnostic | Exam 1 | Exam 2 | Exam 3 | Exam 4 | Exam 5 | Exam 6 | Exam 7 | Exam 8 | Exam 9 | Exam 10 |
|---|---|---|---|---|---|---|---|---|---|---|---|
| 100 | | | | | | | | | | | |
| | | | | | | | | | | | |
| 90 | | | | | | | | | | | |
| | | | | | | | | | | | |
| 80 | | | | | | | | | | | |
| | | | | | | | | | | | |
| 70 | | | | | | | | | | | |
| | | | | | | | | | | | |
| 60 | | | | | | | | | | | |
| | | | | | | | | | | | |
| 50 | | | | | | | | | | | |
| | | | | | | | | | | | |
| 40 | | | | | | | | | | | |
| | | | | | | | | | | | |
| 30 | | | | | | | | | | | |
| | | | | | | | | | | | |
| 20 | | | | | | | | | | | |
| | | | | | | | | | | | |
| 10 | | | | | | | | | | | |

## APPENDIX A:  REVISED TEST ANXIETY SCALE

*The following items refer to how you feel when taking a test.  Answer the following questions 1 through 20 as honestly as you can.  Then go to the chart and fill it in based on your responses.*

*1 = almost never*          *2 = sometimes*          *3 = often*          *4 = almost always*

1. Thinking about my grade in a course interferes with my work on tests          1 2 3 4

2. I seem to defeat myself while taking important tests.          1 2 3 4

3. During tests, I find myself thinking about the consequences of failing.          1 2 3 4

4. I start feeling very uneasy just before getting a test paper back.          1 2 3 4

5. During tests I feel very tense.          1 2 3 4

6. I worry a great deal before taking an important exam.          1 2 3 4

7. During tests, I find myself thinking of things unrelated to the material being tested.          1 2 3 4

8. While taking tests, I find myself thinking how much brighter the other people are.          1 2 3 4

9. I think about current events during a test.          1 2 3 4

10. I get a headache during an important test.          1 2 3 4

11. While taking a test, I often think about how  difficult it is.          1 2 3 4

12. I am anxious about tests.          1 2 3 4

13. While taking tests, I sometimes think about being somewhere else.          1 2 3 4

14. During tests, I find I am distracted by thoughts of upcoming events.          1 2 3 4

15. My mouth feels dry during a test.          1 2 3 4

16. I sometimes find myself trembling before or during tests.          1 2 3 4

17. While taking a test, my muscles are very tight.          1 2 3 4

18. I have difficulty breathing while taking a test.          1 2 3 4

19. During the test, I think about how I should have prepared for the test.          1 2 3 4

20. I worry before the test because I do not know what to expect.          1 2 3 4

Benson, J. L. and N. El-Zahhar.  "Further refinement and validation of the revised test anxiety scale." *Structural equation modeling 1*, 3 (1994): 203-221.

**CHARTING YOUR RESPONSES**

Using the chart below, record your responses. If, for example, you circled "3" for Item 1, "Thinking about my grade in a course interferes with my work on tests," then write a "3" in the space below next to Item 1. Then add up your points for each block (going across) and write your score in the box on the far right titled Total Points. Last, add up all the boxes on the far right (going down) for Your Grand Total Points.

| REVISED TEST ANXIETY SCALE | | | | | | |
|---|---|---|---|---|---|---|
| **Dimensions** | **Item Responses** | | | | | **Total Points** |
| **Tension** Max = 20 pts Min = 5 pts | Item 4 | Item 5 | Item 6 | Item 12 | Item 20 | | |
| **Worry** Max = 24 pts. Min = 6 pts. | Item 1 | Item 2 | Item 3 | Item 8 | Item 11 | Item 19 | |
| **Bodily Symptoms** Max = 20 pts. Min = 5 pts. | Item 10 | Item 15 | Item 16 | Item 17 | Item 18 | | |
| **Test-Irrelevant Thinking** Max = 16 pts. Min = 4 pts. | Item 7 | Item 9 | Item 13 | Item 14 | | | |
| | | | | | | **Your Grand Total Points___** (Estimated Test Anxious Level = 40 points and above) |

Unlike many tests, on this test *the lower your score the better*. According to research, students who failed the Regents' Reading Test showed an average score of 45 on this scale (Stallworth-Clark, et. al., 2000). Therefore, if you scored 45+, you will probably want to practice some strategies for coping with test anxiety.

Perhaps one of the best things you can do for yourself before taking the Regents' Reading Exam is exactly what you are doing now: that is, preparing yourself. In addition to that, there are several resources at your disposal: 1) contact the counseling center at your college; they may have handouts or counseling sessions available; 2) contact the academic success center at your college; they may give workshops on strategies for coping with test anxiety; 3) contact your Learning Support Department; teachers in this department have unequalled expertise in test taking strategies; and 4) contact student affairs at your college; they may have peer and tutoring sessions designed to address test taking.

# APPENDIX B:  SOURCES*

**UNIT ONE**

## CHAPTER ONE:  OVERVIEW

*Georgia Southern University Catalogue.*  Statesboro: Georgia Southern University, 2003-2004.

University System of Georgia, Board of Regents' Web site.  Internet address: www.gsu.edu/
    ~www.rtp/index94.html.

## CHAPTER TWO: VOCABULARY

Discovery Channel, passage adapted from the broadcast of "Nefertiti Resurrected," July, 2006 and from
    www.touregypt.net/featurestories/nefertiti.htm.

Parker, Derek and Julia Parker.  *Dreaming.*  New York: Prentice Hall, 1985.

Peterson, M. S. and K. J. Rigby.  *Interpreting Earth History.*  Dubuque:  Wm. C. Brown Company, 1982.

Solberg, Curtis, David Morris and Anthony Koeninger.  *A People's Heritage: Patterns in United States
    History.*  Second edition.  Dubuque: Kendall/Hunt Publishing Company, 2000.

Tolkien, J. R. R.  *The Lord of the Rings: The Return of the King.*  New York: Ballantine Books, 1955.

## CHAPTER THREE: LITERAL COMPREHENSION

Ebert, Charles H. V.  *Disasters.*  Second edition.  Dubuque: Kendall/Hunt, 1993.

Henslin, James M.  *Sociology: A Down-to-Earth Approach.*  Sixth edition.  New York: Allyn and Bacon, 2003.

Kestner, Jane, William Fry, Steve Ellyson, Jeffrey Coldren, and Peter Beckett.  *General Psychology.*  Dubuque:
    Kendall/Hunt Publishing Company, 2001.

Martin, James Kirby, et. al.  *America and Its Peoples: A Mosaic in the Making.*  Fifth edition.  New York:
    Pearson Longman, 2004.

Solberg, Curtis, David Morris and Anthony Koeninger.  *A People's Heritage: Patterns in United States
    History.*  Second edition.  Dubuque: Kendall/Hunt Publishing Company, 2000.

Wassman, Rose and Lee Ann Rinsky.  *Effective Reading in a Changing World.*  Englewood Cliffs: Prentice-
    Hall, Inc. 1993.

---

**\*Some passages were adapted to facilitate reading.**

**CHAPTER THREE** continued

*Webster's New World Dictionary.* Second college edition. New York: Simon and Schuster, 1982.

## CHAPTER FOUR: INFERENCE

Arthur, Linda and Mark Dallas. *Reading for College: Georgia Reading Exams.* Dubuque: Kendall/Hunt
    Publishing, 2003.

Balin, Beverly. *King in Hell.* New York: Coward-McCann, Inc., 1971

Beasley, Deena. "Stressed Women Would Rather Make Friends Than Fight." Internet address:
    http://home.att.net/~potsweb/uclastudy.html.

*Business Week.* "Hayao Miyazaki." Internet address: www.businessweek.com/magazine/content/
    02_27/b3790630.html.

Kestner Kestner, Jane, William Fry, Steve Ellyson, Jeffrey Coldren, and Peter Beckett. *General Psychology.*
    Dubuque: Kendall/Hunt Publishing Company, 2001.

Seitz, John. *Global Issues: An Introduction.* Second edition. Oxford: Blackwell Publishers, 2002.

Seton, Anya. *The Mistletoe and the Sword.* New York: Avon, 1955.

The Smithsonian. "Why Did Women Fight in the Civil War?" *The Smithsonian Associates Civil
    War E-Mail Newsletter,* Volume 1, Number 8. Internet address: http://civilwarstudies.org/
    articles/Vol_1/women.htm.

visitnepal.com. "Kumari Devi: The Living Goddess." Internet address: www.visitnepal.com/nepal_
    information/kumari.html.

Wassman, Rose and Lee Ann Rinsky. *Effective Reading in a Changing World.* Englewood Cliffs: Prentice-
    Hall, Inc. 1993.

## CHAPTER FIVE: ANALYSIS

Adams, Thomas M., II. *Concepts of Health-Related Fitness.* Dubuque: Kendall/Hunt Publishing Company,
    2002.

Arthur, Linda L. and Mark Dallas. *Reading for College: Georgia Reading Exams.* Dubuque: Kendall/Hunt
    Publishing Company, 2003.

Auel, Jean M. *Valley of the Horses.* New York: Crown Publishers, Inc., 1980.

Bush, George W. State of the Union Address. January 29, 2002. Internet address: www.cnn.com/
    2002/ALLPOLITICS/01/29/bush.speech.text/index.html.

**CHAPTER FIVE** continued

CNN. "Survey: Teachers See Selves as Scapegoats." Internet address: www.cnn.com/education.

Hewitt, Paul G. *Conceptual Physics: A New Introduction to Your Environment.* Boston: Little, Brown and Company, 1981.

Hockstader, Lee. "International Education Matters," *Washington Post*, November 11, 2003.

Katzenstein, Gary. *Funny Business.* New York: Prentice Hall, 1989.

Kestner, Jane, et. al. *General Psychology.* Dubuque: Kendall/Hunt Publishing Company, 2001.

Layton, Donald. *World War II: A Global Perspective.* Second edition. Dubuque: Kendall/Hunt Publishing, 1998.

*Let's Go Greece.* (Nora B. Morrison, editor). New York: St. Martin's Press, 2001.

McAlpine, William and Helen McAlpine. *Japanese Tales and Legends.* Oxford: Oxford University Press, 1996.

Mulholland, Kate. *The King's Shilling.* Lancashire: Devereux Publishing, 1999.

Royal Thai Government, Office of the Prime Minister. *Thailand in the 1990s.* Thailand: National Identity Office, 1991.

Sapa, AP. "Boffin Sees Similarities between Earth, Mars." Internet address: www.iol.co.za.

Seton, Anya. *The Mistletoe and the Sword.* New York: Avon, 1955.

Solberg, Curtis, David Morris and Anthony Koeninger. *A People's Heritage: Patterns in United States History.* Second edition. Dubuque: Kendall/Hunt Publishing Company, 2000.

Valentine, Michael. *Difficult Discipline Problems: A Family-Systems Approach.* Dubuque: Kendall/Hunt Publishing, 1988.

## CHAPTER SIX:  READING RATE

Golden, Arthur. *Memoirs of a Geisha.* New York: Vintage Books, 1997, pp. 36-37

Grizzard, Lewis. *Shoot Low, Boys—They're Ridin' Shetland Ponies.* New York: Ballantine Books, 1985, pp. 216-219

Morgan, Tom. *Saints.* San Francisco: Chronicle Books, 1994, pp. 38-40.

Samuel, Robert T. *The Samurai: The Philosophy of Victory.* New York: Barnes and Noble, 2004.

Seton, Anya. Adapted from *Green Darkness.* Boston: Houghton Mifflin Company, 1972, pp. 22-25.

## UNIT TWO*

### SIMULATED DIAGNOSTIC EXAM

Angelfire.com. "The Autobiography of Mother Jones: Chapter I: Early Years." Internet address: www.angelfire.com.

Barcs, Emery. In Fodor's. *Australia, New Zealand, and the South Pacific.* New York: Fodor's Travel Publications, Inc., 1989.Clark, Constance. *In the Line of Duty: The Service and Sacrifice of America's Finest.* Potomac Publishing, 1989.

Clark, Constance. *In the Line of Duty: Service and Sacrifice of America's Finest.* Potomac Publishing, 1989.

Evans, Patricia. *The Verbally Abusive Relationship.* Holbrook, MA: Adams Media Corporation, 1996.

Kehoe, Thomas J., Harold E. Damerow, and Jose M. Duvall. *Exploring WesternCivilization: To 1648.* Dubuque: Kendall/Hunt Publishing Company, 1997.

Kestner, Jane, William Fry, Steve Ellyson, Jeffrey Coldren, and Peter Beckett. *General Psychology.* Dubuque: Kendall/Hunt Publishing Company, 2001.

Solberg, Curtis, David Morris and Anthony Koeninger. *A People's Heritage: Patterns in U.S. History.* Second edition. Dubuque: Kendall/Hunt Publishing Company, 2000.

Thoele, Sue Patton. *The Woman's Book of Soul.* New York: MJF Books, 1998.

Wallace, Ann and Gabrielle Taylor. *Royal Mothers: from Eleanor of Aquitaine toPrincess Diana.* London: Piatkus Publishers, 1987

### SIMULATED EXAM ONE

"The Black Death, 1348." (2001). EyeWitness: History through the eyes of those who lived it. Internet address: www.ibiscom.com.

Duke, David A. *History of the Political Economy of the United States.* Dubuque: Kendall/Hunt Publishing Company, 2001.

Harrington, Fred H. "What's in a Howl?" (2000). Internet address: www.pbs.org/wgbh/nova/ wolves/howl.html.

Kestner, Jane, William Fry, Steve Ellyson, Jeffrey Coldren, and Peter Beckett. *General Psychology.* Dubuque: Kendall/Hunt Publishing Company, 2001.

Smith, Catherine. "He Was Sent to us From Heaven to Invent the Architectural Form." Student paper. Athens, GA: University of Georgia, Department of Fine Art, 2003.

---

**\*Some passages were adapted to facilitate reading.**

## SIMULATED DIAGNOSTIC EXAM continued

Tolkien. J. R. R. *The Lord of the Rings: The Fellowship of the Ring.* New York: Ballantine Books, 1954.

Ward, Allen. "The Movie *Gladiator* in Historical Perspective." (2001). Internet address: www. ablemedia.com.

## SIMULATED EXAM TWO

The Columbia Electronic Encyclopedia. "Massacre of Saint Bartholomew's Day." Internet address: www.factmonster.com.

Condon, John C. *With Respect to the Japanese: A Guide for Americans.* Yarmouth, MA: Intercultural Press Inc., 1984.

Gaidos, Susan. "New Course Introduces Students to Crime Scene Investigation." *Purdue News.* Internet Address: www.purdue.edu/UNS/html.

Kehoe, Thomas J., Harold E. Damerow, and Jose M. Duvall. *Exploring Western Civilization: To 1648.* Dubuque: Kendall/Hunt Publishing Company, 1997.

Kestner, Jane, William Fry, Steve Ellyson, Jeffrey Coldren, and Peter Beckett. *General Psychology.* Dubuque: Kendall/Hunt Publishing Company, 2001.

"Native American Spirituality." Internet Address: www.religiousmovements.lib.virginia.edu.

New Advent Catholic Encyclopedia. "Saint Bartholomew's Day." Internet address: www.newadvent.org.

Plaidy, Jean. *Indiscretions of the Queen.* London: The Book Club, 1970.

## SIMULATED EXAM THREE

Amsterdam Promotion Foundation. "Amsterdam: Living History, Business, Into the Future," Internet address: www.amsterdampromotion.nl/living/guide.php.

Arthur, Linda L. "Study Abroad: The Basic Facts." Statesboro, GA: Center for International Studies, Georgia Southern University, 2001.

Cowie, Peter. *Swedish Cinema, from Ingeborg Holm to Fanny and Alexander.* Stockholm: Stellan Stals Tryckerier AB, 1985.

Duke, David A. *History of the Political Economy of the United States.* Dubuque: Kendall/Hunt Publishing Company, 2001.

Kehoe, Thomas J., Harold E. Damerow, and Jose M. Duvall. *Exploring Western Civilization: To 1648.* Dubuque: Kendall/Hunt Publishing Company, 1997.

**SIMULATED EXAM THREE** continued

Peyser, Marc. "Doctor Phil." *Newsweek*, September 2, 2002.

Rhoades, Robert E. *Bridging Human and Ecological Landscapes*. Dubuque: Kendall/Hunt Publishing Company, 2001.

U. S. Department of State. Office of the Coordinator for Counterterrorism. "Patterns of Global Terrorism." (2002). Internet address: www.state.gov.

Yeager, Janet. "Harry Potter." Internet address: www.biermans.com.

## SIMULATED EXAM FOUR

Dames, Noelle. "Biogeography of the Pacific Seahorse." Internet address: www.bss.sfsu.edu/Geog/bholzman/courses/Fall00Projects/Seahorse.html.

Ebert, Charles H. V. *Disasters*. Second edition. Dubuque: Kendall/Hunt Publishing Company, 1993.

Elgin, Suzette Haden. *You Can't Say That To Me!* New York: John-Wiley & Sons, Inc., 1995.

Holton, Ed. "The Critical First Year on the Job." Bethlehem, PA: College Placement Council, Inc., 1995.

Layton, Donald L. *World War II: A Global Perspective*. Dubuque: Kendall/Hunt Publishing Company, 1998.

Millman, Dan. *The Way of the Peaceful Warrior*. Tiburon, CA: H J Kramer, Inc., 1984.

Noffke, Suzanne. *Catherine of Siena: The Dialogue*. New York: Paulist Press, 1980.

Peterson, James W. Lee M. Allen, and Nolan J. Argyle. *Political Science: An Overview of the Field*. Second edition. Dubuque: Kendall/Hunt Publishing Company, 1997.

Sellers, Patricia. "The Business of Being Oprah." *Fortune*, April 1, 2002.

## SIMULATED EXAM FIVE

Berardinelli, James. "Lord of the Rings: The Fellowship of the Ring." (2001). Internet address: www.movie-reviews.colossus.net.

Brooke, Michael. *The Concrete Wave: The History of Skateboarding*. Ontario: Warwick Communications, Inc., 1999.

Ebert, Charles H. V. *Disasters*. Second edition. Dubuque: Kendall/Hunt Publishing Company, 1993.

GAO. "Weapons of Mass Destruction: Report to the Chairman." Washington: Subcommittee on Foreign Operations, May 2001.

**SIMULATED EXAM FIVE** continued

Layton, Donald L. *World War II: A Global Perspective*. Dubuque: Kendall/Hunt Publishing Company, 1998.

New Advent. "Mystical Stigmata." (1908). Internet address: www.newadvent.org.

Seton, Anya. *Katherine*. Boston: Houghton Mifflin Company, 1954.

Solberg, Curtis, David Morris and Anthony Koeninger. *A People's Heritage: Patterns in U.S. History*. Second edition. Dubuque: Kendall/Hunt Publishing Company, 2000.

U. S. Department of State. "Consular Information Sheet: China." (2003). Washington: Bureau of Consular Affairs. Internet address: www.travel.state.gov/China.html.

## SIMULATED EXAM SIX

Ancestry.com. "Double Helix Genealogy." Internet address: www.ancestry.com/view/ancmag/

Arthur, Linda. Based on Tiger Woods Home Page (2003) . Internet address: www.allstarz/org/tigerwoods/ profile.html.

Ceaser, James W. *American Government: Origins, Institutions, and Public Policy*. Seventh edition. Dubuque: Kendall/Hunt Publishing Company, 2002.

D'Cook, Davey D. "The History of Hip Hop." (1985). Internet address: www.daveyd. com/raptitle.html.

DNA-view. "Did President Jefferson Have Children with a Slave Mistress?" Internet address: www.dna-view.com/jeffers.html.

Horne, Charles F. "The Code of Hammurabi." Internet address: www.lawresearch.com.

Kehoe, Thomas J., Harold E. Damerow, and Jose M. Duvall. *Exploring Western Civilization: To 1648*. Dubuque: Kendall/Hunt Publishing Company, 1997.

Layton, Donald L. *World War II: A Global Perspective*. Dubuque: Kendall/Hunt Publishing Company, 1998.

NCJRS. "In the Spotlight: Club Drugs." National Criminal Justice Reference Service. Internet address: www.ncjrs.org/club_drugs/summary.html.

Seton, Anya. *Green Darkness*. Boston: Houghton-Mifflin, 1954.

Throckmorton, George J. Forensic analysis in *Salamander: The Story of the Mormon Forgery Murders*. Linda Sillitoe and Allen Roberts. Salt Lake City: Signature Books, Inc., 1988.

Auel, Jean M. *The Clan of the Cave Bear*. New York: Crown Publishers, Inc., 1980.

Diamond, Harvey and Marilyn Diamond. *Fit for Life*. New York: Warner Books, 1985.

## SIMULATED EXAM SEVEN

Elliot, Elisabeth. *The Path of Loneliness*. Nashville: Thomas Nelson Publishers, 1988.

Epstein, Perle. *Kabbalah: The Way of the Jewish Mystic*. New York: Barnes & Noble Books, 1998.

Katzenstein, Gary J. *Funny Business*. New York: Prentice Hall Press, 1989.

Keppler Associates, Inc. "John Walsh: Living with a Mission." Internet address: www.keppler associates.com/speakers/walshjohn.asp.

Kushner, Harold S. *How Good Do We Have to Be?* Boston: Little, Brown, & Company, 1996.

Laney, Ronald. Interview for *Juvenile Justice*. "Reason to Hope: On the Front Lines with John Walsh." Internet address:  www.ojidp/ncjrs.org/jjjournal/jjjournal598/hope.html.

Layton, Donald L. *World War II: A Global Perspective*. Dubuque: Kendall/Hunt Publishing Company, 1998.

Peterson, James W., Lee M. Allen, and Nolan J. Argyle. *Political Science: An Overview of the Field*. Second edition. Dubuque: Kendall/Hunt Publishing Company, 1997.

## SIMULATED EXAM EIGHT

Duke, David A. *History of the Political Economy of the United States*. Dubuque: Kendall/Hunt Publishing Company, 2001.

FDA. "Non-Corrective Decorative Contact Lenses Dispensed Without a Prescription." U.S. Food and Drug Administration, October, 2002. Internet address: www.fda.gov.

Freeman, Arthur and Rose DeWolf. *The 10 Dumbest Mistakes Smart People Make*. New York: Harper Perennial, 1993.

Lappe, Frances M. and Joseph Collins. *World Hunger: Twelve Myths*. New York: Grove Weidenfeld, 1986.

Munsterberg, Hugo. *The Folk Arts of Japan*. Tokyo: Charles E. Tuttle company, 1958.

Preidt, Robert. "Seeing Beyond Eye Fashion." *Health Scout News Reporter*. Internet address: www.healthscourt.com/static/news/509172.html.

Ronan, Stephen. "History of Vegetarianism: On Henry Salt's 'Animal Rights'." Internet address: www. ivu.org/history/salt/rights.html.

Silverman, Harold M. *The Pill Book*. Tenth edition. New York: Bantam Books, 2002.

Sugrue, Thomas. *There is a River: The Story of Edgar Cayce*. Virginia Beach, VA: A.R.E. Press, 1973.

Watts, Alan W. *The Wisdom of Insecurity*. New York: Vintage Books, 1951.

## SIMULATED EXAM NINE

Adams, Thomas M.  *Concepts of Health-Related Fitness*.  Dubuque: Kendall/Hunt Publishing Company, 2002.

Gabaldon, Diana.  *Dragonfly in Amber*.  New York: Dell Publishing, 1992.

Gartenberg, Gerry.  "Advertising that Never Goes Out of Style."  Internet address: www.findarticles.com.

Hartman, Gertrude.  *Medieval Days and Ways*.  New York: The Macmillan Company, 1961.

Holt, Victoria.  *My Enemy, the Queen*.  Garden City, NY: Doubleday & Company, Inc., 1978.

Jong, Erica.  *Fear of Fifty*.  New York: HarperCollins Publishers, 1994.

Layton, Donald L.  *World War II: A Global Perspective*.  Dubuque: Kendall/Hunt Publishing Company, 1998.

Philbin, Tom and Steve Ettinger.  *The Complete Illustrated Guide to Everything Sold in Hardware Stores*.  New York: MacMillan Publishing Company, 1988.

Pipher, Mary.  *Reviving Ophelia: Saving the Selves of Adolescent Girls*.  New York: Ballantine Books, 1994.

## SIMULATED EXAM TEN

Baylis, Maggie.  *House Plants for the Purple Thumb*.  San Francisco: 101 Productions, 1973.

Ceaser, James W.  *American Government: Origins, Institutions, and Public Policy*.  Seventh edition.  Dubuque: Kendall/Hunt Publishing Company, 2002.

Corrigan, Timothy.  *A Short Guide to Writing about Film*.  New York: HarperCollins College Publishers, 1994.

Duke, David A.  *History of the Political Economy of the United States*.  Dubuque: Kendall/Hunt Publishing Company, 2001.

Forward, Susan and Craig Buck.  *Obsessive Love: When Passion Holds You Prisoner*.  New York: Bantam Books, 1991.

Garrett, Franklin M.  *Yesterday's Atlanta*.  Miami: E. A. Seemann Publishing, Inc., 1974.

Matthiessen, Peter.  *Under the Mountain Wall: A Chronicle of Two Seasons in the Stone Age*.  New York: Ballantine Books, 1972.

Starr, Linda.  "Hazing: It's Not Just a College Problem Anymore!"  Education World, Inc., 2000.  Internet address: www.education-world.com.

Strachey, Lytton.  *Elizabeth and Essex: A Tragic History*.  Harmondsworth, England: Penguin Books, 1971.

# APPENDIX C: ANSWER KEY FOR CHAPTERS

**CHAPTER TWO**

*Exercise 1*  Answers will vary.

*Exercise 2*

| | |
|---|---|
| obi | wide sashes |
| lucid | clear |
| charismatics | magnetic personalities |
| condiments | a seasoning/relish for food |
| raw score | number of correct answers |
| meticulous | detailed |
| garrulous | talkative |
| penury | poverty |
| oxidized | rusted |
| ebullient | bubbly |

*Exercise 3*  Answers will vary.

*Exercise 4*  Suggested meanings:

1. meaning of <u>pungent</u>:  *strong, distinctive, sharp, acrid*
key words/phrases/punctuation: *skunk*
context clue: *Common Sense or Cause-Effect*

2. meaning of <u>shrouded</u>: *draped*
key words/phrases/punctuation: *dressed as ghosts/commas*
context clue: *Definition/Description*

3.  meaning of <u>disheveled</u>: *messy, out of order*
key words/phrases/punctuation: *colon*
context clue: *Direct Definition/Description*

4.  meaning of <u>circa</u>: *around, about*
key words/phrases/punctuation: *not clear/dash*
context clue: *Direct Definition*

5.  meaning of <u>facilitate</u>: *make easy*
key words/phrases/punctuation: *however/make difficult*
context clue: *Contrast*

**ANSWER KEY: CHAPTER TWO**

6. meaning of <u>succulent</u>: juicy
key words/phrases/punctuation: *and*
context clue: *Directly Equate*


7. meaning of <u>regress</u>: *go backward*
key words/phrases/punctuation: *but*
context clue: *Contrast*

8. meaning of <u>eluding</u>: *avoiding, evading*
key words/phrases/punctuation: *commas*
context clue: *Listing*


9. meaning of <u>audible</u>: *able to be heard*
key words/phrases/punctuation: *barely/uproar*
context clue: *Cause-Effect*


10. meaning of <u>imminent</u>: close, threatening
key words/phrases/punctuation: *colon/two or more sentences/"winds increasing," "uprooted,"*
     *"power lines swaying," sky darkening"*
context clue: *Long Explanation*


*Exercise 5*   Same as above.

*Exercise 6*

1. a (sketchy)
key words/phrases/punctuation: *on the other hand/well-documented*
context clue: *Contrast*

2. b (sharpness)
key words/phrases/punctuation: *scurried back to safety*
context clue: *Cause-Effect*

3. a (ship)
key words/phrases/punctuation: *Form of the verb "to be"*
context clue: *Direct Definition/Description*

4. a (excited about)
key words/phrases/punctuation: *not/never*
context clue: *Cause-Effect/Common Sense*


**ANSWER KEY: CHAPTER TWO**

5.  c (poor)
key words/phrases/punctuation: *and/commas*
context clue: *Directly Equate*


6.  b (killing)
key words/phrases/punctuation: *or*
context clue: *Direct Definition*


7.  c (curbed)
key words/phrases/punctuation: *snake*
context clue: *Cause-Effect/Common Sense*

8.  c (payment)
key words/phrases/punctuation: *like cash, check*
context clue: *Example*


9.  a  (keep away)
key words/phrases/punctuation: *two or more sentences/martial arts, police academy, pepper spray*
context clue: *Long Explanation*

10.  c  (begged)
key words/phrases/punctuation: *judge/divorce/child*
context clue: *Common Sense/Cause-Effect*


*Exercise 7*

1.  meant
2.  psychiatrist
3.  dreams
4.  doubt
5.  impressive
6.  everyone
7.  continents
8.  levied upon
9.  confronted with
10. school board
11. disastrous
12. evacuated
13. interned


**ANSWER KEY: CHAPTER TWO**

*Exercise 8.*

| | | | | | |
|---|---|---|---|---|---|
| 1. | 2 | 5. | 3 | 9. | 2 |
| 2. | 3 | 6. | 4 | 10. | 2 |
| 3. | 1 | 7. | 1 | | |
| 4. | 3 | 8. | 1 | | |

*Exercise 9*

1. killing of fetus
2. killing of life, especially microorganisms
3. killing of elephants
4. killing of brother(s)
5. killing of insects
6. killing of people/ethnic, national groups
7. killing of man
8. killing of mother
9. killing of pests/insects
10. killing of parents

*Exercise 10*

1. i
2. c
3. b
4. g
5. j
6. h
7. e
8. a
9. d
10. f

*Exercise 11*

1. not
   see
   not easily seen
2. not
   through
   resistant
3. all
   power
   all powerful
4. see
   glasses

5. between
   come
   come between
6. good
   good, not mean
7. self
   writing
   signature
8. climb
   increased

9. not
   death
   live forever
10. not
    belief
    full of
    not believable

**ANSWER KEY:  CHAPTER TWO**

## CHAPTER THREE

*Exercise 1*

1. Peshtigo
2. Wisconsin
3. 1,152
4. debris
5. Mt. Fuji
6. Mt. Pelee
7. 20,000
8. kidney disease, leukemia, respiratory illnesses, cancer
9. Carter
10. $1.00
11. 1942
12. New York
13. Odor, oily substances, chemical smells
14. 21,800
15. Board of Education
16. 500 to 600 per year
17. 1973
18. Texas, Oklahoma, Kansas
19. False
20. 912

*Exercise 2*

Answers will vary.

*Exercise 3*

1. False
2. False
3. True
4. False
5. False
6. False
7. True
8. False
9. True
10. True

*Exercise 4*

1. b
2. a
3. c
4. a
5. c
6. c
7. b
8. a
9. b
10. c

*Exercise 5*

1. dentist office visit
2. words, sentences, paragraphs

*Exercise 6*

1. Larson
2. *Geology of National Parks*
3. Yes
4. 8
5. 01/15/04
6. 8
7. *Step By Step Literature*
8. 2005
9. 4
10. SW

**ANSWER KEY: CHAPTER THREE**

*Exercise 7*

1. murderer - musculature
2. 2
3. Tennessee
4. 4
5. adjective
6. French
7. Oman
8. grape
9. Kola
10. river

*Exercise 8*

1. b
2. a
3. c
4. b
5. False
6. False
7. True
8. False
9. False
10. True

**CHAPTER FOUR**

*Exercise 1*

Answers will vary.

*Exercise 2*

1. b    clues: "by necessity she worked under brutal conditions"
2. c    clues: "instead of taking a job for pennies a day . . ."
         "When she learned she could earn $13 per month . . ."
3. a    clues: "I enjoy myself first-rate."
4. c    clues: "instead of taking a job for pennies a day. . . she dressed as a man"

*Exercise 3*

Answers will vary.

**ANSWER KEY:  CHAPTER FOUR**

*Exercise 4*

Answers will vary

*Exercise 5*

Answers will vary.

*Exercise 6*

A.  Step One:

> -Bothwell's smile froze;
> -shocked when he saw Queen;
> -many questions–would she be angry?

Step Two:

> -Bothwell was unsure.

Step Three:

> Main Idea sentence:  Bothwell was unsure whether or not Queen Mary would receive him graciously.

B.  Step One:

> -clung to him;
> -sobs;
> -"You will never forget me."
> -"No, I will always remember this day."

Step Two:

> -They are lovers and care about each other.

Step Three:

> Main Idea sentence: Bothwell and Queen Mary truly care for one another.

C.  Step One:

> -risky/recklessness;
> -she ran to him;
> -crazy?
> -wife

**ANSWER KEY:  CHAPTER FOUR**

Step Two:

-she wants to marry; he can't

Step Three:

Main Idea sentence:  Bothwell was stunned that Queen Mary suggested they marry because he already had a wife.

*Exercise 7*

A.  Step One:

-India
-mid 1970s
-compulsory sterilization when 2+ children
-male vasectomy program

Step Two:

-drastic measures to curb population

Step Three:

-Main Idea sentence: India has taken drastic measures to curb its population.

Step Four:

The answer is c.

B.  Step One:

-take credit, good grade
-find external reason for bad grade
            instructor, didn't study, distracted during test

Step Two: don't want bad grade to affect self-image

Step Three:

-Main Idea sentence: We make excuses when we fail so our self-image doesn't suffer.

Step Four:

The answer is b.


**ANSWER KEY:  CHAPTER FOUR**

## CHAPTER FIVE

*Exercise 1*

1. b
2. c
3. a
4. c
5. b
6. b
7. a
8. c
9. b
10. c

*Exercise 2*

1. b: psychologists, social workers, counselors, method, community-based family-systems approach

2. c: "They assumed . . ."; "they believed. . ."; "they tried to work. . ."; "they tried to change . . ."

3. a:   the passage gave facts, names, dates, numbers

4. c: "like a pet through a pet doorway"; "they can stay—up to five minutes"

5. b: "put up with"; "not true"; "woefully inadequate"

*Exercise 3*

1. a
2. c
3. a
4. b

*Exercise 4*

1. Definition:
        verb "to be"
        repetition of the word "love"
2. Contrast:
        "In the early part of the twentieth century" vs. "Today"

**ANSWER KEY:  CHAPTER FIVE**

3. Persuasion:
   "All nations should know";
   The words/phrases "deliberate," "necessary," "not wait," "not stand by," "not permit to threaten"
   The sentence, "My hope is that all nations will heed our call."
4. Example:
   "For example,"
5. Description:
   Lots of adjectives:
   "placid, long, tree-lined," "congested," "glitzy," "concrete," "hip-clipped," "golden," "floating"
6. Narrative:
   Use of quotation marks
   Use of dialogue
7. Comparison:
   Two entities being compared: Mars and Earth
   The words: "similar," "identical," and "both"


**CHAPTER SIX**


| Passage One | Passage Three |
|---|---|
| 1. c | 1. T |
| 2. a | 2. F |
| 3. b | 3. F |
| 4. c | 4. T |
| 5. a | 5. F |
| 6. T | 6. T |
| 7. F | 7. F |
| 8. T | 8. T |
| 9. F | 9. T |
| 10. T | 10. T |

| Passage Two | Passage Four | Passage Five |
|---|---|---|
| 1. T | 1. T | 1. T |
| 2. F | 2. T | 2. F |
| 3. F | 3. F | 3. F |
| 4. T | 4. T | 4. F |
| 5. T | 5. T | 5. T |
| 6. F | 6. F | 6. F |
| 7. F | 7. T | 7. T |
| 8. F | 8. T | 8. T |
| 9. T | 9. F | 9. F |
| 10. F | 10. T | 10. T |

**ANSWER KEY: CHAPTER SIX**

# APPENDIX D:  ANSWER KEYS FOR SIMULATED EXAMS

**SIMULATED DIAGNOSTIC EXAM**

| | | | |
|---|---|---|---|
| 1. 2 | | 31. 3 | |
| 2. 3 | | 32. 3 | |
| 3. 4 | | 33. 4 | |
| 4. 3 | | 34. 1 | |
| 5. 2 | | 35. 3 | |
| 6. 3 | | 36. 4 | |
| 7. 4 | | 37. 4 | |
| 8. 3 | | 38. 3 | |
| 9. 2 | | 39. 4 | |
| 10. 1 | | 40. 1 | |
| 11. 3 | | 41. 4 | |
| 12. 4 | | 42. 2 | |
| 13. 3 | | 43. 2 | |
| 14. 4 | | 44. 3 | |
| 15. 2 | | 45. 1 | |
| 16. 1 | | 46. 4 | |
| 17. 3 | | 47. 2 | |
| 18. 1 | | 48. 3 | |
| 19. 3 | | 49. 4 | |
| 20. 4 | | 50. 3 | |
| 21. 2 | | 51. 1 | |
| 22. 1 | | 52. 2 | |
| 23. 3 | | 53. 3 | |
| 24. 4 | | 54. 4 | |
| 25. 1 | | | |
| 26. 3 | | | |
| 27. 2 | | | |
| 28. 3 | | | |
| 29. 1 | | | |
| 30. 1 | | | |

**ANSWER KEY: DIAGNOSTIC EXAM**

**SIMULATED EXAM ONE**

| | | | |
|---|---|---|---|
| 1. 2 | | 31. 1 |
| 2. 3 | | 32. 2 |
| 3. 1 | | 33. 3 |
| 4. 4 | | 34. 4 |
| 5. 1 | | 35. 4 |
| 6. 3 | | 36. 2 |
| 7. 1 | | 37. 1 |
| 8. 4 | | 38. 3 |
| 9. 1 | | 39. 4 |
| 10. 3 | | 40. 2 |
| 11. 4 | | 41. 4 |
| 12. 2 | | 42. 2 |
| 13. 3 | | 43. 1 |
| 14. 4 | | 44. 4 |
| 15. 3 | | 45. 2 |
| 16. 1 | | 46. 2 |
| 17. 2 | | 47. 3 |
| 18. 2 | | 48. 4 |
| 19. 4 | | 49. 2 |
| 20. 1 | | 50. 4 |
| 21. 3 | | 51. 3 |
| 22. 2 | | 52. 4 |
| 23. 4 | | 53. 2 |
| 24. 3 | | 54. 1 |
| 25. 4 | | |
| 26. 4 | | |
| 27. 3 | | |
| 28. 2 | | |
| 29. 1 | | |
| 30. 2 | | |

**ANSWER KEY:  SIMULATED EXAM ONE**

**SIMULATED EXAM TWO**

| | |
|---|---|
| 1. 1 | 31. 3 |
| 2. 4 | 32. 3 |
| 3. 3 | 33. 4 |
| 4. 2 | 34. 2 |
| 5. 4 | 35. 4 |
| 6. 1 | 36. 1 |
| 7. 1 | 37. 2 |
| 8. 4 | 38. 1 |
| 9. 2 | 39. 3 |
| 10. 4 | 40. 2 |
| 11. 3 | 41. 1 |
| 12. 1 | 42. 3 |
| 13. 3 | 43. 2 |
| 14. 2 | 44. 4 |
| 15. 4 | 45. 3 |
| 16. 4 | 46. 1 |
| 17. 1 | 47. 4 |
| 18. 2 | 48. 2 |
| 19. 4 | 49. 3 |
| 20. 1 | 50. 1 |
| 21. 3 | 51. 4 |
| 22. 2 | 52. 4 |
| 23. 4 | 53. 4 |
| 24. 3 | 54. 1 |
| 25. 3 | |
| 26. 4 | |
| 27. 2 | |
| 28. 2 | |
| 29. 4 | |
| 30. 2 | |

**ANSWER KEY: SIMULATED EXAM TWO**

**SIMULATED EXAM THREE**

| | | | |
|---|---|---|---|
| 1. | 1 | 31. | 4 |
| 2. | 2 | 32. | 2 |
| 3. | 4 | 33. | 4 |
| 4. | 3 | 34. | 3 |
| 5. | 2 | 35. | 1 |
| 6. | 4 | 36. | 4 |
| 7. | 3 | 37. | 3 |
| 8. | 3 | 38. | 3 |
| 9. | 4 | 39. | 2 |
| 10. | 2 | 40. | 4 |
| 11. | 1 | 41. | 1 |
| 12. | 2 | 42. | 3 |
| 13. | 4 | 43. | 2 |
| 14. | 4 | 44. | 2 |
| 15. | 3 | 45. | 1 |
| 16. | 2 | 46. | 3 |
| 17. | 4 | 47. | 2 |
| 18. | 4 | 48. | 4 |
| 19. | 1 | 49. | 3 |
| 20. | 3 | 50. | 3 |
| 21. | 4 | 51. | 2 |
| 22. | 2 | 52. | 4 |
| 23. | 1 | 53. | 1 |
| 24. | 3 | 54. | 4 |
| 25. | 3 | | |
| 26. | 4 | | |
| 27. | 3 | | |
| 28. | 3 | | |
| 29. | 1 | | |
| 30. | 2 | | |

**ANSWER KEY:  SIMULATED EXAM THREE**

**SIMULATED EXAM FOUR**

| | |
|---|---|
| 1. 4 | 31. 3 |
| 2. 3 | 32. 4 |
| 3. 1 | 33. 3 |
| 4. 3 | 34. 1 |
| 5. 4 | 35. 4 |
| 6. 3 | 36. 2 |
| 7. 1 | 37. 3 |
| 8. 4 | 38. 3 |
| 9. 2 | 39. 1 |
| 10. 3 | 40. 2 |
| 11. 4 | 41. 3 |
| 12. 4 | 42. 1 |
| 13. 4 | 43. 4 |
| 14. 3 | 44. 1 |
| 15. 4 | 45. 3 |
| 16. 1 | 46. 2 |
| 17. 2 | 47. 4 |
| 18. 4 | 48. 1 |
| 19. 1 | 49. 1 |
| 20. 2 | 50. 4 |
| 21. 4 | 51. 2 |
| 22. 3 | 52. 3 |
| 23. 4 | 53. 3 |
| 24. 3 | 54. 2 |
| 25. 2 | |
| 26. 3 | |
| 27. 1 | |
| 28. 3 | |
| 29. 2 | |
| 30. 4 | |

**ANSWER KEY: SIMULATED EXAM FOUR**

**SIMULATED EXAM FIVE**

| | | | |
|---|---|---|---|
| 1. | 4 | 31. | 4 |
| 2. | 2 | 32. | 3 |
| 3. | 3 | 33. | 1 |
| 4. | 2 | 34. | 2 |
| 5. | 1 | 35. | 3 |
| 6. | 4 | 36. | 4 |
| 7. | 4 | 37. | 4 |
| 8. | 1 | 38. | 2 |
| 9. | 4 | 39. | 3 |
| 10. | 2 | 40. | 1 |
| 11. | 3 | 41. | 4 |
| 12. | 2 | 42. | 3 |
| 13. | 4 | 43. | 2 |
| 14. | 2 | 44. | 1 |
| 15. | 1 | 45. | 4 |
| 16. | 4 | 46. | 3 |
| 17. | 1 | 47. | 4 |
| 18. | 3 | 48. | 3 |
| 19. | 1 | 49. | 2 |
| 20. | 2 | 50. | 4 |
| 21. | 3 | 51. | 1 |
| 22. | 4 | 52. | 3 |
| 23. | 4 | 53. | 1 |
| 24. | 1 | 54. | 4 |
| 25. | 4 | | |
| 26. | 2 | | |
| 27. | 4 | | |
| 28. | 3 | | |
| 29. | 1 | | |
| 30. | 3 | | |

**ANSWER KEY:  SIMULATED EXAM FIVE**

**SIMULATED EXAM SIX**

| | |
|---|---|
| 1. 2 | 31. 4 |
| 2. 1 | 32. 3 |
| 3. 4 | 33. 1 |
| 4. 1 | 34. 2 |
| 5. 3 | 35. 4 |
| 6. 2 | 36. 3 |
| 7. 1 | 37. 4 |
| 8. 4 | 38. 3 |
| 9. 1 | 39. 4 |
| 10. 3 | 40. 2 |
| 11. 4 | 41. 4 |
| 12. 2 | 42. 2 |
| 13. 3 | 43. 4 |
| 14. 2 | 44. 3 |
| 15. 1 | 45. 2 |
| 16. 4 | 46. 1 |
| 17. 3 | 47. 1 |
| 18. 1 | 48. 4 |
| 19. 4 | 49. 1 |
| 20. 2 | 50. 3 |
| 21. 4 | 51. 2 |
| 22. 1 | 52. 4 |
| 23. 4 | 53. 3 |
| 24. 3 | 54. 2 |
| 25. 4 | |
| 26. 3 | |
| 27. 2 | |
| 28. 1 | |
| 29. 4 | |
| 30. 2 | |

**ANSWER KEY:  SIMULATED EXAM SIX**

**SIMULATED EXAM SEVEN**

| | | | |
|---|---|---|---|
| 1. 4 | | 31. 4 | |
| 2. 3 | | 32. 2 | |
| 3. 2 | | 33. 3 | |
| 4. 1 | | 34. 1 | |
| 5. 3 | | 35. 4 | |
| 6. 1 | | 36. 3 | |
| 7. 4 | | 37. 3 | |
| 8. 2 | | 38. 3 | |
| 9. 4 | | 39. 1 | |
| 10. 1 | | 40. 2 | |
| 11. 2 | | 41. 3 | |
| 12. 3 | | 42. 1 | |
| 13. 3 | | 43. 1 | |
| 14. 1 | | 44. 3 | |
| 15. 4 | | 45. 4 | |
| 16. 2 | | 46. 3 | |
| 17. 4 | | 47. 2 | |
| 18. 2 | | 48. 1 | |
| 19. 2 | | 49. 1 | |
| 20. 4 | | 50. 2 | |
| 21. 1 | | 51. 3 | |
| 22. 1 | | 52. 4 | |
| 23. 2 | | 53. 3 | |
| 24. 4 | | 54. 4 | |
| 25. 3 | | | |
| 26. 4 | | | |
| 27. 2 | | | |
| 28. 1 | | | |
| 29. 2 | | | |
| 30. 3 | | | |

**ANSWER KEY: SIMULATED EXAM SEVEN**

**SIMULATED EXAM EIGHT**

| | | | |
|---|---|---|---|
| 1. 3 | | 31. 3 | |
| 2. 1 | | 32. 4 | |
| 3. 3 | | 33. 4 | |
| 4. 4 | | 34. 2 | |
| 5. 3 | | 35. 1 | |
| 6. 1 | | 36. 2 | |
| 7. 2 | | 37. 2 | |
| 8. 4 | | 38. 4 | |
| 9. 3 | | 39. 4 | |
| 10. 1 | | 40. 3 | |
| 11. 4 | | 41. 1 | |
| 12. 2 | | 42. 3 | |
| 13. 1 | | 43. 4 | |
| 14. 4 | | 44. 2 | |
| 15. 2 | | 45. 1 | |
| 16. 2 | | 46. 3 | |
| 17. 3 | | 47. 2 | |
| 18. 1 | | 48. 1 | |
| 19. 4 | | 49. 3 | |
| 20. 2 | | 50. 2 | |
| 21. 2 | | 51. 1 | |
| 22. 4 | | 52. 3 | |
| 23. 1 | | 53. 4 | |
| 24. 3 | | 54. 2 | |
| 25. 2 | | | |
| 26. 3 | | | |
| 27. 2 | | | |
| 28. 1 | | | |
| 29. 3 | | | |
| 30. 4 | | | |

**ANSWER KEY:  SIMULATED EXAM EIGHT**

**SIMULATED EXAM NINE**

| | | | |
|---|---|---|---|
| 1. 3 | | 31. 2 |
| 2. 4 | | 32. 3 |
| 3. 2 | | 33. 4 |
| 4. 1 | | 34. 1 |
| 5. 2 | | 35. 2 |
| 6. 3 | | 36. 1 |
| 7. 3 | | 37. 2 |
| 8. 2 | | 38. 3 |
| 9. 1 | | 39. 1 |
| 10. 1 | | 40. 4 |
| 11. 4 | | 41. 2 |
| 12. 3 | | 42. 2 |
| 13. 3 | | 43. 3 |
| 14. 2 | | 44. 1 |
| 15. 1 | | 45. 4 |
| 16. 4 | | 46. 4 |
| 17. 3 | | 47. 3 |
| 18. 1 | | 48. 2 |
| 19. 2 | | 49. 4 |
| 20. 3 | | 50. 2 |
| 21. 1 | | 51. 4 |
| 22. 4 | | 52. 1 |
| 23. 1 | | 53. 4 |
| 24. 1 | | 54. 3 |
| 25. 1 | | |
| 26. 2 | | |
| 27. 3 | | |
| 28. 2 | | |
| 29. 4 | | |
| 30. 3 | | |

**SIMULATED EXAM NINE**

**SIMULATED EXAM TEN**

| | | | |
|---|---|---|---|
| 1. 3 | | 31. 2 |
| 2. 2 | | 32. 1 |
| 3. 4 | | 33. 4 |
| 4. 4 | | 34. 3 |
| 5. 3 | | 35. 4 |
| 6. 2 | | 36. 3 |
| 7. 2 | | 37. 3 |
| 8. 1 | | 38. 3 |
| 9. 4 | | 39. 4 |
| 10. 3 | | 40. 1 |
| 11. 2 | | 41. 2 |
| 12. 3 | | 42. 2 |
| 13. 3 | | 43. 1 |
| 14. 2 | | 44. 2 |
| 15. 1 | | 45. 3 |
| 16. 2 | | 46. 4 |
| 17. 4 | | 47. 1 |
| 18. 2 | | 48. 3 |
| 19. 4 | | 49. 1 |
| 20. 1 | | 50. 3 |
| 21. 4 | | 51. 4 |
| 22. 3 | | 52. 2 |
| 23. 2 | | 53. 3 |
| 24. 3 | | 54. 1 |
| 25. 4 | | |
| 26. 1 | | |
| 27. 3 | | |
| 28. 2 | | |
| 29. 4 | | |
| 30. 1 | | |

**SIMULATED EXAM TEN**

# ANSWER KEYS: GRAPHICS

An Irish proverb states a simple truth: "Even a small thorn causes pain." How often, out of thoughtlessness or lack of attention, do we inflict pain, even though we don't want or mean to? We yearn to live gently, and yet gentleness–especially toward ourselves–seems so difficult in our fast paced lives. When we are frantically trying to abide by a timetable that is at odds with our natural ebb and flow, the ability to breathe deeply and choose our reaction is diminished. Before we know it, a thorny comment is automatically launched.

Lost in the acceleration of our pace is the energy and time for supporting ourselves and our loved ones. But with intention, we can cultivate the art of gentleness. However, we will need to make a strong commitment to living gently and adopt an attitude that supports our decision. And as usual, we'll need to start this attitude adjustment by treating ourselves gently. What a thought!

Of course we expect ourselves to be gentle with others, but aren't we supposed to drive ourselves and be our own severest critic? No. In reality, learning to be gentle with ourselves enhances our ability to treat others with respect. Being unforgiving of ourselves and treating ourselves harshly bruises us and in the long run may cause us to bruise others. By being sensitive to ourselves, we are better and safer friends and family members.

-Thoele, pp. 122-123

1. This passage would be classified as

    emphasizes a 'way of being'

1. religion.
②. philosophy.
3. science.
4. anthropology.

2. It is implied that most people react

1. after taking a deep breath.
2. purposefully.
③. in haste.
4. with patience.

3. The proverb would best be restated as

1. "thorns are dangerous."
2. "pain is a part of life."
3. "sticks and stones may break my bones, but words can never harm me."
④. "even the most insignificant comment can hurt if said harshly."   first paragraph

4. A main idea for the third paragraph is that

1. we purposefully cause pain in other people's lives.
2. thorny comments are automatically launched.
③. being gentle with ourselves enables us to treat others with respect.
4. we should not be forgiving when someone treats us badly.

5. When the author asks the reader to consider the underlined question in paragraph three, she is being

1. sympathetic.
②. ironic.
3. apathetic.
4. ridiculous.

6. The purpose of this selection is to

1. describe Irish culture and its literary elements.
2. entertain the reader by discussing how frantic humans get.
③. persuade the reader to be gentler to him/herself and others.
4. inform the reader of the latest research on stress.

**DIAGNOSTIC EXAM, PASSAGE ONE**

*The following is an excerpt from Mother Jones' autobiography written in 1925:* #11

From 1886 workers in the city of Chicago were involved in a movement for an eight-hour day. The city was divided into two angry camps. The working people were on one side—jobless, hungry, cold, fighting police with bare hands. On the other side were the employers, experiencing neither hunger nor cold, supported by the newspapers and by the police.

Extremists took advantage of the discontent to preach their doctrines. Speakers Used to address huge crowds on the windy shore of Lake Michigan. Although I never endorsed the philosophy of chaos, I often attended the meetings.

A bitterly cold winter set in in 1886. Long unemployment resulted in terrible suffering. Bread lines increased. Soup kitchens could not handle the masses. On Christmas day, hundreds of poverty-stricken people in rags, paraded down Prairie Avenue before the mansions of the their employers, carrying a black flag (symbolizing the motto "never surrender.") I thought the parade an insane move as it only served to make the police more savage—and the public less sympathetic.

The first of May ushered in the eight-hour day uprising. The newspapers had done everything to alarm the people. All over the city there were strikes and walkouts. Employers quaked in their boots. They saw revolution. The workers in the McCormick Harvester Works gathered outside the factory. Bricks were thrown. Windows were broken. Some one turned in a riot call.

The police without warning charged down upon the workers, shooting into their midst. Many were trampled under horses' feet, and young men and young girls were shot.

Time marched on. On November 11, the leaders of the extremists in the eight-hour day movement were hanged. Even though the dead were buried, their cause was not. The struggle for more human conditions in the workplace still lives on.

—angelfire, internet

7. It is implied that the extremists' main protest centered on

1. police brutality.
2. unfair newspaper coverage.
3. unemployment.
4. unreasonably long work hours.

8. We can infer that Mother Jones attended the speeches on the lake because

1. she endorsed chaos.
2. her friends were the extremists.
3. she was interested in the movement. *she kept up-to-date*
4. she wanted to express her discontent. *with their activities*

9. Mother Jones' attitude toward the parade on Christmas Day was one of

1. sympathy.
2. skepticism.
3. condescension.
4. understanding.

10. The protesters paraded on Prairie Avenue because

1. that was the street where the rich employers lived.
2. that was where the soup kitchens were located.
3. it was the main avenue in Chicago.
4. the police would not attack them in a family neighborhood.

11. The selection is written from the point of view of

1. the workers.
2. the police.
3. Mother Jones.
4. the newspaper editor.

12. The events depicted in the selection took place in

1. the early 1900's.
2. before the writer was born.
3. after the death of the writer.
4. the late 1800's.

The great prophet of Islam is Muhammad who was born about 570 AD in Mecca, a city in western Arabia. Muhammad's father died before he was born, and the boy's mother died when he was six years old, so Muhammad was raised in the care of relatives.

Mecca was located along a caravan route used for transporting goods from Asia to Syria and other parts of the Middle East. Muhammad was involved in this trade and became the business agent of a wealthy widow, Khadijah, whom he married when he was about twenty-five (she was forty).

Muhammad appears to have spent much time fasting and praying. In 610 he received a revelation from the angel Gabriel that he was to be the Messenger of God—to recite the words of God for his people. These recitations were later collected into the holy book of Islam, the Koran.

While pagan polytheism was the predominant religious belief of Arabia, there were Christians and Jews there with whom Muhammad had come into contact. Muhammad preached a message that there was but one God, Allah, and Muhammad was his prophet. He warned of a judgment day and urged the Meccans to renounce false idols and to accept the bounty and compassion of the one God. The dominant Quraysh tribe rejected his message. They feared that Mecca would lose its place as a pilgrimage center where numerous gods could be worshiped in an ancient building known as the Kaaba. Muhammad became subject to a boycott. He was nevertheless safe as long as his uncle, who was head of a clan associated with the Quraysh tribe, offered him protection. But in 619 both his uncle and his wife, Khadijah, died. The new clan leader refused to grant Muhammad protection. In 622 Muhammad and about 70 of his followers decided to flee Mecca and go to Medina which is located about 250 miles to the north.

Muhammad had been invited to Medina to act as a peace arbitrator among the feuding tribes. Medina was a city with three Jewish clans as well as a large Arab population. Muhammad made himself the leader of the Arabs of the city and eventually eliminated the Jews (some by execution) who resisted his efforts at conversion. Later he began attacks on Mecca and in 630 he marched into Mecca with little bloodshed. He granted a general amnesty and made Mecca the center of worship of his new religion. When Muhammad died in 632, Islam was the religion of the greater part of the Arabian peninsula.                -Kehoe, et. al, pp. 275-6

**13. As is stated in the passage, Muhammad was**

1. born in Medina.
2. raised in a caravan.
3. cared for by relatives.
4. left at an orphanage.

**14. The Quraysh tribe**

1. believed in one God.
2. feared Muhammad.
3. believed in Muhammad.
4. rejected Muhammad's message.

**15. The passage implies that Muhammad's uncle**

1. was not influential with the Quraysh tribe.
2. cared about Muhammad.
3. thought Muhammad was crazy.
4. was a Christian.

**16. Polytheism, as used in paragraph two, most nearly means belief in**

1. many gods.
2. multiple wives.
3. Christianity.
4. Islam.

**17. We can infer that**

1. Muhammad had a large Jewish following.
2. Mecca was more progressive than Medina.
3. Muhammad felt threatened by the Jews of Medina.
4. Islam could never replace polytheism.

**18. The author's purpose in writing the selection is to**

1. inform.    biographical material
2. persuade.
3. classify.
4. contrast.

**DIAGNOSTIC EXAM, PASSAGE THREE**

19. The style of writing employed is

1. informal.
2. scientific.
3. (academic.) historical and biographical selection,
4. argumentative. including dates, names, places

**DIAGNOSTIC EXAM, PASSAGE THREE**

For many of us, sleep is a fairly routine phenomenon. It is true that the amount of sleep that allows us to function most efficiently may vary across individuals. It is also true that the amount of sleep we experience each night tends to decrease as we move into adulthood and old age.

Most of us are also likely to have found that some nights getting to sleep seems harder than normal. However, most of the time, we probably don't think much about sleep. For some individuals, however, sleep is not typically a routine process.

Insomnia, which is variously described as a lack of sleep, a loss of sleep, or poor sleep, is one commonly reported sleep disorder. Many people who believe that they have problems sleeping turn to sleep medications for help. Mendleson estimated that 20 million prescriptions for sleep medications are written per year, with large numbers of additional people seeking help from over-the-counter medications. However, many psychologists, like Carlson, consider sleeping aids to be one of the main causes of sleeping problems. People develop a tolerance to these medications, requiring larger doses as time goes on.

A second sleep disorder is sleep apnea. A person suffering from sleep apnea stops breathing during sleep, which results in a build-up of carbon dioxide, which causes the person to wake up gasping for air. Sleep apnea may be related to narrow airways, more common in obese people, especially men. The frequency of sleep apnea also increases among the elderly, where the cause is often a malfunction of the brain mechanisms that control respiration. In infants, sleep apnea may be a possible cause of sudden infant death syndrome.

Narcolepsy is another common sleep disorder. It appears to occur because certain components of sleep are activated at inappropriate times. The disorder may run in families. The sudden overwhelming urges to sleep, called sleep attacks, which a

narcoleptic experiences at various times during waking hours, constitute the primary symptom of narcolepsy.

-Kestner, et. al., pp. 87-8

20. The reader can infer that Mendelson

1. is a professor.
2. believes sleep aids are unnecessary.
3. had a child who died due to sleep apnea.
4. is interested in the number of people taking sleep aids.

21. Contrary to popular thinking, Carlson believes that

1. sleep medications are lethal.
2. sleep medications complicate existing sleeping problems.
3. doses of sleep medications remain the same over time.
4. it is possible to reduce dosages of sleep medications over time.

22. A person with sleep apnea

1. stops breathing during sleep.
2. builds up oxygen while sleeping.
3. remains asleep during the night.
4. has wider airways.

23. Sleep attacks are best described as

1. tossing and turning.
2. insomnia.
3. narcolepsy. *direct explanation*
4. fitfulness.

24. In the passage, the author

1. contrasts types of sleep disorders.
2. attempts to persuade the reader to consider his views on narcolepsy.
3. prioritizes sleep disorders.
4. classifies types of sleep disorders. *types listed: insomnia apnea narcolepsy*

25. Insomnia can be described as all of the following except

1. sleep walking. *process of elimination*
2. loss of sleep.
3. poor sleep.
4. lack of sleep.

**DIAGNOSTIC EXAM, PASSAGE FOUR**

Verbal abuse is a kind of battering which does not leave evidence comparable to physical battering. It can, however, be just as painful, and recovery can take much longer. The abuser often cloaks his attack in a "what's wrong with you, making a big thing out of nothing" attitude. Often, for the verbally abused woman, there is no other witness to her reality and no one who can understand her experience. Friends and family may see the abuser as a nice guy and, certainly, he sees himself as one.

The victim of abuse lives in a confusing world. In public she is with one man, in private he may become another. Behind doors common occurrences may include: 1) subtle diminishing; 2) angry outbursts; 3) cool indifference; 4) one-upmanship; 5) witty sarcasm; 6) silent withholding; r 7) unreasonable demands.

Many women try every approach to improve their relationship: explaining, overlooking, asking, begging, living their lives independently, or not asking for too much. Nothing seems to work. Evans, a writer in this area, indicates that none of these tactics work because verbal abuse is an issue of control, a means of holding power over another. The abuser is not interested in making the relationship better: s/he is interested in power over the victim and in a tactic called "crazy-making."

The effects of verbal abuse are primarily qualitative. That is, they cannot be seen like the effects of physical abuse. There are no physical signs of injury—no black eyes or broken bones. The intensity of anguish which the victim suffers determines the extent of the injury.

Evans states that we should remember three critical aspects of verbal abuse when attempting to analyze it: one, the abuse most often takes place behind closed doors; two, the abuser denies the abuse; and three, physical abuse is always preceded by verbal abuse.
                                                                    -Evans, pp. 17-19

26. According to the selection, the general public at first glance considers the verbal abuser as

1. mentally unstable.
2. a physical abuser.
3. a nice guy.
4. somewhat aggressive.

27. In the context of this passage, it is implied that crazy-making (paragraph three) involves

1. the victim making the abuser crazy.
2. the abuser making the victim crazy.
3. women believing men are crazy.
4. friends viewing the couple as incompatible.

28. The reader can conclude that the reason women's approaches to improving their relationships do not work is that

1. women do not try hard enough.
2. the victim is too aggressive.
3. the abuser pretends the relationship is fine the way it is.
4. the approaches have not been tested scientifically.

29. Qualitative, as underlined, most nearly indicates that the effects of verbal abuse

1. can not be seen. *direct explanation*
2. are clearly visible.
3. are hazy and clouded.
4. are indeed minimal.

30. Evans would agree with which of the following statements?

1. Physical abuse may follow verbal abuse.
2. Verbal abuse is always followed by physical abuse.
3. Physical abuse is the same as verbal abuse.
4. Verbal abuse is not as harmful as physical abuse.

31. The main idea of the selection is best expressed by the first sentence of which paragraph?

1. 4th paragraph
2. 2nd paragraph
3. 1st paragraph *1st sentence*
4. 3rd paragraph

The American landscape was radically altered by "suburban sprawl." A pioneer in this development was William Levitt, who in 1949 built the first subdivision of homes on Long Island—17,500 of them, all exactly alike. Due to memories of inadequate housing during the war, young married couples stood in line for four days to purchase one of his basic four-room houses which sold for less than $10,000, including everything from landscaping to kitchen appliances. Now the American Dream seemed within the grasp of ordinary Americans: they could now build their own nests.

And nests they were. The home became child-centered, and family size was on the rise. One sociological study reported in the late 1940s that a wife was impregnated every seven seconds. The 37.5 million households in 1945 had increased to 53 million by 1960, largely the result of masses of subdivisions mushrooming across the nation. Moreover, women's magazines like *Ladies'Home Journal* began to promote the woman's role as a homemaker, gardener, and den mother. In 1954 *McCall's* coined the word "togetherness" to describe the new commitment to a close family.

Eager for the approval of others, young people were as sedate and conservative in their values as their parents. One observer wrote that the "dedication of bourgeois America to personal security" had produced "a generation with strongly middle-aged values." By 1955 twenty-two percent of all college students majored in business, emulating their parents' desire for the job, the home, and the station wagon filled with kids. One poll in the 1950s revealed that three of youth's greatest heroes were Joe DiMaggio, Doris Day, and Roy Rogers.

-Solberg, et al, pp. 245-7

32. It is stated that couples stood in line to purchase basic houses because

1. the homes were cheaper because appliances were not included.
2. they wanted to say they were first to buy a subdivision home.
3. they remembered the inadequate housing situation during the war.
4. they wanted homes with appliances included.

33. The phrase, within the grasp of ordinary Americans, most nearly means

1. Americans could now be ordinary.
2. couples now had more than $10,000.
3. Americans now had a yard.
4. most Americans could now buy their own homes.

*direct explanation :*

34. We can infer from the passage that in the late 1940s the population

1. increased.
2. decreased.
3. stayed the same.
4. was not important.

35. The main idea of the last paragraph is that young people of the 1950s

1. were liberal-minded.
2. majored in business.
3. were like their parents.
4. popularized Joe DiMaggio.

36. The author illustrates his point in paragraph two by

1. contrasting *Ladies Home Journal* and *McCall's* magazines.
2. telling a story.
3. giving personal testimony.
4. describing the American household. *information on*
   *1. family size*
   *2. woman's role*
   *3. new term coined*

One by one, the names were called out, names of law enforcement officers who died in the line of duty in 1988. And as each name was read, a widow, or a mother, or a child would step forward and place a flower in a gigantic wreath.

Some were stoic, as if they had learned to manage their pain, at least in public. Some wept. Some needed assistance in returning to their seats. Around them, the colleagues of their loved one stood proudly in uniform for two hours, impervious to the soaking rain.

Mourners placed 161 flowers in the wreath, each representing a death that had taken place the year before—the loss of a man or woman who willingly undertook risks most of us would never even consider taking.

As members of "the thin blue line," they risked their lives every day to protect their communities and their nation from the terror and destruction of crime. Yet our nation seems to have simply forgotten their service—and their sacrifice.

Of course, these fallen heroes are remembered by their families and friends. But, as years pass, the newspaper clippings yellow and crumble. The flowers so carefully saved from the funeral spray turn to dust.

As Chairman of the National Law Enforcement Officers Memorial Fund, I believe that people do care—but that many of us, busy with our own preoccupations, overlook the need to pay homage to those who give their lives in our service.

Though an estimated 30,000 law enforcement officers have died in the line of duty since America's beginnings, we as a nation have created no monument to honor their sacrifices. There's no stately building or peaceful garden dedicated to their memory.
                                          -Clark, pp. 1-2

37. The phrase the thin blue line refers to

1. funeral procession.
2. police force.
3. national law enforcement memorial fund.
4. the margin of risk a police officer takes.

38. Overall, the writer uses which of the following to get her point across?

1. journalistic reporting
2. definition
3. persuasion      *invoking sympathy through*
4. comparison      *description to show officers have been forgotten*

39. The word colleagues (paragraph two) most nearly means

1. college mates.
2. relatives.
3. superiors.
4. fellow officers.   *description*

40. The tone of the passage is

1. somber.      *use of adjectives and verbs*
2. distrustful.      *"stoic"*
3. suspenseful.      *"wept"*
4. impartial.      *"fallen heroes"*

41. Since America's beginnings how many officers have died in the line of duty?

1. 3,000,000.
2. 300.
3. 3,000,
4. 30,000.

42. The writer implies that police officers who have fallen

1. are remembered by no one.
2. should receive more recognition.
3. usually have no family to pay for burial.
4. are given elaborate funereal services.

Anne Hyde was appointed a maid of honor at the court of Mary, Princess of Orange. There Anne met James, the brother of the princess (and King), for the first time.

It was an unpopular match from the start. Strongest opposition came from James's mother, the Queen Dowager, who did everything in her power to prevent her second son's marriage with a commoner. It was totally unacceptable. Indeed, if James's older brother, King Charles, were to die without an heir, then Anne (a commoner) would become Queen. The Queen Dowager even tried to stop the wedding and reprimanded her son for "having such low thoughts as to wish to marry such a woman." The situation was unthinkable. But James was unmoved. The Queen Dowager's pleadings did nothing but strengthen James's resolve—and, anyway, Anne was already pregnant.

They were married by the chaplain privately around midnight. No sooner had the wedding taken place than James began to have misgivings about his wife and looked for ways to reverse the situation. But James needed grounds to break the marriage. Conveniently, there were rumors that the child was not his.

Princess Mary, who not long before had welcomed Anne into her household, was less than amused and pressed her brother to end the marriage. Even Anne's own father, Edward Hyde, refused to support his daughter. He felt that to incur the wrath of the royal family could easily endanger his own position in the government. Anne's father even suggested to Charles, the King, that he should send his daughter to the Tower and have her executed by act of Parliament for such behavior. The King, having reluctantly given his consent to his brother's marriage, would not go back on his word.

—Wallace & Taylor, p. 104

43. Reprimanded her son most nearly means

1. talked to him.
2. scolded him. *Queen Dowager angry*
3. provoked him.
4. begged him.

44. The Queen Dowager did not want James to marry because she believed

1. Anne was already married.
2. her other son, Charles, was in love with Anne.
3. he was marrying beneath his position.
4. she would lose influence over him.

45. The Queen Dowager's attitude toward Anne was

1. venomous and condescending. *"commoner" "low"*
2. loving and caring. *"unacceptable"*
3. sympathetic but strict. *"unthinkable"*
4. undisturbed and indifferent.

46. The passage implies that James was going to marry Anne

1. to spite the king.
2. for her money.
3. to protest social customs.
4. because she was pregnant.

47. After the marriage, everyone supported James's desire for annulment except

1. Anne's father.
2. the King.
3. the Queen Dowager.
4. Princess Mary.

48. Based on the information given in the last paragraph, we can conclude that

1. James got the annulment.
2. Anne was sent to the Tower.
3. Anne remained married to James. *The King would not*
4. Anne was executed. *Consent to an annulment*

**DIAGNOSTIC EXAM. PASSAGE EIGHT**

Whether one calls Australia the world's smallest continent or the largest island, it is a land of fascinating contrasts. Almost the size of the U.S., Australia has a population of under 18 million. Australia is also the only continent inhabited by a single nation, although one in five Australians was born overseas.

In Australia, untamed nature is never far from technological civilization. While this proximity is a major attraction to the visitor, it also poses risks that may not be obvious: sharks may lurk in the blue waters of the golden beaches which stud the coastline; the innocent-looking bush stretching from the roadside is likely to be a treacherous thicket. Hardly a weekend goes by without search parties seeking bush walkers—often allegedly experienced—who have become lost in the maze. Mostly they are found. Also, the Australian countryside rarely radiates mellow serenity. More often it appears harsh and alien at first sight. Indeed, one's first encounter with nature in Australia may evoke a feeling of puzzlement, even dismay. After all, the first Europeans who landed there were shocked when they surveyed their surroundings.

While the major resort areas or the big cities provide maximum creature comforts for the most demanding visitor, trips off the beaten track or to the sparsely populated hinterland, called the Outback, need careful preparation by competent experts, for there the traveler will be left very much alone.

These are sensible warnings only. They are not intended to dampen the traveler's interest in surfing or exploring the bush. On the contrary, by using common sense and readily available advice, the visitor will enjoy a safe Australian vacation, eventually falling in love with the melancholy beauty of much of the continent.

-Barcs, pp.43-44

DIAGNOSTIC EXAM, PASSAGE NINE

49. The purpose of the first paragraph is to

1. persuade the reader to visit Australia.
2. contrast Australia to the U.S.
3. prove that most Australians are not born there.
4. give some facts about Australia.

50. Hinterland, as underlined, is best described as

1. urban.
2. relaxing.
3. uninhabited. *direct explanation*
4. gloomy.

51. Maze, as used in the second paragraph, is a referent for

1. treacherous thicket. *long explanation*
2. bush walker.
3. studded coastline.
4. technological civilization.

52. The author suggests that the "untamed nature" of Australia

1. is serene.
2. may be dangerous.
3. is unattractive in appearance.
4. swallows up all who try to experience it.

53. In the last paragraph, the writer attempts to

1. dampen the traveler's interest.
2. warn the reader of dangers lurking.
3. ease the reader's mind about visiting.
4. encourage the reader not to visit Australia.

54. In the first paragraph, the reader can infer Australia is unique because

1. it is inhabited by 18 million people.
2. it houses major resort areas.
3. it has more visitors than any other continent.
4. the continent is inhabited by a single nation.

*"it is the only continent..."*

Because human beings are so remarkably adept at using language and because they also are reasonably accurate at predicting how others will respond, they acquire the ability to lie. Children usually have a lot to learn about lying and can easily be caught when they fib. With adults, however, it's not so easy to detect the person who is not telling the truth. Is an employer able to determine whether a job applicant is concealing his or her past? Can police investigators tell whether the suspect is truthful when they claim total innocence? In spite of the pride that many people take at being able to spot liars, even well trained interrogators are not much better at telling who is lying, and who is telling the truth.

Employers and law enforcement personnel may use a polygraph (commonly known as a lie detector) in their quest to gain the truth. Traditional polygraphs measure a person's heart rate, blood pressure, breathing rate, and skin conductivity, based on perspiration. Other forms of lie detectors attempt to measure audible and inaudible frequencies in the words that a person speaks. The assumption behind all of these forms of lie detection is that not telling the truth will create some emotional reactions. Machines that record biological arousal can measure these emotional reactions.

Unfortunately (from law enforcement's point of view) using a lie detector is not that simple For some people, just being "hooked up" to a machine can cause stress that makes truth versus untruth indistinguishable. Questions asked of the suspect might also be personally embarrassing, causing an emotional reaction in an innocent person.

On the other hand, guilty people may beat the polygraph: some might feel no emotion, and show no autonomic arousal when they lie. Delusional people who have lost contact with reality may actually believe their lies.

It would be nice to have a simple way of finding the truth; unfortunately, there's not one. Research on the validity of polygraph results documents their unreliability.

-Kestner, et. al., pp. 376-377

1. It is implied that polygraphs are more likely to be used by

1. psychologists.
2. law enforcement.
3. personal assistants.
4. judges.

2. The main idea of the passage is that

1. polygraph results are reliable.
2. autonomic arousal can occur for many reasons.
3. polygraph results are not very reliable. *last sentence*
4. human beings have acquired the ability to lie.

3. The word quest as used in the passage most nearly means

1. search. *signal word = truth*
2. agenda.
3. road.
4. negligence.

4. Most professionals who utilize lie detectors assume that someone telling a lie

1. does not react emotionally or physically.
2. can be detected easily.
3. can not even answer baseline questions without reacting.
4. responds emotionally when hooked up to a lie detector.

5. The author of the selection would probably agree that

1. an individual's blood pressure changes when s/he is lying.
2. an individual's blood pressure does not change when s/he is lying.
3. an individual's blood pressure goes down when s/he is lying.
4. physical reactions are not considered when measuring whether or not a person is lying.

6. The underlined phrase delusional people most nearly means

1. individuals grounded in reality.
2. individuals who take drugs.
3. individuals grounded in fantasy.
4. individuals interested in facts and statistics.

**SIMULATED EXAM ONE, PASSAGE ONE**

Frodo took it from his breeches-pocket and handed it slowly to the wizard. Gandalf held it up. "Can you see any markings on it?" He asked.

"No," said Frodo. "There are none; it is quite plain."

"Well, then, look!" To Frodo's astonishment the wizard threw it suddenly into the glowing corner of the fire.

"Wait!" he commanded, giving Frodo a quick look from under his bristling brows. Gandalf got up, closed the shutters, and drew the curtains. The room became dark and silent, except for the clack of Sam's shears, now nearer to the window.

For a moment the wizard stood looking at the fire; then he stooped and removed the ring with the tongs, and grasped it in his hands.

"Take it," boomed Gandalf. "It is quite cool. Hold it up. And look closely."

As Frodo did so, he now saw fine lines—lines of fire that formed piercingly bright letters. "I cannot read the fiery letters," said Frodo in a quivering voice.

"No, but I can," replied Gandalf. "The letters are Elvish, of an ancient <u>mode</u>, but the language is that of Mordor, which I will not utter here. But in common tongue they say: *One Ring to bring them all and in the darkness bind them.*

Last night I told you of Sauron, the Dark Lord. This is the One Ring that he lost many ages ago, and he must *not* get it."

Frodo sat silent and motionless. Fear seemed to stretch out a vast hand. "I wish the ring had never come to me."

"So do I," said Gandalf, "and so do all who live to see such times. But that is not for them to decide. All we have to decide is what to do with the time that is given us."

-Tolkien, pp. 54-56

7. The author implies that Sauron can be compared to

1. the devil.
2. an angel.
3. God.
4. a goblin.

8. From the last two paragraphs, the reader can conclude that

1. Gandalf is not a very powerful wizard.
2. Frodo is too fearful to act.
3. Gandalf is afraid of Sauron.
4. Frodo must make a decision.

9. The passage emphasizes

1. storytelling. *< dialogue and action*
2. religious teachings.
3. persuasive techniques.
4. argumentative writing.

10. The underlined word, <u>it</u>, in the first sentence refers to

1. the wizard.
2. the markings.
3. the ring.
4. Frodo's pocket.

11. In this context the word <u>mode</u>, as underlined, most probably means

1. Elf.
2. common tongue.
3. jewelry.
4. style. *< signal word = "letters"*

12. An overriding theme of this selection could be titled

1. good, evil, and Sauron.
2. Gandalf, Frodo, and the ring. *< each is threaded throughout the passage*
3. Frodo confronts Sauron.
4. elves have a language of their own.

13. From the selection, the reader can assume that Sam is

1. Frodo's friend.
2. an elf.
3. the gardener.
4. a wizard.

**SIMULATED EXAM ONE, PASSAGE TWO**

The idea, that some stimuli can not be consciously perceived but can still affect our behavior, first received national attention in the 1950s. James Vicary claimed that when he flashed the messages "Buy Popcorn" and "Drink Coca-Cola" on the movie screen at very short durations during a movie, popcorn and soft-drink sales increased significantly. The idea that people were being unconsciously controlled by subliminal messages became a concern for many, including the Federal Communications Committee.

The issue in the 1980s was the controversy of whether or not subliminal information involving satanic and other antisocial messages was being used to influence teenagers. It was claimed that certain popular heavy-metal groups were imbedding these messages in the music by recording backwards. Parents, clergy, and government officials voiced great concern over subliminal persuasion. A study designed specifically to evaluate the ability of listeners to identify the meaning of backward statements found no evidence that the meaning of the backward speech recordings was understood (Vokey & Read).

The most recent interest in subliminal perception has been generated by the marketing of so-called subliminal audio tapes. These tapes, which appear to contain only relaxing sounds, are claimed to contain subliminal messages for helping people improve things like memory or self-esteem, or to aid in weight loss. The idea is that if one plays the tape while asleep, the subliminal message will have its claimed effect. In a well controlled experiment to test the effects of such tapes, Greenwald and others found no evidence that the subliminal content of the tapes had any effect.

-Kestner, et. al., p. 112

14. Subliminal perception was first discussed in

1. the 1980s.
2. the mid 1990s.
3. the early 1990s.
4. the 1950s.

15. It was claimed that satanic messages were imbedded in

1. federal communications.
2. subliminal audio tapes.
3. music recordings.
4. ads in movie theaters.

16. The author's opinion is that

1. subliminal messaging has little effect.
2. subliminal messaging makes an impact.
3. satanic messages in music are acceptable.
4. audio tapes help people lose weight.

17. In the context of the passage, the advertising of "Buy Popcorn" and "Drink Coca-Cola" was

1. traditional in its technique.
2. subliminal in its technique.
3. recorded backwards.
4. put on audio tapes.

18. We can infer that James Vicary

1. owned stock in Coca-Cola.
2. believed subliminal advertising worked.
3. was trying to cheat the public.
4. was a member of the Federal Communications Committee.

19. In the second paragraph the word issue most nearly means

1. edition.
2. offspring.
3. information.
4. concern. &lt; signal words = verb "to be"
                              controversy
              context clue = direct definition

**SIMULATED EXAM ONE, PASSAGE THREE**

Coming out of China, the Black Death reached the shores of Italy in the spring of 1348 unleashing a rampage of death across Europe. By the time the epidemic played itself out three years later, up to fifty percent of Europe's population had fallen victim to the pestilence.

One form derived its name from the swellings or buboes that appeared on a victim's neck, armpits or groin. Although some survived the painful ordeal, the manifestations of these lesions usually signaled the victim had a life expectancy of up to a week. Infected fleas that attached themselves to rats and then to humans spread this bubonic plague.

A second variation, pneumatic plague, attacked the respiratory system and was spread by merely breathing the exhaled air of a victim. It was much more virulent than its bubonic cousin: life expectancy was measured in one or two days.

The Italian writer Giovanni Boccaccio lived through the plague as it ravaged the city of Florence in 1348. Boccaccio wrote a graphic description of the effects of the epidemic on his city: "The symptoms were not the same as in the East, where a gush of blood from the nose was the plain sign of inevitable death; but it began with certain swellings in the groin or under the armpit. They grew to the size of a small apple or an egg. . . . and were vulgarly called tumors. In a short space of time these tumors spread all over the body. Soon after this, black or purple spots appeared on the body, a certain sign of death.

The violence of this disease was that it was highly contagious. No doctor's advice, no medicine could alleviate this disease. Very few recovered; most people died within about three days of the appearance of the tumors."

-The Black Death, internet

20. According to the passage, once a victim noticed buboes on his body

1. he only had up to a week to live.
2. he would soon be well.
3. his respiratory system would fail.
4. he would only live for two days.

21. In paragraph two, these lesions refers to

1. neck, armpits or groin.
2. manifestations.
3. buboes. *referent found in first sentence of second paragraph*
4. pestilence.

22. Virulent, as underlined, is best defined as

1. pneumatic.
2. vicious.   *signal: : = direct explanation*
3. controversial.
4. innocuous.

23. According to the passage, in regard to the plague that ravaged Florence, a certain sign of death was

1. a swelling the size of an egg.
2. a gush of blood.
3. an infected rat living in the house.
4. a black spot.

24. We can infer that the Black Death also ravaged

1. the West.
2. Russia.
3. China. *first sentence*
4. the U.S.

25. Alleviate, as used in the last paragraph, most nearly means

1. enhance.
2. worsen.
3. propagate.
4. make bearable.

Ask anyone about wolf vocalizations and the howl invariably springs to mind. It is howling that defines the wolf and fascinates us.

The center of a wolf's universe is its pack and howling keeps the pack together. Some have speculated that howling strengthens the social bonds between packmates; that may be so, but chorus howls can also end in nasty quarrels between packmates. Some members, usually the lowest-ranking, may actually be punished for joining in the chorus. Whether howling together actually strengthens social bonds among wolves, or just reaffirms them, is unknown.

We do know, however, that howling keeps packmates together physically. Because wolves range over vast areas to find food, they are often separated from one another. Of all their calls, howling is the only one that works over great distances. Its low pitch and long duration are well-suited for transmission
#30 in forests and across tundra.

When a wolf howls, not only can its packmates hear it, but so can any other wolf within range. These other wolves may be members of hostile adjacent packs that are competitors for territory and prey. (Pups, especially those under four months of age, love to howl and will usually reply to any howling they hear, even that of total strangers). In northern Minnesota where wolves are protected from humans, the primary cause of death for adult wolves is being killed by wolves from other packs.

There is one member of the pack who will
#26 tend to howl more boldly: the alpha male. The alpha male is the dominant male of the pack and father of the pups. He is most likely to howl and even approach a stranger—often with confrontation on his mind. One sign of this aggressiveness can be heard in his voice: his howls become even lower-pitched.

-Harrington, internet

26. According to the passage, the boldest of a wolf pack is

1. the pregnant female.
2. a pup.
3. the lowest-ranking male.
4. the alpha male. *see last paragraph*

27. According to the passage, howling serves in all of the following ways except to

1. keep members of the pack together physically.
2. locate lost pups.
3. keep hostile wolves away.
4. reaffirm social bonds.

28. In the second paragraph, them, refers to

1. wolves.
2. social bonds. *strengthens social bonds or reaffirms them*
3. members.
4. lowest-ranking packmates.

29. The main idea of paragraph three is

1. howling keeps members of the pack in close contact.
2. wolves range over vast areas to find food.
3. wolves live in forest and tundra.
4. wolves are often separated from one another.

30. As used in the passage, tundra, most probably means

1. forest.
2. treeless plains. *signal word = "across," indicating an expanse*
3. woodland.
4. oceans.

31. The author of this passage uses a style which is

1. informal but informative.
2. formal and informative.
3. scientific and analytical.
4. argumentative and persuasive.

**SIMULATED EXAM ONE, PASSAGE FIVE**

Cognitive theories of dreaming, like Cartwright's problem-solving theory, view dreams as having important psychological functions. The main function of dreams in Cartwright's theory is to help individuals solve their ongoing problems. Thus, rather than viewing the content or images in dreams as basically random selections from the various information stored in memory, Cartwright suggests that the images are selected to tell a story. They relate to recent experiences, especially experiences which have an emotional component. Dreams during the course of a night's sleep often have re-peated images, suggesting that these images are being activated by ongoing concerns rather than by some random process. Dream meaning relates to the status of our ongoing needs, and dreams function to assimilate new data and reorganize related memories. In #37 > times of stress or personal turmoil, when your emotions run high, the same parts of memory are likely to be activated during REM sleep. Thus, the effects of personal concerns on dreams are most likely to be seen by studying people under stress.

Data relevant to Cartwright's theory were thus provided by studies of dreaming in individuals undergoing a divorce. These studies have shown that depressed people going through a divorce are likely to enter their first REM state earlier than nondepress-ed individuals, and to stay in REM longer. The work of Cartwright and her colleagues also suggests that by incorporating what is stressing you into your dream and experi-encing the emotions that go with these sources of stress, the dream provides a way to work through and overcome what is troubling you.                    -Kestner, et. al., pp. 86-7

33. According to Cartwright, dreams relate to

1. a solitary experience.
2. experiences that have a rational component.
3. recent emotional experiences.
4. random selections from memory.

34. As underlined in the selection, assimilate most nearly means

1. delete.
2. isolate.
3. disregard.
4. absorb. <signal word - "and"

35. The passage states that the effects of personal concerns on dreams are most likely to be seen by

1. examining well adjusted people.
2. testing an individual's memory while awake.
3. analyzing individuals who have been married for many years.
4. studying people under stress.

36. The central focus of the passage is that

1. dreams attempt to make sense out of physiological activities in the brain.
2. dreams provide a way for individuals to work through their troubles.
3. Cartwright is the most well-known dream researcher.
4. divorced persons have the most insightful dreams.

37. The word turmoil most likely means

1. strife. <signal word = "or"; key word = stress
2. tranquility.
3. divorce.
4. harmony.

32. We can infer that REM refers to

1. Random-Effect-Memory.
2. a stage of dreaming <signal word = "sleep"
3. stress factors.
4. a problem-solving theory.

**SIMULATED EXAM ONE, PASSAGE SIX**

Amidst the Medieval and Gothic structures and the unique city scape filled with a mystique all its own, Florence embraces some of the most exemplary architectural masterpieces created during the Renaissance era. The name, which directly translates as "rebirth," led the way to the development of a new architectural form in thought that spanned from the 15th through the 16th centuries. Viewed as the greatest achievement attainable in the arts, these buildings were introduced by Italian architects. The structures were fashioned from a restored interest in classical Roman and Greek theories in art and architecture.

The one man credited with the rise of the Italian style in Renaissance architecture, is a Florentine son by the name of Filippo Brunelleschi. Standing at the threshold of Gothic and Renaissance, Brunelleschi began his artistic existence as a goldsmith and sculptor, but soon after he turned to architecture.

Perhaps one of the structures Brunelleschi is most noted for is the dome of Florence's cathedral. This is a masterful rendering of Brunelleschi's brilliance and ingenuity. With a drum already in existence, the Florentine community was faced with the problem of creating a dome structure that spanned the 140-foot diameter base. Not fearful of such a challenge, Brunelleschi solved this engineering dilemma. Since the space was too large for wooden supports and there was no room for buttressed walls, these traditional methods were tossed. In their place Brunelleschi created new methods as well as the machinery to execute them. The dome was created around an octagonal section made of twenty-four ribs. The dome was encased by a thin double shell that reduced the weight of the structure. To anchor the structure, a "lantern" was placed at the top.

Although Brunelleschi was credited with Renaissance ingenuity and aesthetics, this dome was not truly reflective of his own architectural style. In fact, his solutions to the massive structure derived from Gothic building principles. This fact only emphasizes

Brunelleschi's grandest achievement: he created the first successful representation of a merging of both Gothic and Roman building methods.
                                                                    -Smith

38. Renaissance, as used in the first paragraph, means

1. architecture.
2. era.
3. rebirth. *direct definition: next sentence*
4. masterpiece.

39. In the context of this passage, the buildings of Florence were based

1. solely on Brunelleschi's theories.
2. theories of sculpture.
3. on previous Florentine works.
4. on classical Roman and Greek theories.

40. According to the passage, Brunelleschi's grandest achievement was

1. the cathedral itself.
2. merging Gothic and Roman building methods.
3. his work as a sculptor.
4. creating a lantern to fortify the dome.

41. The reader can infer that during the Renaissance, Florence was considered

1. a rural community.
2. a village.
3. a region of city-states.
4. an urban environment. *signal phrase = "city scape" first sentence*

42. Brunelleschi's attitude toward building the dome was one of

1. fear.
2. enthusiasm.
3. indifference.
4. hopelessness.

One needs to recall that the expansionist period into the New World was dominated by different countries at different times. The Portuguese were the first great explorers and began their explorations in the African continent before they went into South America. Then they moved into the area of present-day Brazil; there they introduced the concept of African slavery. The Portuguese influence remained in Brazil; even today, the official language of Brazil is Portuguese.

The Spanish challenged Portugal's dominance and began to dominate the New World in a quest for gold. They solely were influential, controlling South and Central America, Mexico and a vast portion of the present-day United States. The Spanish plundered so much gold from the Native Americans that inflation was the result. There was so much gold in Spain after the Aztec, Maya and Incas were conquered that the Spanish actually cast their gold pieces with more gold than the piece was actually worth.

*#43* After 1588, with the sinking of the Spanish Armada, the Spanish influence in the New World waned. By this time England and France were competing for a piece of the New World wealth but the days of gold were gone. New commodities would have to replace the fabulous riches of gold.

For the French, dealing with the Native Americans for fur was a mainstay of their economic base; but the English, unlike the Spanish and French, were initially interested in permanent settlements, rather than trading and plundering. Whereas the Spanish and French tended to intermarry among the Native population, English men were accompanied by English women. By their settlement patterns, the European powers each left their legacy, or imprint, in the New World.

-Duke, pp. 7-8

*signal word*

43. Waned most nearly means

1. decreased. < *signal word: "sinking"*
2. increased.                    *cause and effect*
3. remained constant.
4. fluctuated.

44. A central theme of the passage is that during the expansionist period

1. Spain dominated the new World.
2. the French traded for furs with the Native Americans.
3. the English were marrying Native American women.
4. the New World was dominated at different times by different countries.

45. We can infer from the selection that the Spaniards

1. traded for gold.
2. stole the gold.
3. mined for the gold.
4. married into the tribes for gold.

46. According to the passage, all of the following statements are true about the French except

1. they married Native American women.
2. they took home vast amounts of gold. < *process of elimination*
3. fur trading was their economic base.
4. they came to the New World after the Spanish.

47. Imprint, as used in the last sentence, most nearly means

1. indentation.
2. document.
3. legacy.
4. seal.

48. According to the passage, the official language of Brazil is

1. Spanish.
2. Brazilian.
3. Mayan.
4. Portuguese.

**SIMULATED EXAM ONE, PASSAGE EIGHT**

The movie, *Gladiator*, though entertaining, does not accurately portray history, particularly when viewed through the roles of Commodus and Lucilla.

Commodus, who became emperor of Rome in 180, was not of average build, dark-haired, nor did he fight with his right hand as in the movie version. In reality, he had a strong physique, sported golden-blond hair, and fought with his left hand. Also, he was not always single: at the age of sixteen, he married Bruttia Crispina (whom he soon after executed for adultery).

In the movie version, Lucilla is the sister that Commodus lusts after. The picture of Commodus as a man starved for affection has some support in historical sources. In *Historia Augusta* the sexual excesses that are typically ascribed to a tyrannical ruler are true of the emperor's behavior. In historical sources, however, Lucilla is the only sister with whom Commodus is *not* accused of incestuous relations.

Not many of the facts of Lucilla's life were revealed in the movie: Lucilla is shown as a once-married mother with a son who is heir to the throne. Historically speaking, Lucilla was fourteen when she married, and she bore three children before she was widowed in her late teens. Her father forced her to remarry immediately. Lucilla had nothing in common with her new husband. Always in consultation with her mother, both Lucilla and her mother bitterly resented the marriage: she was only nineteen, and he was over fifty.

As the movie indicates, Lucilla plotted to kill Commodus in 182. Nothing happened to her in the movie, but we know from history books that she was summarily executed for her part in the plot.

As for Commodus, in the *Gladiator* he was killed in the arena in front of all of Rome. Actually, he did not die by a gladiator's hand; he was assassinated by assailants of his own court.

One needs to be wary of historical fiction, whether it is read or viewed on screen.

-Ward, internet

49. The author gets his point across through the use of

1. narration.
2. contrast. *movie vs. history*
3. description.
4. persuasion.

50. The author's tone is

1. mostly nostalgic.
2. extremely persuasive.
3. somewhat sarcastic.
4. a bit argumentative. *presents refutations using historical sources*

51. Ascribed to, as underlined, most nearly means

1. unrelated to.
2. discredited.
3. associated with.
4. inscribed.

52. The reader can infer that Commodus

1. was married for many years.
2. had many children.
3. was never married.
4. was married only for a short time.

53. The main idea of the selection is that

1. Commodus was like a dictator.
2. one needs to be wary of historical fiction.
3. you can not trust anyone, not even relatives.
4. Roman emperors were barbarians.

54. The phrase wary of most nearly means

1. cautious about *entire passage shows flaws in*
2. sure of. *historical fiction (i.e, movie)*
3. surprised by.
4. bored with.

**SIMULATED EXAM ONE. PASSAGE NINE**

Imagine the following <u>scenario</u>. You go to the supermarket one day to buy a half gallon of milk. You are in a hurry and pick up the milk and head over to the express checkout line where it is clearly stated on a sign that the line is for customers purchasing 12 items or less. You get in line and notice that the person in front of you has more than the maximum number of items. You count the items in that person's cart, all the way up to 18. You look at the sign above the checkout – it says 12 items maximum, and cash only. As you are counting again, the person behind the register starts scanning the items. Then you see the person in front of you pulling out a checkbook. What do you think? Can't they read? Can't they count? You look at the person and say to yourself, "This person is inconsiderate. I have to wait because the person in front of me is a jerk." All these thoughts indicate that you see this person's behavior as evidence of his or her inner traits—bad things are done by bad people, after all.

Now imagine a different <u>scenario</u>. The semester is coming to an end. Being the wonderful person that you are, you have invited all of your classmates to your place for a spaghetti dinner. On the day of the dinner, at about 5:00 p.m., you suddenly remember that you are hosting a dinner! You rush to the supermarket to get what you need. You buy four large jars of spaghetti sauce, four boxes of spaghetti, two packets of cheese, five loaves of garlic bread, two bags of tossed salad and a jumbo bottle of salad dressing. You now have 18 items and you rush to the checkout lines. They are jammed with people and their overflowing carts. You glance at the express checkout and see it's empty. So you rush over and quickly start putting your items on the belt. The check-out person scans the first couple of items and just then three people show up behind you with one or two items each.

Kestner, et. al. pp 438-9

1. <u>Scenario</u>, as used in the passage, most nearly means

1. situation. *long explanation - entire paragraph is a scenario*
2. landscape.
3. view.
4. problem.

2. The "you" in the first paragraph is irritated because

1. the cashier scanned the items without counting them.
2. the express lane closed as "you" approached it.
3. there was no milk.
4. someone got in the express lane who had more than 12 items.

3. The author gets his point across through the use of

1. sarcasm.
2. metaphor.
3. irony. *opposite of what is expected; you would not expect "you" to get in the*
4. figurative language. *express lane*

4. The reader can assume that "you" is a

1. teacher.
2. student.
3. cashier.
4. bad person.

5. The main idea of the passage is

1. don't do your friends any favors.
2. you can use the express lane under certain conditions.
3. a lot of jerks shop at the grocery store.
4. we give ourselves the benefit of the doubt, but we don't do the same for others. *conclude by contrasting the two scenarios.*

6. From the information we are given in the second scenario, the narrator

1. slows down the express lane.
2. calls the man behind him a jerk.
3. politely gives his place to the people behind him.
4. thinks that he, himself, is being a jerk.

**SIMULATED EXAM TWO, PASSAGE ONE**

As a growing number of students traveled to cities like Paris, Bologna, and Salerno in search of the best teachers, they unofficially established themselves in rented halls or rooms, hired the professors, and set the terms and conditions of their apprenticeship. These included the length and content of the lectures, the length of the academic terms, the fines the masters would have to pay for absence, for not covering the text in the required time, or for drawing less than five students to their lectures. At the University of Bologna, formally established by Emperor Barbarossa in 1158, the corporation of students controlled the university.

Not unlike university students of today, the all male medieval students attended lectures, took notes, studied for examinations, learned the art of oral disputation (questioning and thinking on one's feet). However, there were notable differences. Classes were taught in Latin, the universal language of the Church and scholarship, not in the everyday tongue. Every student who entered the university was expected to be well versed in classical Latin grammar and literature. For lectures, professors read authoritative texts, such as the Bible or the work of Aristotle, and made comments on these texts.

The curriculum consisted of studying the seven liberal arts. Upon the completion of the liberal arts curriculum after three or four years, if the student passed rigorous, comprehensive examinations, he would be awarded a baccalaureate degree. A significant difference between then and now is that students were examined orally and in public.

-Kehoe, pp. 324-5

7. We can assume from the passage that students during this era

1. were in control of their education.
2. had limited educational opportunities.
3. were more intelligent than students today.
4. never studied for a Master's degree.

8. According to the passage, students held professors accountable for all of the following *except*

1. the content of the course.
2. absences.
3. number of students in the classes.
4. writing of supplemental materials. *process of elimination paragraph one*

9. The University of Bologna was established by

1. the Church.
2. the emperor.
3. Aristotle.
4. a corporation of students.

10. According to the passage,

1. the majority of professors were women.
2. men believed women should stay at home and have children.
3. women were not taught Latin.
4. women did not study at university.

11. A major difference between students today and students of the 1150s is that students today

1. do not take notes during lectures.
2. are examined publicly.
3. are not taught in Latin.
4. do not attend university.

12. As used in the second paragraph, oral disputation most likely means

1. public debate. *signal = ( ) parentheses*
2. private submission.
3. private agreement.
4. public broadcasting.

Some of the same questions are asked over and over by Americans who become interested in Japan and things Japanese. Here are two of those questions, along with the answers.

*Hasn't Japan become "Americanized' in recent years?* It was about 125 years ago that Japan opened up to the outside world after a long period of seclusion. From that period (the Meiji era), Japanese delegations traveled everywhere, learning Western forms of every kind of institution: from schooling to transportation to sports. Baseball has been played in Japan for more than a century, for example. So while it is true that there has been a tremendous Western influence exerted in recent years, even as there has been something of a Japanization in the United States, it is not something new. Moreover, Americans are likely to think that such changes are continuous and cumulative, so that every day Japan is somehow less Japanese and more Western; but this has not been the case in the past and is not likely to be so in the future.

*Don't most people in Japan speak English?* The study of English is required in schools, but in the past and even today, a foreign language is studied mostly for the purpose of reading and, to a lesser extent, writing. Speaking a foreign language has not been important. This is because the chances of being able to speak with a foreigner were remote in the past. Also, in Japan what is written has always been valued in a way that speaking has not.

—Condon, pp. 75–6

14. In the context of this passage, Japanization (paragraph two) means that

1. Japan incorporated ideas from the U.S.
2. the U.S. incorporated ideas from Japan.  *transfer same idea of westernization*
3. U.S. citizens traveled to Japan.
4. Japan retained the good from outsiders and disregarded the bad.

15. The author would probably agree that

1. Western institutions are better than Japanese institutions.
2. Americanization of Japan is a new concept.
3. A complete Americanization of Japan will occur within the next century.
4. Japan will always remain Japanese.

16. It can be inferred from the passage that

1. English has always been taught in Japanese schools.
2. in Japan, English has become more important than the Japanese language.
3. if you want to speak English in Japan, look for an International School.
4. English conversation is not widely taught in Japan.

17. The author's style is

1. formal.
2. rigid.
3. chatty  *< Q&A question and answer format*
4. sarcastic.

18. The main idea of the passage is that

1. English is prevalent in Japan.
2. foreigners sometimes have the wrong idea about Japan.  *< existing ideas about Japan are refuted —*
3. it is difficult for Westerners to visit Japan.  *through question and answer format*
4. baseball is as popular in Japan as it is in the United States.

13. According to the article, Japan opened up to the world

1. when the United States was Japanized.
2. after the first baseball game was played.
3. over a century ago.
4. before the Meiji era.

**SIMULATED EXAM TWO, PASSAGE THREE**

The Prince swayed as he walked into the Chapel Royal. The two unmarried Dukes on either side of him moved closer. There was a hushed silence throughout the chapel and all attention was focused on two brilliant figures. The Prince swayed again, magnificent in his blue velvet but, as many noticed, looking confused and uneasy: and Caroline of Brunswick, shimmering in her bejewelled white satin with the diamond coronet on her head, looked a true Princess.

But the Prince kept his face turned from her. He was thinking of that other ceremony which had taken place in Mrs. Fitzherbert's house in Park Street. That was a real marriage; this was a farce; and he yearned for Maria, whom he knew he should never have left. If he had left her for marriage to this woman, it would have been a different matter, for this could be blamed on the exigencies of State. But he had deserted her for Lady Jersey whom he was discovering to be worthless.

And here he was at the altar about to be married to a woman he didn't know. He could see no virtue in her. To him she was unattractive, and even the fumes of brandy which dulled his senses could not free him from the future he visualized.

How different that ceremony in Park Street and the ecstasy which had followed.

Is it too late? But of course it was too late. Here he was, kneeling at the altar, and the Archbishop of Canterbury was about to conduct the ceremony.

He stumbled to his feet. He must get away. He could not go on with this. There was a sudden silence in the chapel. All eyes were on the Prince of Wales; all wondered what drama they were about to witness.

-Plaidy, pp. 130-132

20. The reader can deduce that the wedding is

1. for royalty.
2. a dream come true for the bride and groom.
3. a simple affair.
4. being held for the common folk.

21. Two brilliant figures (first paragraph) refers to

1. the two unmarried Dukes.
2. Mrs. Fitzherbert and Maria.
3. the Prince and Caroline of Brunswick.
4. Lady Jersey and the Prince of Wales.

22. As underlined in the passage, farce most nearly means

1. fact.
2. fake. contrast
3. luxury.
4. festival.

23. The Prince can be described as

1. exultant.
2. argumentative.
3. indifferent.
4. depressed.

24. The last paragraph leaves the reader with a sense of

1. ecstasy.
2. romance.
3. suspense.
4. hope.

19. We can infer from the selection that the Prince did not want to marry Caroline because

1. he was homosexual.
2. Caroline was a foreigner.
3. he was married to Lady Jersey.
4. he wanted to be with Maria.

**SIMULATED EXAM TWO, PASSAGE FOUR**

Covert behavior falls under the subject of psychology. One question that we face is how can one scientifically study a behavior that is private, implicit, and not publicly observed? For example, many people are involved in a romantic relationship. In such a relationship, it is very common for a person to express his or her love for the other person. Love is a wonderful emotion to experience, but can it be studied scientifically? In other words, how can we as psychologists test or prove that one person loves another? As an emotion, love is experienced as a private, internal event in one person. Do you take it on faith, or the other person's word? A scientist studying love would want proof or evidence that can be counted. He would want to define love in terms that may be seen and counted by another person. What could be measured? How about simply counting the number of times that one person tells the other "I love you"? Or hooking the person up to a machine that measures physiological responses like respiration, heart beat, blood pressure, or skin temperature. Or measuring the frequency of kissing, the amount of money one person spends on the other, or the duration that the couple spends time together. In fact, all of these measures could actually be graphed. Now, you might be saying to yourself, "That's not love; love is more complicated than all that and more personal."

In order to be studied scientifically, love or any other behavior has to be defined in terms that are open, unambiguous, public, and measurable. Therefore, when we think about science we have to remember one important point: science does not have all the answers for us.

-Kestner, et. al., pp. 4-5

26. The author conveys his point by

1. defining the field of "psychology."
2. describing a psychological event.
3. giving a testimonial.
4. presenting an example.

27. The reader can deduce from the information in the passage that

1. love does not exist.
2. love may never be studied in purely scientific terms.
3. all feelings are overt.
4. only scientists should study love.

28. In regard to a couple's relationship, all of the following can be measured except

1. kissing.
2. loving        *process of elimination*
3. time spent together.
4. money spent on one another.

29. A main focus of the passage is that

1. love can easily be defined.
2. science can measure covert behavior.
3. an individual should accept love on faith.
4. science does not always have the answers.

30. Most probably the author is a(n)

1. journalist.
2. psychologist.
3. sociologist.
4. expert on love.

25. The word implicit most nearly means

1. public.
2. illegal.
3. indirect.    *signal word = "private"*
4. not complicated.    *signal indicator = ,*

**SIMULATED EXAM TWO, PASSAGE FIVE**

Anorexia nervosa is an eating disorder that involves the relentless pursuit of thinness through starvation and/or extreme exercise behavior. It can eventually lead to death if it is not treated. It primarily affects females during adolescence and early adulthood, with the most common age (at onset) of 12 to 18; only about five percent of anorexics are male. Anorexia is rarely reported outside the Western industrialized countries of the world. Most anorexics are young, white females who are often bright, talented perfectionists usually preoccupied with feeling in control. Typically, they come from well-educated, middle-income, and upper-income families.

Although anorexics avoid eating, they do have a high interest in food. They cook for others, they talk about food, and they may insist on watching others eat. Anorexics have distorted body images, thinking that they will become attractive only when they become skeletal in appearance. As self-starvation continues and the fat content of the body drops to a bare minimum, menstruation usually stops for females.

Numerous causes of anorexia have been proposed including societal, psychological, and physiological factors. The societal factors most often cited are the current fashion trend and glorification of thinness. Psychological factors include motivation for attention, desire for individuality, and denial of sexuality. Physiological causes involve the hypothalamus, which becomes abnormal. There are long-term effects such as infertility, loss of muscle mass, brittle bones, and internal organ damage.

Death results in somewhere between two percent to ten percent of all anorexics.

-Kestner, et. al., pp. 364-5

31. It is suggested in the passage that anorexia is

1. found most often in Asian nations.
2. never found in a nonindustrialized country.
3. particularly evident in countries such as Australia, the United States, and England.
4. widespread throughout the world.

32. Anorexia is rarely found among

1. teenagers.
2. white females.
3. young males. *process of elimination*
4. well-educated young women.

33. All of the following are characteristics of an anorexic except

1. they have a high interest in food.
2. they become skeletal.
3. if female, they stop menstruating.
4. they have high self-esteem. *< process of elimination paragraph two*

34. According to the selection, infertility is an example of a

1. psychological effect of anorexia.
2. physiological effect of anorexia.
3. societal effect of anorexia.
4. mental effect of anorexia.

35. Physiological causes, as cited in the passage, most nearly relate to

1. emotions.
2. physics.
3. mental ability.
4. physical health. *Signal word = hypothalamus definition by example*

36. The author's tone is

1. factual. *< facts and scientific terms*
2. emotional.
3. immature.
4. dramatic.

The diversity of American Indian tribes precludes a unification of their religions and their belief systems. Anthropologists have compiled a huge trove of information detailing practices and beliefs of many different tribes. While there is an abundance of popularized versions of Native American spirituality by some researchers, the versions are not the products of the tribes or their members.

The origins of contemporary Native American religion can be traced back 30,000 to 60,000 years with the arrival of the first groups of people from northeast Asia. The religion of Native Americans has developed from the hunting taboos, animal ceremonialism, beliefs in spirits, and shamanism embraced by those early ancestors. Since these peoples settled in America slowly and in small groups over several thousand years, we still lack precise immigration knowledge.

The Native American Church, or Peyote Church, illustrates a trend of manipulating traditional Native American spirituality. It incorporates Christianity while moving away from tribal-specific religion. Christianity has routinely penetrated Native American spirituality in the last century. And in the last few decades, New Age spirituality has taken advantage of that trend. New Agers and charlatans alike have radically revised traditional Native American religions: in today's world, "Star Beings" (rather than buffalo) are pondered. Outraged Native Americans continue to expose those they see exploiting traditional Native American spirituality.

– "Native American Spirituality," internet

37. The word, precludes, in the first sentence most nearly means

1. makes easy.
2. prevents. *Contrast*
3. comes before.
4. comes after.

38. We can infer from the passage that popularized versions of Native American spirituality

1. have not correctly portrayed Native American religions and belief systems.
2. present accurate information about the immigration patterns of Native Americans.
3. do not give enough information to summarize Native American religions.
4. mostly emphasize how Christianity relates to Native American religion.

39. The author believes the Native Americans

1. descend from shamanism.
2. know the history of their migration.
3. migrated from Asia.
4. traveled from North America.

40. The author's attitude toward the Native American Church is one of

1. admiration.
2. skepticism. *signal word = "manipulating"*
3. neutrality.
4. exaltation.

41. The author uses "Star Beings" as an example of

1. the absurdity of New Agers making claims on Native American spirituality.
2. an advertising slogan for Native American religions.
3. traditional shamanistic practices.
4. a famous quote.

42. The purpose of the last paragraph is to

1. describe Christianity.
2. praise New Age spirituality.
3. expose manipulators of Native American spirituality.
4. condone New Agers' actions.

**SIMULATED EXAM TWO, PASSAGE SEVEN**

*#48*

With the onslaught of the many 'Crime TV' shows which focus on forensic science, such as *CSI: Crime Scene Investigation*, there has been a dramatic rise in the enrollment in forensics courses at the college level nationwide. One example of this phenomena is the interest shown by the student body at Purdue University in Indiana.

"Introduction to Forensic Science" is being offered for the first time Fall, 2003. The course introduces students to topics ranging from forensic crime scene techniques to entomology (interestingly, knowledge of the life cycles of insects help investigators determine the time and location of death). In addition, when investigating a crime, forensic scientists often draw upon the fields of biology, physics, botany, and computer science. Trace evidence, court room involvement, and new trends in forensic investigations are also covered in the course. Because analyzing and reconstructing a crime often requires expertise from medical examiners, such as psychologists and psychological profilers, students are exposed to guest lecturers in those fields. Neal Haskell, who established the UT Forensic Anthropology Facility to study human decomposition, is one such lecturer.

Other highlights of the course are: 1) opportunities for students to meet professionals in forensics, including crime laboratory investigators from local, state, and federal agencies; 2) provisions for students to review the cases solved by these professional crime scene investigators ; and 3) viewings of clips from television shows such as *CSI* and *Justice Files* which illustrate crime investigations in progress.

Aiming to satisfy student curiosity about crime investigations while providing information on the real-life science and technology used to solve crimes, the introductory course promises to be an important addition to the university curriculum.
-Gaidos, internet

43. Entomology is most integral to the field of forensics in regard to determining

1. who the victim is.
2. the time of death of the victim.
3. who the perpetrator is.
4. how the victim died.

44. The course "Introduction to Forensic Science" is being offered

1. at the University of Tennessee.
2. on television.
3. by guest lecturers from the local, state, and federal levels.
4. through Purdue University.

45. The central focus of the passage is

1. *CSI* is the most popular crime TV show.
2. new trends are covered in introductory forensics courses.
3. the enhanced forensic course will be an important addition to the Purdue University curriculum.
4. students view clips of crime TV shows during class.

46. The word onslaught, as used in the first sentence, most nearly means

1. sudden increase. *<signal word= "many"*
2. slow decrease.
3. canny advertising.
4. ongoing discussion.

47. The author illustrates his point by using

1. contrast.
2. argumentation.
3. narration.
4. example.

48. The reader can infer that

1. students take forensics classes to earn an easy "A."
2. crime TV shows are the reason students are now interested in forensics classes. *<first sentence*
3. guest lecturers have not been invited to forensic classes in the past.
4. traditionally, there has been wide interest in forensics classes across the country.

**SIMULATED EXAM TWO, PASSAGE EIGHT**

A mass murder of French Protestants in Paris sprang from the attempted murder of one man, Admiral Coligny, during the feast of Saint Bartholomew. The assassination order was given by a powerful woman, Catherine de' Medici, the Catholic king's mother. It was because the attack made on Coligny August 22 had failed that Catherine conceived the idea of a general massacre. She saw in this decision a means of preserving her influence over the king. Also, she wanted to prevent the vengeance of the Protestants who were outraged by the attack made on the Admiral.

Because the wedding of Henry of Navarre was being held that same week, many Protestants were in Paris, thus presenting the opportunity for mass murder. Toward midnight the troops took up arms in and around the Louvre, and Coligny's abode was surrounded. Besme, a man loyal to the Queen Mother, plunged a dagger into the admiral's breast and flung his body out the window. Coligny was the first victim; his death was followed by the killing of minor leaders and of all Protestants within reach of the soldiery. On the following morning blood flowed in streams; houses of the rich were pillaged regardless of the religious opinions of their owners. Some of the corpses were buried by grave-diggers of the Cemetery of the Innocents, but most were thrown into the Seine. The massacre continued even after a royal order to stop, and it spread from Paris into other regions of France.

News of the massacre was welcomed by the Pope and the King of Spain. Protestants however were horrified; the massacre continued into October, and an estimated 70,000 were killed in all of France. The killings rekindled the ill-will between Protestants and Catholics, and consequently there was a resumption of civil war.

-The Columbia Electronic Encyclopedia & New Advent, internet

49. We can infer that the King of Spain was

1. a Protestant.
2. related to the Pope.
3. a Catholic.   Signal word = "and"
4. married to Catherine de' Medici.

50. The massacre began

1. the week of the wedding of Henry Navarre.
2. a week after the assassination of the admiral.
3. in October.
4. upon the resumption of civil war.

51. Resumption most nearly means

1. end.
2. truce.
3. origination.
4. restart.  < signal word= "rekindled"

52. In paragraph two, the author makes her point through the use of

1. definition.
2. contrast.
3. analytical reasoning.
4. description. < Strong language; graphic portrayal of massacre

53. The reader can infer from the passage that Catherine de' Medici gave the assassination order on Coligny

1. because Coligny had ignored her.
2. to make amends with the Protestants.
3. because Henry of Navarre was getting married.
4. because he was a threat to her relationship with her son.

54. Besme was probably a(n)

1. soldier.
2. Protestant.
3. grave-digger.
4. outlaw.

#51

**SIMULATED EXAM TWO, PASSAGE NINE**

History will record 2001 as a watershed year in the international fight against terrorism. The events of September 11 of that year galvanized civilized nations as no other event has. The President's call to arms outlined a global campaign along multiple fronts: Diplomatic, Intelligence, Law Enforcement, and Military, among others.

First, State Department officials immediately began working with foreign officials to forge a coalition to support a response. The President and the Secretary of State met with leaders from more than 50 nations. In addition organizations such as the European Union and NATO took steps to enhance information sharing, to tighten border security, and to combat terrorist financ- ing. Public diplomacy remains in the forefront; the Department of State is aggressively seeking to counter distorted views of the United States overseas.

Second, cooperation among intelligence agencies around the world has expanded to unprecedented levels. Sharing of intelligence about terrorist movements and their planned attacks is an absolute prerequisite for success- ful interdiction. Such information is extremely valuable in identifying terrorist cells before they have a chance to act.

Third, law enforcement professionals have launched a global dragnet to identify, arrest, and bring terrorists to justice. The FBI has led the law-enforcement engagement, working with all federal, state, and local agencies. To date, more than 7,000 FBI agents have worked diligently to unravel the plans of Al-Qaida cells.

Last, on September 12, the UN Security Council condemned the attacks and reiterated the inherent right of collective self-defense in accordance with the UN Charter. NATO reiterated that "an armed attack on one or more of the allies in Europe or North America shall be considered an attack against them all." Consequently 136 countries offered a range of military assistance, 89 granted overflight authority, and 76 granted landing rights for U.S. military aircraft.

-U S Department of State, internet

**SIMULATED EXAM THREE, PASSAGE ONE**

1. The reader can infer that the President

1. understands that he needs support of other nations in the war against terror.
2. wants to unilaterally fight terrorism.
3. believes the European Union has done enough to fight terrorism.
4. doesn't care about the image of the U.S. overseas when it comes to fighting terrorism.

2. U.S. and foreign officials forged a coalition

1. because of the State Department.
2. to fight terrorism on all fronts.
3. to support a response to the President.
4. to create NATO.

3. Galvanized, as used in paragraph one, most nearly means

1. separated.
2. neutralized.
3. angered.
4. startled. < signal = "September 11"

4. The author would probably agree that

1. no Al-Qaida cells exist except in the Middle East.
2. the CIA should head all aspects of counter-terrorism efforts.
3. there are Al-Qaida cells in the U.S.
4. sharing of intelligence with other nations is dangerous.

5. In the last paragraph, the author uses the UN Security Council's condemnation as an example of a(n)

1. diplomatic support.
2. military support.
3. law-enforcement support.
4. intelligence support.

6. The phrase collective self-defense most likely means that if there is an attack on a European or North American ally,

1. nations will collectively vote on war strategies.
2. one nation will respond upon agreement from all.
3. only the nation attacked can respond.
4. an attack on one elicits a response from all.

7. The word interdiction most nearly means

1. solutions.
2. accusations.
3. prohibition. < signal phrase: "before they have a chance to act"
4. attacks.

What, then, was the Renaissance and why did it begin in Italy? One can often define an age by contrasting it to another. The Middle Ages revolved around the Age of Faith. The religion of Christianity gave definition to the Middle Ages. The search for salvation was the primary motivation for most people within Christendom. Individuals during the Middle Ages were God-centered. During the Middle Ages, society was predominantly agrarian. It was ruled by a warrior nobility. The Roman Catholic Church with its priests, monks, and bishops formed the First Estate. The pope was not only a spiritual leader but a powerful political force. In contrast, the Renaissance was man-centered. It was secular rather than spiritual. This does not mean that religion and salvation were not important, but they were not the focal point of most people's lives.

The Renaissance started in Italy because of four basic reasons. First, Italy exuded an independence and freedom: urban life had never disappeared entirely in Italy, the way it had in the many places in Europe.

Second, for some time, Venice had outfitted the crusaders and was the conduit for the silk and spice trade from India and China. Merchant banking families, like the Medici in Florence, were able to profit from these commercial endeavors and became the ruling elite. These wealthy bankers were able to finance and patronize the arts, providing employment for the famous painters, sculptors and architects of the time.

Furthermore, the Byzantines and Moslems cross-fertilized the urban city-states with their cultural ideas.

Last, Italy had many reminders of the Roman past: the road network, the aqueducts, the public buildings, the monuments.

In conclusion, the freedom of the urban elite, wealth, new ideas, and a standing heritage from the past—all of these factors contributed to a shift in attitude that made the Renaissance. —Kehoe, pp. 414-5

8. Overall, in paragraphs two through five, the author makes his point through

1. definitions.
2. examples.
3. reasons.
4. sarcasm.

9. The Renaissance period focused on

1. the search for salvation.
2. faith.
3. agrarian issues.
4. man.

10. The word secular, as used in the passage, most nearly means

1. religious.
2. worldly. *contrast*
3. sectional.
4. mystical.

11. According to the passage, the Medicis were

1. bankers.
2. crusaders.
3. commoners.
4. artists.

12. The Renaissance started in Italy for all of the following reasons except that

1. Italy exuded independence.
2. the common man in Italy supported it. *also process of*
3. Italy had historical landmarks and *elimination*
   infrastructures.
4. the Moslems brought in new ideas.

13. In the first paragraph, the author illustrates his point through

1. description.
2. persuasion.
3. religious referents.
4. contrast.

**SIMULATED EXAM THREE, PASSAGE TWO**

In February, 1895, the Edison "Kinetoscope" was unveiled to audiences in Stockholm, and from that date, Swedes have had a growing interest in cinema.  In fact, there is no more stirring phenomena in the entire history of silent film than the Swedish achievements between 1913 and 1921. Although the Swedes allowed the Americans a head-start of at least ten years, from 1913 the world looked to Stockholm for craftsmanship and imagination in cinema.

The beginnings were cautious and somewhat ponderous, like many a Scandinavian response to new artistic movements. One man set Swedish cinema on its auspicious course. Charles Magnusson had, as a young man of 19, attended the first exhibition of Lumiere films in Malmo in 1896 and resolved to become a cameraman. By 1905 he was starting to make a name as a newsreel photographer of great integrity and courage. In 1909 he joined a youthful company known as Svenska Bio in Kirstianstad (in southern Sweden). From the start, Svenska Bio bolstered its activity by acquiring up to twenty movie theaters, thus providing a ready outlet for its own productions (a tradition that continues to this day in Sweden). Consequently, Kristianstad became the main center of film activity in the country.

Magnusson later became a producer, and his pronouncements reveal him as a rare visionary. He realized that the public must be absorbed in what was happening on the screen: "The action is the motion picture's Alpha and Omega. It should give opportunities for intensely exciting and interesting situations.  The film producer must be supreme ruler. He alone decides; but after he has given the starting signal, he should leave the director in peace. If the director is unworthy of this confidence, he is not fit to be a director."

-Cowie. pp. 5-6

14. It can be inferred that American silent film began

1. when the world was looking to Stockholm.
2. in 1931.
3. about 1923.
4. around 1900.

15. According to the passage, Svenka Bio was established in

1. Stockholm.
2. Malmo.
3. southern Sweden.
4. northern Sweden.

16. The author suggests that Swedes approach unestablished art forms

1. overzealously.
2. timidly.
3. flippantly.
4. too seriously.

17. The word, phenomena, used in the second sentence, most likely means

1. definition.
2. silent films.
3. American film work.
4. events. < signal word = "achievements"

18. According to the passage, one of the innovative, enterprising actions Svenka Bio took was to

1. exhibit at Malmo.
2. utilize Edison's Kinetoscope.
3. hire newsreel photographers.
4. buy its own theaters.

19. According to the passage, Magnusson was all of the following except a

1. director. < process of elimination
2. cameraman.
3. producer.
4. photographer.

**SIMULATED EXAM THREE, PASSAGE THREE**

The Harry Potter series is clearly an unprecedented success. *The Sorcerer's Stone, The Chamber of Secrets*, and the *Prisoner of Azkaban* have concurrently occupied the top three positions on the *New York Times* best seller list. They seem to be unparalleled among any other series for children or for adults. Even educators have noted that "after a decade of despair over a generation lost to video games and television, Harry Potter books have lured huge numbers of school children to the printed page."

Nonetheless, the Harry Potter phenomenon is not without controversy. In at least eight states, parent protesters want to pull the books from school libraries, or at least stop them from being read in classrooms. These protesters have argued that the books are harmful to children. The Harry Potter series has been denounced as "a handbook for witchcraft and violence," "anti-Christian," and "evil and dangerous." This situation has led to quite a quandary for educators. Because some parents want to ban the same books that have encouraged children to read, school districts seem forced to choose between respecting parental authority and furthering the learning process.

Members of the library profession have questioned the validity of the complaints surrounding the series. Reacting to the controversy, Krug, director of the American Library Association Office for Intellectual Freedom responded with the question "what book did the parents read?" The implication is that the protestors have not read the books at all and have simply been projecting their own assumptions onto the books without understanding the content.                    -Yeager, Internet

21. The reader can infer from the passage that the Harry Potter series is unique because

1. it won the *New York Times* award for "best selling series."
2. the series appeals to elementary school children.
3. it has already been made into video games.
4. all three titles were on the bestseller list concurrently.

22. According to the author, the Harry Potter series protests mainly come from

1. school children.
2. parents.
3. the school board.
4. teachers.

23. The author of this article would agree that the Harry Potter series

1. is controversial.
2. is harmful but should remain on the bookshelves.
3. should be banned.
4. promotes witchcraft and violence.

24. The word denounced most nearly means

1. promoted.
2. sold.
3. condemned.
4. ridiculed.

25. Members of the library profession

1. agree with the protesters.
2. question the validity of the Harry Potter series.
3. are skeptical of the protestors' complaints.
4. believe the protesters are illiterate.

20. In the first paragraph, the Harry Potter series refers to a series of

1. magazines.
2. short stories.
3. books.
4. films.

**SIMULATED EXAM THREE, PASSAGE FOUR**

During Hoover's presidency attempts were made to aid the economy. The Reconstruction Finance corporation provided $3 billion in loans to some industries, and banks and the Federal Farm Board provided $500 million to farmers. But the two programs were too little and too late. The failure of the economy was blamed on Hoover and not the economic forces. It was his public relations and reactions, however, which hurt his bid for re-election.

Hoover, having realized that part of the economic woes were due to faith in the economy, attempted to restore that faith by having lavish dinners in the White House. The public reacted negatively to the campaign and considered Hoover callous to flaunt lavish dinners when so many were hungry. When the veterans of World War I camped in Washington, D. C. and demanded their veteran's bonus early, Hoover responded by sending MacArthur, Patton, and Eisenhower into the streets with the army, tanks, and tear gas. That spectacle caused Roosevelt to correctly believe that he, himself, would win the election early.

When Roosevelt entered office he and his staff believed drastic measures were necessary to restore faith in the economy and to forestall the worsening depression. One of the first financial acts under the new administration in 1933 was a closure of all the national banks for one week. The measure could have ignited more panic but instead a festive mood seemed to envelop the country. The intent of the bank closures was to audit the banks, close the weak ones, and shore up the stable banks. One week did not allow a thorough auditing process, but the shakiest banks were closed.

-Duke. p. 125

27. Who was president after Hoover?

1. Patton
2. MacArthur
3. Roosevelt
4. Eisenhower

28. According to the passage, Roosevelt believed Hoover would not win re-election because

1. Eisenhower campaigned against him.
2. Hoover held lavish dinners at the White House.
3. Hoover sent troops against veterans of World War I.
4. Roosevelt had more money with which to campaign.

29. The word lavish, as used in the selection, most nearly means

1. luxurious. (signal phrase = "White House"
2. delicious.
3. religious.
4. genteel.

30. We can infer from the passage that Roosevelt

1. did not accomplish much in terms of the economy.
2. accomplished more than Hoover did in regard to the economy.
3. was a weak president.
4. had been a banker before he became President.

31. One result from the closure of the banks was that

1. none of the banks were audited.
2. the public panicked.
3. all the banks were closed for good.
4. the unstable banks were closed for good.

26. Why was the economic aid from Hoover not effective?

1. It was given too late.
2. It was not enough money.
3. It was given only to manufacturers.
4. It was too little money, too late.

**SIMULATED EXAM THREE, PASSAGE FIVE**

When the last millennium was still quite young, a handful of adventurers floated down the river Amstel in hollowed-out logs. They built a dam and began to exact toll money from passing traders. In 1275 Count Floris of Holland granted Amsterdam special toll privileges, and in 1300 the town got its first charter.

Amsterdam is a human-sized city, with a compact layout and a resident population of just 750,000. You can cross the city center in half an hour on foot. The mixed, open, tolerant atmosphere is an important part of the city's heritage. Greater Amsterdam is a bustling cosmopolitan region with 140 nationalities represented. Over 44% of Amsterdam's residents are of non-Dutch origin. Amsterdam is a city open to foreign influence in all respects. Flexibility and tolerance of other cultures are keys to Amsterdam's success. Over the centuries, the city has been a haven to many waves of refugees and all have contributed to its style and prosperity. For example, Protestant and Jewish people fleeing to Amsterdam laid the foundations of the diamond cutting industry and brought valuable news of trade routes to the East.

South of the city center is Amstelveen, a 'green municipality' of which only about one-third is built up. Recreational facilities such as parks, sports fields together with water and woods, make up more than 20% of the municipality's surface area. Amstelveen enjoys spacious, low-density housing, and is especially popular with families.

Amsterdam may be a small city but it packs a big punch. Rembrandt, Van Gogh, and the Royal Concertgebouw Orchestra are all well known. The city is an international meeting-point of culture, business, and science. It is a city that is on the go, but where quality of life still counts.

-Amsterdam Promotion Foundation, internet

32. The main reason Amsterdam is successful is due to its

1. River Amstel.
2. international flavor.
3. its Jewish population.
4. famous artists.

33. In the second paragraph, the author gets his point across through

1. comparison and contrast.
2. description and definition.
3. narration and persuasion.
4. example and statistics.

34. It is implied that Amstelveen is unique because

1. it is packed with modern housing.
2. 2/3 of the town is commercialized.
3. 2/3 of the town is green.
4. only families are allowed to live there.

35. The phrase packs a big punch most nearly means

1. is impressive.
2. is effective.
3. has political importance.
4. has many artists.

36. The phrase, when the last millennium was still quite young, refers to

1. 1275.
2. recently.
3. the early 1900s.
4. the early 1000s. signal phrase= "last millennium" also refers to date 1275

37. The author's attitude toward Amsterdam is one of

1. surprise.
2. nostalgia.
3. admiration.
4. sympathy.

**SIMULATED EXAM THREE, PASSAGE SIX**

Have you ever thought about traveling to a country you have held only in your imagination? Or perhaps you would like to return to a country you have already visited? Study abroad programs in the state of Georgia may provide you with that opportunity, and you may draw more benefits from your experience than you thought possible.

There are several myths that surround studying overseas. First, it is natural to wonder whether or not you would be able to afford a study abroad program. In regard to financing, there are many scholarships available. In Georgia, for instance, the HOPE scholarship pays tuition costs and allots money toward book expenses. It is a good idea for students to consult with the International Office or the Financial Aid office at their home institution because most monies from loans can be applied to study abroad and will cover program costs.

Students also have the idea that they have to speak a foreign language to study abroad. The reality is that there are just as many, if not more, programs that are taught in English. The University System of Georgia offers programs to France, Italy, Russia, and Greece which do not require any language skills.

Third, sometimes students are worried that the credits will not fit their curriculum. Because universities have reciprocity agreements, credits transfer easily. The International Office coordinator will work with your advisor to ensure that you receive appropriate academic credit for your overseas work.

Fourth, the idea of being homesick can be overwhelming. Any professor who has worked with a study abroad program can tell you that you will make new, lifelong friends. Or, you may consider convincing your best friend, who might be attending a university elsewhere, to enroll in the program too.

As you can see, the myths that surround study abroad are just that—myths! They are not the reality.

-Arthur

38. The author of this article is probably

1. a photo journalist.
2. the president of a college.
3. a study abroad advisor. *has broad knowledge of attitudes toward study abroad*
4. a travel agent.

39. The purpose of the passage is to

1. entertain.
2. persuade.
3. argue.
4. narrate.

40. The main idea of the passage is that

1. studying abroad does not enhance a student's resume.
2. students do not have to speak a foreign language to study abroad.
3. students will make lifelong friends when they study overseas.
4. myths about study abroad are not the reality.

41. The author makes her point across by

1. refuting myths about study abroad. *presents compelling arguments against myths*
2. describing specific study abroad programs.
3. contrasting study abroad to studying at a home institution.
4. narrating her own study abroad experience.

42. The state of Georgia is used

1. as an analogy.
2. as a symbol.
3. as an example. *signal phrase = "for instance"*
4. figuratively.

43. It can be inferred that the author believes

1. students are not worried about receiving academic credit for study abroad.
2. many students who want to study abroad don't speak a foreign language.
3. studying overseas is not a viable option for university study.
4. there are no myths that surround study abroad.

During the past decade, the mountain and hillside ecosystems of the world have become a primary concern of national and international agencies. As a result of the Earth Summit, an increasing number of projects and initiatives are oriented toward global mountain environments.

This emphasis on mountains is not without justification. Mountains and uplands constitute about one-fifth of the earth's terrestrial surface and are directly or indirectly relevant for well over half of the world's population. Although about 10 percent of the world's population live in high mountains, a much larger population, which constitute the bulk of humanity, reside in hilly piedmont regions and adjacent lowlands. This wider population benefits from the supply of mountain food, water, wood, and minerals. The mountains are the water towers of planet earth—indeed without them the Amazon Basin or the Gangetic Plains would transform into deserts. Their massive watersheds are crucial for providing irrigation water, hydro-electric power, and nutrients to populations down stream. Mountains also harbor most of the world's wild species of our major food crops and medicinal plants. Correspondingly, mountains are the homelands of most of the world's remaining tribal groups known for their *in situ* maintenance of plant and animal genetic resources. Along with the Hindu Kush Himalayan Region of Asia, the Andes of South America claims the largest, most diverse, most economically and ecologically important mountain setting in the world.          -Rhoades, p. 6

45. When the author writes that the mountains are the water towers of planet earth he is making use of

1. figurative language. *mountains ≠ towers*
2. contrastive phrasing.
3. sarcasm.
4. humor.

46. The author is most likely a professor of

1. biology.
2. geography.
3. ecology.
4. physics.

47. According to the passage, what percent of the earth's land surface is composed of mountains and uplands?

1. 10
2. 20
3. 30
4. 40

48. Most likely, the discussion that follows the last paragraph focuses on

1. international agencies.
2. deserts, such as the Gobi.
3. natural resource management.
4. the Andes.

49. The word, harbor, as used in the selection, most nearly means

1. pier.
2. injure.
3. shelter. *signal word= "homelands"*
4. classify.

44. The author of this article would probably agree that

1. mountains do not affect the ecosystem to any great degree.
2. the public is not aware of the important role mountains have as a water resource.
3. flatlands are more crucial than mountains and uplands.
4. more people should reside in mountainous areas.

**SIMULATED EXAM THREE, PASSAGE EIGHT**

## TEST THREE

Dr. Phil McGraw talked his way onto a spot as a therapist on "Oprah." Thanks to his appearances every Tuesday, viewership of Oprah is 24 percent higher for that day than the rest of the week. Now in 2002 he is the hottest talk-show commodity to come along since Oprah herself. Dr. Phil is famous for his blunt, take-no-prisoners style of therapy. "People are used to being coddled," he says. "It's so much easier to tell people what they want to hear instead of what they need to hear." Although he has a Ph.D. in clinical psychology, McGraw has a way of offering advice that sounds like something you might hear from a good ole Texas boy, which McGraw, 51, just happens to be.

McGraw has a sort of X-ray vision when it comes to analyzing people's problems. He sometimes sounds more like a trial lawyer than a therapist in the way he interrogates people, digging deeper into their lives until they almost confess the answer to their problems. It's not always pretty to watch. McGraw tends to see the world in black and white—his favorite catch phrase is "you either get it or you don't"—and he doesn't have a lot of patience for people who don't get it, who refuse to take a hard look at their own lives.

Americans have long had a fascination with self-help experts, from Ben Franklin's Poor Richard ("Early to bed . . .") to the positive thinking of Norman Vincent Peale. But in the last few decades, gurus like Marianne Williamson have turned self-help from a stick into a crutch, with the emphasis on "codependency" and the dreaded "find your inner child"—ideas built on blaming someone else for your troubles. Maybe McGraw's tough take on personal responsibility is what people are demanding now.
                                             -Peyser, pp. 50-52

50. According to the article, the characteristic that distinguishes Dr. Phil is

1. that he has a Ph.D in psychology.
2. that he tells people what they want to hear.
3. his no-nonsense way of talking.
4. that he appeared first on "Oprah."

51. The author implies that Dr. Phil

1. refuses to take a hard look at his own
       life.
2. does not have a lot of patience.
3. has long been a guru.
4. only works on Tuesdays.

52. The author's attitude toward Marianne Williamson is one of

1. admiration.
2. impartiality.
3. enthusiasm.
4. disrespect.

53. The purpose of paragraph two is to

1. describe Dr. Phil. = blunt, Ph.D., Texas, 51
2. relate that Dr. Phil is a guru.
3. contrast Dr. Phil's style with Oprah's
       style.
4. define psychotherapy.

54. We can infer from the last paragraph that

1. Norman Vincent Peale has a psychology degree.
2. having a crutch is not such a bad idea.
3. blaming someone else for your troubles will
       help in the healing process.
4. the public is tired of the self-help
       approach of the last few decades.

*also refer to #52 for contrast*

**SIMULATED EXAM THREE, PASSAGE NINE**

# SCANTRONS

| | LAST NAME | | FIRST NAME | MI |
|---|---|---|---|---|

# SIMULATED DIAGNOSTIC EXAM

1 ①②③④   11 ①②③④   21 ①②③④   31 ①②③④   41 ①②③④   51 ①②③④

2 ①②③④   12 ①②③④   22 ①②③④   32 ①②③④   42 ①②③④   52 ①②③④

3 ①②③④   13 ①②③④   23 ①②③④   33 ①②③④   43 ①②③④   53 ①②③④

4 ①②③④   14 ①②③④   24 ①②③④   34 ①②③④   44 ①②③④   54 ①②③④

5 ①②③④   15 ①②③④   25 ①②③④   35 ①②③④   45 ①②③④

6 ①②③④   16 ①②③④   26 ①②③④   36 ①②③④   46 ①②③④

7 ①②③④   17 ①②③④   27 ①②③④   37 ①②③④   47 ①②③④

8 ①②③④   18 ①②③④   28 ①②③④   38 ①②③④   48 ①②③④

9 ①②③④   19 ①②③④   29 ①②③④   39 ①②③④   49 ①②③④

10 ①②③④   20 ①②③④   30 ①②③④   40 ①②③④   50 ①②③④

## SKILLS ANALYSIS

| Vocabulary | Literal Comprehension | Inference | Analysis |
|---|---|---|---|
| 16, 23, 27, 29, 33, 37, 39, 43, 50, 51 | 3, 9, 10, 11, 12, 13, 14 21, 22, 25, 26, 32, 41, 47 | 7, 8, 15, 17, 20, 28, 30, 34, 42, 44, 45, 46, 48, 52, 53, 54 | 1, 2, 5, 6, 18, 19, 24, 36, 38, 40, 49 |
| | Main Idea 4, 31, 35 | Main Idea | |

# SIMULATED EXAM
# TWO

| LAST NAME | | FIRST NAME | MI |
|---|---|---|---|

(Name grid bubbles A–Z)

1 ①②③④   11 ①②③④   21 ①②③④   31 ①②③④   41 ①②③④   51 ①②③④

2 ①②③④   12 ①②③④   22 ①②③④   32 ①②③④   42 ①②③④   52 ①②③④

3 ①②③④   13 ①②③④   23 ①②③④   33 ①②③④   43 ①②③④   53 ①②③④

4 ①②③④   14 ①②③④   24 ①②③④   34 ①②③④   44 ①②③④   54 ①②③④

5 ①②③④   15 ①②③④   25 ①②③④   35 ①②③④   45 ①②③④

6 ①②③④   16 ①②③④   26 ①②③④   36 ①②③④   46 ①②③④

7 ①②③④   17 ①②③④   27 ①②③④   37 ①②③④   47 ①②③④

8 ①②③④   18 ①②③④   28 ①②③④   38 ①②③④   48 ①②③④

9 ①②③④   19 ①②③④   29 ①②③④   39 ①②③④   49 ①②③④

10 ①②③④   20 ①②③④   30 ①②③④   40 ①②③④   50 ①②③④

| SKILLS ANALYSIS | | | |
|---|---|---|---|
| Vocabulary | Literal Comprehension | Inference | Analysis |
| 1, 12, 22, 25, 35, 37, 46, 51 | 4, 6, 8, 9, 13, 21, 28, 32, 33, 34, 43, 44, 50 | 2, 7, 10, 11, 14, 16, 19, 20, 23, 24, 27, 29, 30, 31, 38, 39, 48, 49, 53, 54 | 3, 15, 17, 26, 36, 40, 41, 42, 47, 52 |
| | Main Idea 45 | Main Idea 5, 18 | |

| LAST NAME | FIRST NAME | MI |
|---|---|---|

# SIMULATED EXAM
# THREE

1 ①②③④   11 ①②③④   21 ①②③④   31 ①②③④   41 ①②③④   51 ①②③④

2 ①②③④   12 ①②③④   22 ①②③④   32 ①②③④   42 ①②③④   52 ①②③④

3 ①②③④   13 ①②③④   23 ①②③④   33 ①②③④   43 ①②③④   53 ①②③④

4 ①②③④   14 ①②③④   24 ①②③④   34 ①②③④   44 ①②③④   54 ①②③④

5 ①②③④   15 ①②③④   25 ①②③④   35 ①②③④   45 ①②③④

6 ①②③④   16 ①②③④   26 ①②③④   36 ①②③④   46 ①②③④

7 ①②③④   17 ①②③④   27 ①②③④   37 ①②③④   47 ①②③④

8 ①②③④   18 ①②③④   28 ①②③④   38 ①②③④   48 ①②③④

9 ①②③④   19 ①②③④   29 ①②③④   39 ①②③④   49 ①②③④

10 ①②③④   20 ①②③④   30 ①②③④   40 ①②③④   50 ①②③④

## SKILLS ANALYSIS

| Vocabulary | Literal Comprehension | Inference | Analysis |
|---|---|---|---|
| 3, 6, 7, 10, 17, 24, 29, 35, 36, 49 | 2, 5, 9, 11, 12, 15, 16, 18, 19, 20, 22, 26, 27, 28, 31, 47, 50 | 1, 14, 21, 23, 25, 30, 34, 43, 44, 46, 51 | 4, 8, 13, 33, 37, 38, 39, 41, 42, 45, 48, 52, 53, 54 |
| | Main Idea 32, 40 | Main Idea | |

| LAST NAME | FIRST NAME | MI |
|---|---|---|

# SIMULATED EXAM FOUR

1 ① ② ③ ④   11 ① ② ③ ④   21 ① ② ③ ④   31 ① ② ③ ④   41 ① ② ③ ④   51 ① ② ③ ④

2 ① ② ③ ④   12 ① ② ③ ④   22 ① ② ③ ④   32 ① ② ③ ④   42 ① ② ③ ④   52 ① ② ③ ④

3 ① ② ③ ④   13 ① ② ③ ④   23 ① ② ③ ④   33 ① ② ③ ④   43 ① ② ③ ④   53 ① ② ③ ④

4 ① ② ③ ④   14 ① ② ③ ④   24 ① ② ③ ④   34 ① ② ③ ④   44 ① ② ③ ④   54 ① ② ③ ④

5 ① ② ③ ④   15 ① ② ③ ④   25 ① ② ③ ④   35 ① ② ③ ④   45 ① ② ③ ④

6 ① ② ③ ④   16 ① ② ③ ④   26 ① ② ③ ④   36 ① ② ③ ④   46 ① ② ③ ④

7 ① ② ③ ④   17 ① ② ③ ④   27 ① ② ③ ④   37 ① ② ③ ④   47 ① ② ③ ④

8 ① ② ③ ④   18 ① ② ③ ④   28 ① ② ③ ④   38 ① ② ③ ④   48 ① ② ③ ④

9 ① ② ③ ④   19 ① ② ③ ④   29 ① ② ③ ④   39 ① ② ③ ④   49 ① ② ③ ④

10 ① ② ③ ④   20 ① ② ③ ④   30 ① ② ③ ④   40 ① ② ③ ④   50 ① ② ③ ④

| SKILLS ANALYSIS | | | |
|---|---|---|---|
| Vocabulary | Literal Comprehension | Inference | Analysis |
| 7, 11, 16, 22, 31, 40, 44, 53 | 3, 5, 6, 10, 15, 18, 21, 24, 26, 28, 35, 41, 43, 45, 50 | 1, 2, 9, 13, 19, 20, 27, 32, 38, 39, 42, 46, 48, 49, 52, 54 | 4, 12, 14, 17, 23, 25, 29, 30, 33, 34, 47, 51 |
| | Main Idea 8, 36 | Main Idea 37 | |

| LAST NAME | FIRST NAME | MI |
|---|---|---|

# SIMULATED EXAM
# FIVE

1 ①②③④    11 ①②③④    21 ①②③④    31 ①②③④    41 ①②③④    51 ①②③④

2 ①②③④    12 ①②③④    22 ①②③④    32 ①②③④    42 ①②③④    52 ①②③④

3 ①②③④    13 ①②③④    23 ①②③④    33 ①②③④    43 ①②③④    53 ①②③④

4 ①②③④    14 ①②③④    24 ①②③④    34 ①②③④    44 ①②③④    54 ①②③④

5 ①②③④    15 ①②③④    25 ①②③④    35 ①②③④    45 ①②③④

6 ①②③④    16 ①②③④    26 ①②③④    36 ①②③④    46 ①②③④

7 ①②③④    17 ①②③④    27 ①②③④    37 ①②③④    47 ①②③④

8 ①②③④    18 ①②③④    28 ①②③④    38 ①②③④    48 ①②③④

9 ①②③④    19 ①②③④    29 ①②③④    39 ①②③④    49 ①②③④

10 ①②③④    20 ①②③④    30 ①②③④    40 ①②③④    50 ①②③④

| SKILLS ANALYSIS | | | |
|---|---|---|---|
| Vocabulary | Literal Comprehension | Inference | Analysis |
| 4, 7, 20, 28, 31, 53 | 1, 5, 8, 12, 13, 15, 18, 25, 29, 35, 40, 43, 46 | 6, 9, 11, 14, 16, 19, 21, 22, 23, 26, 27, 34, 36, 38, 39, 41, 44, 47, 52, 54 | 2, 3, 10, 17, 24, 30, 32, 33, 37, 42, 45, 48, 50, 51 |
| | Main Idea | Main Idea 49 | |

# SIMULATED EXAM
## SIX

|  | LAST NAME | FIRST NAME | MI |
|---|---|---|---|

1 ① ② ③ ④   11 ① ② ③ ④   21 ① ② ③ ④   31 ① ② ③ ④   41 ① ② ③ ④   51 ① ② ③ ④

2 ① ② ③ ④   12 ① ② ③ ④   22 ① ② ③ ④   32 ① ② ③ ④   42 ① ② ③ ④   52 ① ② ③ ④

3 ① ② ③ ④   13 ① ② ③ ④   23 ① ② ③ ④   33 ① ② ③ ④   43 ① ② ③ ④   53 ① ② ③ ④

4 ① ② ③ ④   14 ① ② ③ ④   24 ① ② ③ ④   34 ① ② ③ ④   44 ① ② ③ ④   54 ① ② ③ ④

5 ① ② ③ ④   15 ① ② ③ ④   25 ① ② ③ ④   35 ① ② ③ ④   45 ① ② ③ ④

6 ① ② ③ ④   16 ① ② ③ ④   26 ① ② ③ ④   36 ① ② ③ ④   46 ① ② ③ ④

7 ① ② ③ ④   17 ① ② ③ ④   27 ① ② ③ ④   37 ① ② ③ ④   47 ① ② ③ ④

8 ① ② ③ ④   18 ① ② ③ ④   28 ① ② ③ ④   38 ① ② ③ ④   48 ① ② ③ ④

9 ① ② ③ ④   19 ① ② ③ ④   29 ① ② ③ ④   39 ① ② ③ ④   49 ① ② ③ ④

10 ① ② ③ ④   20 ① ② ③ ④   30 ① ② ③ ④   40 ① ② ③ ④   50 ① ② ③ ④

| SKILLS ANALYSIS | | | |
|---|---|---|---|
| Vocabulary | Literal Comprehension | Inference | Analysis |
| 5, 6, 10, 11, 17, 24, 30, 36, 38, 41, 43, 47, 52 | 21, 23, 26, 35, 39, 40 | 4, 7,15, 22, 28, 31, 32, 33, 34, 42, 45, 48, 49, 50, 51 | 2, 3, 8, 9, 13, 14, 16, 18, 19, 20, 27, 29, 37, 44, 53, 54 |
| | Main Idea 12, 46 | Main Idea 1, 25 | |

| LAST NAME | FIRST NAME | MI |
|---|---|---|

# SIMULATED EXAM
# SEVEN

1 ①②③④　11 ①②③④　21 ①②③④　31 ①②③④　41 ①②③④　51 ①②③④

2 ①②③④　12 ①②③④　22 ①②③④　32 ①②③④　42 ①②③④　52 ①②③④

3 ①②③④　13 ①②③④　23 ①②③④　33 ①②③④　43 ①②③④　53 ①②③④

4 ①②③④　14 ①②③④　24 ①②③④　34 ①②③④　44 ①②③④　54 ①②③④

5 ①②③④　15 ①②③④　25 ①②③④　35 ①②③④　45 ①②③④

6 ①②③④　16 ①②③④　26 ①②③④　36 ①②③④　46 ①②③④

7 ①②③④　17 ①②③④　27 ①②③④　37 ①②③④　47 ①②③④

8 ①②③④　18 ①②③④　28 ①②③④　38 ①②③④　48 ①②③④

9 ①②③④　19 ①②③④　29 ①②③④　39 ①②③④　49 ①②③④

10 ①②③④　20 ①②③④　30 ①②③④　40 ①②③④　50 ①②③④

| SKILLS ANALYSIS | | | |
|---|---|---|---|
| Vocabulary | Literal Comprehension | Inference | Analysis |
| 8, 15, 29, 36, 40, 52 | 14, 17, 21, 22, 26, 27, 30, 32, 38, 41, 50 | 3, 9, 10, 11, 12, 13, 25, 28, 34, 35, 39, 46, 47, 51, 54 | 1, 4, 5, 6, 7, 19, 20, 23, 24, 31, 42, 43, 44, 45, 48, 49, 53 |
| | Main Idea 2, 16 | Main Idea 18, 33, 37 | |

| LAST NAME | FIRST NAME | MI |
|---|---|---|

# SIMULATED EXAM EIGHT

1 ① ② ③ ④     11 ① ② ③ ④     21 ① ② ③ ④     31 ① ② ③ ④     41 ① ② ③ ④     51 ① ② ③ ④

2 ① ② ③ ④     12 ① ② ③ ④     22 ① ② ③ ④     32 ① ② ③ ④     42 ① ② ③ ④     52 ① ② ③ ④

3 ① ② ③ ④     13 ① ② ③ ④     23 ① ② ③ ④     33 ① ② ③ ④     43 ① ② ③ ④     53 ① ② ③ ④

4 ① ② ③ ④     14 ① ② ③ ④     24 ① ② ③ ④     34 ① ② ③ ④     44 ① ② ③ ④     54 ① ② ③ ④

5 ① ② ③ ④     15 ① ② ③ ④     25 ① ② ③ ④     35 ① ② ③ ④     45 ① ② ③ ④

6 ① ② ③ ④     16 ① ② ③ ④     26 ① ② ③ ④     36 ① ② ③ ④     46 ① ② ③ ④

7 ① ② ③ ④     17 ① ② ③ ④     27 ① ② ③ ④     37 ① ② ③ ④     47 ① ② ③ ④

8 ① ② ③ ④     18 ① ② ③ ④     28 ① ② ③ ④     38 ① ② ③ ④     48 ① ② ③ ④

9 ① ② ③ ④     19 ① ② ③ ④     29 ① ② ③ ④     39 ① ② ③ ④     49 ① ② ③ ④

10 ① ② ③ ④     20 ① ② ③ ④     30 ① ② ③ ④     40 ① ② ③ ④     50 ① ② ③ ④

| SKILLS ANALYSIS | | | |
|---|---|---|---|
| Vocabulary | Literal Comprehension | Inference | Analysis |
| 3, 10, 17, 22, 30, 40, 47, 51, 53 | 5, 7, 8, 14, 16, 20, 29, 33, 34, 39, 41, 45, 52 | 2, 12, 18, 19, 23, 24, 25, 27, 28, 31, 35, 38, 48 | 1, 4, 6, 11, 13, 15, 21, 26, 32, 36, 37, 42, 44, 46, 49, 54 |
|  | Main Idea | Main Idea 9, 43, 50 |  |

| LAST NAME | FIRST NAME | MI |
|---|---|---|

# SIMULATED EXAM NINE

1 ① ② ③ ④    11 ① ② ③ ④    21 ① ② ③ ④    31 ① ② ③ ④    41 ① ② ③ ④    51 ① ② ③ ④

2 ① ② ③ ④    12 ① ② ③ ④    22 ① ② ③ ④    32 ① ② ③ ④    42 ① ② ③ ④    52 ① ② ③ ④

3 ① ② ③ ④    13 ① ② ③ ④    23 ① ② ③ ④    33 ① ② ③ ④    43 ① ② ③ ④    53 ① ② ③ ④

4 ① ② ③ ④    14 ① ② ③ ④    24 ① ② ③ ④    34 ① ② ③ ④    44 ① ② ③ ④    54 ① ② ③ ④

5 ① ② ③ ④    15 ① ② ③ ④    25 ① ② ③ ④    35 ① ② ③ ④    45 ① ② ③ ④

6 ① ② ③ ④    16 ① ② ③ ④    26 ① ② ③ ④    36 ① ② ③ ④    46 ① ② ③ ④

7 ① ② ③ ④    17 ① ② ③ ④    27 ① ② ③ ④    37 ① ② ③ ④    47 ① ② ③ ④

8 ① ② ③ ④    18 ① ② ③ ④    28 ① ② ③ ④    38 ① ② ③ ④    48 ① ② ③ ④

9 ① ② ③ ④    19 ① ② ③ ④    29 ① ② ③ ④    39 ① ② ③ ④    49 ① ② ③ ④

10 ① ② ③ ④    20 ① ② ③ ④    30 ① ② ③ ④    40 ① ② ③ ④    50 ① ② ③ ④

## SKILLS ANALYSIS

| Vocabulary | Literal Comprehension | Inference | Analysis |
|---|---|---|---|
| 8, 15, 19, 23, 29, 37, 38, 43, 47 | 2, 10, 12, 13, 16, 20, 21, 27, 30, 33, 46, 50, 53 | 4, 5, 9, 11, 17, 18, 22, 31, 32, 35, 36, 41, 44, 45, 49, 51 | 3, 6, 7, 24, 25, 26, 28, 34, 42, 48, 52, 54 |
| | Main Idea 39, 40 | Main Idea 1, 14 | |

| | LAST NAME | FIRST NAME | MI |
|---|---|---|---|

# SIMULATED EXAM
# TEN

1 ① ② ③ ④    11 ① ② ③ ④    21 ① ② ③ ④    31 ① ② ③ ④    41 ① ② ③ ④    51 ① ② ③ ④

2 ① ② ③ ④    12 ① ② ③ ④    22 ① ② ③ ④    32 ① ② ③ ④    42 ① ② ③ ④    52 ① ② ③ ④

3 ① ② ③ ④    13 ① ② ③ ④    23 ① ② ③ ④    33 ① ② ③ ④    43 ① ② ③ ④    53 ① ② ③ ④

4 ① ② ③ ④    14 ① ② ③ ④    24 ① ② ③ ④    34 ① ② ③ ④    44 ① ② ③ ④    54 ① ② ③ ④

5 ① ② ③ ④    15 ① ② ③ ④    25 ① ② ③ ④    35 ① ② ③ ④    45 ① ② ③ ④

6 ① ② ③ ④    16 ① ② ③ ④    26 ① ② ③ ④    36 ① ② ③ ④    46 ① ② ③ ④

7 ① ② ③ ④    17 ① ② ③ ④    27 ① ② ③ ④    37 ① ② ③ ④    47 ① ② ③ ④

8 ① ② ③ ④    18 ① ② ③ ④    28 ① ② ③ ④    38 ① ② ③ ④    48 ① ② ③ ④

9 ① ② ③ ④    19 ① ② ③ ④    29 ① ② ③ ④    39 ① ② ③ ④    49 ① ② ③ ④

10 ① ② ③ ④    20 ① ② ③ ④    30 ① ② ③ ④    40 ① ② ③ ④    50 ① ② ③ ④

| SKILLS ANALYSIS | | | |
|---|---|---|---|
| Vocabulary | Literal Comprehension | Inference | Analysis |
| 6, 11, 15, 24, 29, 35, 42, 45, 48, 49 | 1, 2, 5, 9, 12, 14, 17, 18, 20, 21, 23, 28, 30, 34, 40, 41, 46, 47, 50, 53 | 3, 8, 10, 13, 16, 19, 25, 27, 31, 32, 38, 43, 44, 52, 54 | 4, 22, 26, 33, 36, 37, 39, 51 |
| | Main Idea | Main Idea 7 | |